The
Ribhu Gita

The English Translation
from the Original Sanskrit Epic
Sivarahasyam
Translated by
Dr. H. Ramamoorthy and Nome

Society of Abidance in Truth
Santa Cruz, California
USA

First Edition 1995
Second Edition 2017
Copyright 1995
All Rights Reserved

Society of Abidance in Truth
SAT Temple
1834 Ocean Street
Santa Cruz, California 95060
USA
(831) 425-7287
www.SATRamana.org
email: sat@cruzio.com

ISBN: 9781947154001
Printed in USA

सदाशिवसमारम्भां
ऋभुऋष्यादिमध्यगाम् ।
रमणसद्गुरुपर्यन्तां
वन्दे गुरुपरम्पराम् ॥

sadāśiva-samārambhāṁ
ṛbhu-ṛṣy-ādi-madhyagām |
ramaṇa-sadguru-paryantāṁ
vande guru-paramparām ||

Sadasiva being the beginning,
Ribhu and other sages in between,
Reaching up to Ramana, the Sadguru—
To this lineage of Gurus, prostrations!

Contents

Foreword

"I say unto you, there is only the Supreme Brahman. This world is not born. I am just the state of Existence, only Bliss. This world (jagat) is not created."

Ribhu: 30:1

Salutations to the One Self

Ribhu reveals Himself…

It was the mid-1970's when the young jnani, Nome, came upon some literature published by Sri Ramanasramam containing an English translation of chapter 26 along with a few other verses from the Tamil version of the *Ribhu Gita*. It is said that Sri Bhagavan would often read chapter 26 to devotees at the asramam. Knowing this small part of history about Sri Bhagavan, Nome set out, with the help of devotees, to obtain an original copy of the entire Tamil version of the *Ribhu Gita*. Sri Ramanasramam was contacted and, by the grace of Sri Bhagavan, SAT was able to procure a copy of this holy text. However, this copy would sit, safely and undisturbed, for a good number of years before SAT was able to find a capable translator in the USA, especially one that was within travel distance to SAT, before it would be translated, in its entirety, into the English language.

The genesis of this work was the early 1980's. Satsangs had been taking place for a number of years, the Society of Abidance in Truth was in its infancy, and plans to build the SAT Temple were beginning to coalesce in the minds of devotees. The Tamil *Ribhu Gita* had remained untranslated for many years, but, upon the horizon, it soon would become accessible to English speaking devotees of Self-Knowledge.

Knowledge meets Knowledge...

In 1989, by the Grace of Siva, construction of the SAT Temple was completed, and virtually simultaneously SAT came to know of a scholar translator through Chinmaya Mission by the name of Dr. H. Ramamoorthy. Early in his life, Dr. Ramamoorthy worked for the railways in India. After his retirement, he earned his doctorate in Sanskrit, and came to live in the U.S., spending most of his time with his family, who immigrated to the U.S., in San Jose, California.

Dr. Ramamoorthy was contacted and was delighted to be involved in such a holy endeavor. The alignment of Dr. Ramamoorthy's knowledge of Sanskrit and Nome's Knowledge of the Self was the perfect recipe for the translation of this work.

Nome and Dr. Ramamoorthy soon met, and there was an immediate spiritual connection between them. Nome soon learned from Dr. Ramamoorthy that the Tamil version of the *Ribhu Gita* was derived from the Sanskrit original in the *Sivarahasyam*. Spontaneously, the natural response was to translate both versions! Research to obtain a copy of the Sanskrit version of the Sivarahasyam bore fruit and a copy was procured from the T.M.S.S.M. Library in Thanjavur, India, published in 1983.

For Dr. Ramamoorthy it was a love project as he required no funds for the translations. As a retiree, this was a project sent from Lord Siva, Himself, which would occupy the last stage of his life.

Dr. Ramamoorthy would say that the time spent with Nome at the SAT Temple on the translations was, for him, going to satsang. He would often say, "Ribhu is making himself known." Over the course of a dozen years, meeting once or twice weekly at the SAT Temple and sometimes at longer intervals when Dr. Ramamoorthy was away to visit family on the East Coast, together they translated not only both versions of the *Ribhu Gita,* but many other works by Adi Sankara. The first edition of the English translation of the Sanskrit version was released in 1995, and five years later the English translation of the Tamil version was released.

When the Tamil translation of the *Ribhu Gita (Song of Ribhu)* in English was released by SAT in late 2000, Dr. Ramamoorthy was away. When he returned several months later, Nome presented him with a copy of the *Song of Ribhu*. The look on his face was that of a child receiving a long-awaited, precious gift, and then a peace radiated from him as though he felt he had fulfilled his destiny. When he returned home that evening, he fell ill and was absorbed in Sri Bhagavan one week later.

This second edition does not stray from the original in its translation. A few typographical errors have been corrected and footnotes have been added to give further illumination to some Sanskrit words or phrases. Also added is a chapter containing 108 names of Sri Ribhu. From the lips of the human vehicle from which these were written, he would say, with a sparkle in his eyes and a playful smile, "They are written by Vyasa," indicating that he had no claim to them, but rather, they came from the One, for the One, in the One.

It is no small benefit to humankind to have these sacred works available. Since the first edition of the *Ribhu Gita* was released, aspirants from around the world have requested permission from SAT to publish this scripture in their native language in order to make this text available to more devotees. SAT has happily and with blessings given these devotees permission to do so. To date, this treatise has been published in Korean and Italian, with plans for translations in Russian and Portuguese.

Ribhu says, "Know that Siva is certainly the Self. Siva is the jiva. Siva is Brahman. There is no doubt of this. Whoever reads or hears this explanation, either once or always, is, indeed, liberated. There is no doubt of this. Hearing this even for a minute or half minute, he will become merged (connected, blessed) with Brahman." 35: 51-52

'Whoever reads or hears this explanation will become Brahman or is Liberated.' These words are a common thread throughout the *Ribhu Gita.* As for this writer, had this scripture fallen into hand in young adulthood it would have been incomprehensible. Even when the vague light of the spirit began to flicker in this heart, even then, this treatise would have remained a mystery. It would not be until later in life, by the Grace of Lord Siva, when I met my beloved teacher and husband that the words contained herein would open the center of my being and allow supreme love and absolute trust to rush in revealing the Truth of the words of Ribhu.

Ribhu says, "Whoever is without the grace of Siva will never know the meaning of this text. The Self is to be grasped by the proper attitude and faith. The Supreme is the One, Siva. This is certain." 42:17

Saturated with the purest Advaita, if words could answer Bhagavan Sri Ramana Maharshi's inquiry "Who am I?," the *Ribhu Gita* would surely do so.

—Sasvati

Acknowledgements

Deep appreciation and gratitude are here expressed for Raman Muthukrishnan and Sangeeta Raman for proofreading this book and distribution of SAT publications, for Raymond Teague and Ganesh Sadasivan for proofreading, for Sasvati for design, layout and seeing to the printing, for Richard Schneider and all the SAT Temple devotees whose support of the temple and the publication of these teachings of Self-Knowledge has made the present book possible.

Notes on Translation

In this translation of the *Ribhu Gita* from Sanskrit into English, the approach is to convey the profound spiritual significance of the text while simultaneously translating as literally as possible the actual contents of each verse. Indeed, the English translation is very much in the very order in which the Sanskrit words proceed. Each stanza of the original Sanskrit text has been translated as a unit. Translation, though, is inherently approximate, however close. The contextual connotation in the idiom of the original language may not be appropriately reflected in the new language in a translation that gives only the direct meanings of the individual translated words. Word-wise, phrase-wise, and sentence-wise translation, or a restatement of the idea in the new language, has been adopted as best serves the attempt to convey the contents of the original as closely as possible.

All of the Sanskrit terms used in the English translation can be found in the extensive glossary with accompanying definitions. In a few instances, for ease of reading, a brief definition has also been inserted in parentheses in the text itself immediately following the Sanskrit term. A few Sanskrit terms are employed only once and, if deemed to be not especially pertinent to the knowledge of Advaita Vedanta expounded in this scripture, are briefly defined in parentheses in the text itself, without inclusion in the glossary.

Aside from its usual usage, capitalization has been employed to aid the reader in identifying terms signifying the Absolute, as in the capitalization of the word "That."

Brackets, [ ], signify an insertion made by the translators considered helpful to render the verse comprehensible. Ellipses (. . .), which appear but a few times, indicate missing text in the Sanskrit edition.

The footnotes present alternative meanings to the word or phrase immediately preceding the footnote number or show the Sanskrit word in transliterated form that has been translated into English.

The glossary contains a significant amount of information that is quite necessary for a thorough understanding of the *Ribhu Gita*. Readers, especially those unfamiliar with Sanskrit and Vedanta, are advised to take the opportunity, upon encountering Sanskrit terms or English equivalents with which they are unfamiliar, to read the definitions provided. The definitions present accurate meanings, as well as comments by such great sages as Bhagavan Sri Ramana Maharshi and Adi Sankaracarya, and will well serve the reader who is desirous of a thorough comprehension of the wondrous knowledge expounded in this exalted scripture.

Introduction

Sivarahasyam is a Sanskrit epic that is primarily devoted to the glory of Lord Siva. It describes renowned Saiva centers of pilgrimage, holy rivers, religious observances, spiritual instruction, and other topics in the manner of various Purana-s, such as the love and devotion of great worshippers, divine and otherwise (such as Nandikesvara, Chandikesvara, Bhringi, Upamanyu, Markandeya, Gautama, Suka, Vasishta, Agastya, Sakti, Parasara, Vyasa, Dadhici, Ridhi, Kanva, Visvamitra, Kapila, Durvasa, Bhrigu, Sananda, Sanandana, and Bhagiratha), accounts of the sacred shrines where many devotees obtained salvation from their sicknesses and the results of sinful acts by penances and observances, and jyotirlinga-s (at Kedara, Omkara, Baidyanath, Kusruna, Naganatha, Mahakala, Bhima, Tryambaka, Visvanatha, Srisaila, Gokarna, and Rameswaram, as also other shrines such as Varanasi, Hardwar, Kurukshetra, Prayag, Gangasagar, Pushkar, and others). In the sixth amsa, or part, of this twelve-part tome that consists of about one hundred thousand verses, a dialogue occurs on the slopes of Mount Kedara in the Himalayas about the Supreme Brahman between the sage Ribhu, who is a mind-born son of Brahma, and the sage Nidagha. This dialogue, a self-contained exposition of non-duality, is referred to as *Ribhu Gita.*

Ribhu-Nidagha dialogues on the Self and Brahman also figure in the ancient texts of the traditional anthology of 108 Upanishads. Their dialogues appear in *Tejobindu Upanishad* of *Krishna Yajurveda* (37th in the list), *Mahopanishad* of *Sama Veda* (61st), *Annapoornopanishad* of *Atharva Veda* (70th), and *Varahopanishad* of *Krishna Yajurveda* (98th).

There is reference to Ribhu Gita by Bhagavan Ramana Maharshi in *Talks with Sri Ramana Maharshi.* H.H. Sri Chandrasekharendra Sarasvati, a Sankaracharya of the Kanchi Kamakoti Pitha, stated in glowing terms that the *Ribhu Gita* is to the *Sivarahasyam* what the *Bhagavad Gita* is to the *Mahabharata.* Part VI of the *Sivarahasyam*, along with Parts IV and V, was published in Sanskrit in 1983, though manuscripts of this treatise were known long before this. There is a translation in Tamil of the *Ribhu Gita,* the first edition of which appeared in print more than a hundred years ago. There were also printed publications of the *Ribhu Gita* in the Bengali and Kannada languages decades earlier.

The Knowledge of Brahman is covered in the *Ribhu Gita* in about two thousand verses. The text is a relentless reiteration of uncompromising Advaita—that the Supreme Brahman, "That," is all that exists and exists not, that nothing else exists, that the Self is Brahman and Brahman is the Self, that I am That, I am all, and That is myself. This Awareness is moksha (liberation), which is attained by the way of knowledge and the certitude "I am Brahman." In the *Ribhu Gita's* thorough sweep of Advaita, it brushes aside as unreal the trinity of the gods Brahma, Hari, and Hara, the path of action, the concepts of varna (caste) and asrama-s (the orders of life), and the duties prescribed for these. It delineates the characteristics of a videhamukta (one liberated out of the body), as well as the characteristics of a jivanmukta (one liberated while yet in the body), implying that liberation, being a function of knowledge, occurs with the destruction of avidya (ignorance) and that the continuance of the physical body is in no way incompatible with complete liberation.

Brahman-Realization by a knowledge of negation is reinforced by a profusion of instances of what That is not. That Brahman is all is emphasized by the enumeration of a plenitude of positive examples. The manner of exposition is structured often as a cascade of multiple repetitions to drive home the intended knowledge.

Salutation to Siva, the one Absolute,
Who is identical with Brahman,
Who is inconceivable and ineffable,
Who is immutable and imperishable,
Of the nature of undifferentiated Being,
Of the nature of infinite Consciousness,
Of the nature of limitless Bliss,
And by whose Grace That is realized.

Salutation to Sri Ribhu,
Who is one with Siva,
Who reveals the true nature of Brahman,
Who brings forth this sublime teaching
Of the nature of the purest Advaita,
Of the nature of timeless, spiritual glory,
Of the nature of formless, perfect fullness,
And by whose Grace the Self is realized as That.

Salutation to the Sadguru, Bhagavan Sri Ramana
    Maharshi,
Who is Siva Himself,
Who reveals that Siva, Brahman, and the Self are
    identical,
Who, by silence and explanation, brings about
    the Realization
Of this eternal, supreme Knowledge,
Of the quintessence of Advaita Vedanta,
Of Liberation from all of the imagined bondage,
And by whose Grace is realized that the Self alone is.

That which is known as Brahman, or the Self, is the timeless Truth. Unalloyed Being, it alone is for all eternity. Nonduality is its nature. Advaita Vedanta, consists of the
Knowledge of this immutable Truth. It reveals how the Self
alone is real, one without a second. It is the revelation of Reality. An exposition of Advaita Vedanta unsullied by even the
least trace of a notion of ignorant dualism is the essence and
substance of the teaching proclaimed by the great sage,
Ribhu, that appears, untitled, in the ancient Sanskrit scripture
Sivarahasyam, Later, in the Tamil version, this instruction
by Ribhu was entitled *Ribhu Gita*, the song of Ribhu. In the
form of a dialogue between the great sage, Ribhu, and his
blessed disciple, Nidagha, verse upon verse, chapter upon
chapter, elucidates the nondual Knowledge of the Self, the
Supreme Brahman. With countless negations of all that is of
an unreal nature and declaration after declaration regarding
the sole-existent reality of Brahman, the Self, the Truth is presented, utterly unobscured, by Ribhu in this rare, sacred work.

This Brahman-Knowledge, or Self-Realization, is of the nature of direct experience that transcends all perceptions and notions. In this direct experience, or Realization, there is a complete absence of the delusion of duality, which manifests as the notions of an ego, a mind, a body—which is mistaken to be one's identity or residence— and of an objective world. Sankalpa-s, notions assumed to be valid due simply to lack of inquiry into them, alone constitute all of those illusions. If one frees oneself from such delusions and illusions by absorption of the truth revealed by Ribhu, what remains is the perpetual, direct experience of the ever-present Self.

The Self is self-effulgent Being-Consciousness-Bliss. Nothing else is a knower of the Self; nor is there anything else for the Self to know. There has never been anything else created. The Self alone is. It knows itself by itself. It is never a known or unknown object. It simply is as it is. Being abides in itself; Consciousness knows itself; Bliss reposes in itself. This pure, nondual Realization is what Ribhu teaches, and one who approaches this sacred scripture in the correct manner realizes the same Truth.

Because of the consistent height of the spiritual instruction contained within the *Ribhu Gita,* with its flood of negations of both the secular and concepts of spirituality, inclusive of ideas associated with Vedanta and worship of Siva, the aspirant must approach this sacred teaching in a way that yields the intended fruit, which is Self-Realization. The seeker must be endowed with an intense desire for Liberation. Self-Realization is alone deep, lasting happiness, and attaining it is alone the purpose of life. The aspirant should be endowed with nonattachment. Having discerned what is eternal and the source of happiness, he should be nonattached to all that is transitory, all that is mutable, all that is mere, fleeting, phenomenal appearance, all that depends upon the senses, all that depends on the mind, all that is contained within the states of mind, and all that depends on the individual, or jiva, in order to be experienced.

The aspirant should be endowed with the power of discrimination. He should embrace the inquiry into the real nature of the Self and, disidentifying from the body, senses, prana, mind, and ego, or "I" notion, be one-pointedly immersed in meditation on the Self. He should discriminate between the real and the unreal, so that he realizes that the real ever is and the unreal never comes to be. He should regard all that is transitory, changeful, objective, composed of parts, sporadic, or dependent as unreal. He should realize that that which is eternal, unchanging, nonobjective, indivisible and partless, continuous, and nondependent is the ever-existent Reality.

Abandoning the notions of the external, which give rise to the appearance of the world, and notions of the internal, which give rise to the delusions of a mind and an individual, the aspirant should have full faith in the sacred Knowledge of Advaita Vedanta. Endowed with humility and, also, with full faith in the Guru and in the innate ability to realize—because all are, in truth, the Self—he should imbibe the sublime wisdom of this *Ribhu Gita* and abide in the natural state of Self-Realization.

It is from the great sage, the ever-gracious Bhagavan Sri Ramana Maharshi, that we know of *Ribhu Gita* and its exalted significance. The revered Annamalai Swami said, "Bhagavan often said that we should read and study the *Ribhu Gita* regularly. In the *Ribhu Gita* it is said, 'That bhavana "I am not the body, I am not the mind, I am Brahman, I am everything" is to be repeated again and again until this becomes the natural state.' Bhagavan sat with us every day while we chanted extracts from the *Ribhu Gita*, which affirmed the reality of the Self. It is true that he said that these repetitions are only an aid to Self-enquiry, but they are a very powerful aid."[1]

What is extolled and expounded in *Ribhu Gita* is the identical, supreme Truth evident in the Maharshi's Realization. The ineffable, immortal state, which is transcendent of all, in which there is no differentiation, which is sahaja—the innate, natural state—and beyond which there is nothing else is Sri Bhagavan's. His boundless peace, His supreme happiness, His profound wisdom, and His very presence are what the *Ribhu Gita* describes. The Maharshi says, "I did not yet

know that there was an Essence, or Impersonal Real, underlying everything and that God and I were both identical with
it. Later, at Tiruvannamalai, as I listened to the *Ribhu Gita*
and other sacred books, I learned all this and found that they
were analyzing and naming what I had felt intuitively without
analysis or name."[2] In Sri V. Ganesan's book entitled *Moments Remembered,* Sri M.G. Shanmugam recounts, "Bhagavan would quote from *Ribhu Gita, Kaivalya Navaneetam,
Jnana Vasistha,* and other advaitic texts and explain to me
their greatness. All the while, I was aware I was in the blissful
presence of a Brahmajnani, so highly extolled in all our scriptures."[3] Thus, for the realized sages, a holy text such as *Ribhu
Gita* is an expression or reflection of the ineffable Truth,
which they have realized and are, while, for the seekers of
Liberation, it is a gateway into the infinite space of pure
Being-Consciousness-Bliss, which is Brahman. That such a
scripture, the expression of that from which all words and
thoughts turn back unable to grasp, should exist is a great
blessing. That there is a sage, a knower of Brahman who is
Brahman himself, is inestimable Grace for which we can
never be too thankful.

Whether reading chapter after chapter, immersed in the
floodtide of supreme Knowledge, or verse by verse, phrase
by phrase, plumbing the fathomless depth of this liberating
Knowledge, one should approach this scripture as a profound meditation. This is no mere collection of words or
thoughts, but the revelation of the eternal Self. Indeed, the
knowledge contained herein can be comprehended by the
innermost Consciousness alone; neither the eyes nor the intellect can do so.

The repetition in Ribhu's instruction is intentional and is
for the purpose of inculcating a profound meditative approach and the direct experience of Self-Knowledge described therein. For those who experience this Realization,
the Truth is ever fresh and of perpetual fascination. They who
aspire cannot hear too much of it. To truly understand
Ribhu's teaching is to abide in and as the one Absolute Self.
Sri Ribhu's revelation of the Truth of the Self, Brahman, is
seamlessly, perfectly consistent. Apparent contradictions in

the *Ribhu Gita* are completely dissolved when one realizes the meaning of his declarations. Thus, in some chapters "All is Brahman" is emphasized, while in others "Brahman alone is, and there is no all" is emphasized. If one considers anything else to be or to appear, know that Brahman alone is all that. The formless alone exists as all form without any other factor, thing, or modification existing whatsoever. Therefore, "all" or "everything" is a term with no significance apart from the truly existent Brahman. This is true of all that can be named or conceived. Indeed, Brahman alone is present, and there has never been even a single, objective thing. Nothing has been created. The Self, Brahman, formless and homogeneous and limitless, admits of nothing outside it and nothing inside it. It is as it is, always. A disciple said to the Maharshi, "*Ribhu Gita* speaks of so many objects as unreal, adding at the end that they are all Brahman and thus real." The Maharshi replied, "Yes, when you see them as so many, they are asat, i.e., unreal; whereas when you see them as Brahman, they are real, deriving their reality from their substratum, Brahman." Later in this same dialogue, the disciple asked, "Viveka is said to be discrimination between the Self and the non-Self. What is the non-Self?" The Maharshi, full of Grace and supreme Knowledge, replied, "There is no non-Self, in fact. The non-Self also exists in the Self. It is the Self which speaks of the non-Self because it has forgotten itself. Having lost hold of itself, it conceives something as non-Self, which, after all, is nothing but itself."[4]

In the *Ribhu Gita*, Sri Ribhu negates all that is worldly and of the samsara. He also negates all concepts regarding that which is spiritual, such as various forms of worship, practice, meditation, the gods, and even names given to the Absolute and the realized state. In many instances, Ribhu redefines the meaning of some form to elucidate its profound spiritual significance. The Maharshi has graciously commented abundantly upon this. In *Letters from Sri Ramanasramam,* we read, "Bhagavan got that book *(Ribhu Gita),* read it, and told us the following: 'O Lord! I went all around the world to do pradakshina (circumambulation) to you, but you are in fullness everywhere. How then can I contemplate a second? I shall worship you as "kutastha akhila rupa" (immovable, entire form of the world). (Alternative translation: the immovable and immutable that is the nature of the whole.) That is the only pradakshina to you.' Namaskar also means the same thing. The merging of the mind in the Self is namaskar and not the mere act of prostrating whenever you get up or sit down or whenever you go that side or come this side."[5]

In *Day by Day with Bhagavan*, we read, "The proper pradakshina is going around the Self or, more accurately, to realize we are the Self and that within us all the countless spheres revolve, going around and around, as described in the following stanza of the *Ribhu Gita*, Tamil version (Chapter 3, verse 39):

Reflecting, 'I am the all-blissful Self'
Is worship as with words and flowers.
True circumambulation is the thought
'In me the million universes roll;'
He who knows all beings bow to Him
And He to none,
He bows before the Mahalinga-Self.[6]

In *Talks with Sri Ramana Maharshi*, the Maharshi again references Ribhu, thus, "Says the *Ribhu Gita*, 'I remain fixed, whereas innumerable universes, becoming concepts within my mind, rotate within me. This meditation is the highest pradakshina (circumambulation).'"[7]

In the passage from *Day By Day with Bhagavan*, cited above, the Maharshi proceeds to clearly explain the relation of the wise to the forms of spiritual practice and worship and alludes to the same instruction contained in the *Ribhu Gita*: "The jnani, though he knows that meditation on the Self is the best worship, will join in all the other kinds of worship for the good of others and as an example to them. In fact, he may observe all the other ways even more correctly and steadfastly than those who follow only those paths and know nothing of jnana. That is referred to in the following verse, also occurring in *Ribhu Gita*. The gist is, 'If the Guru refers to dvaita (duality) when teaching advaita (nonduality) to the disciple, it is not to be regarded as his real teaching any more than one should regard as real the grief of one who weeps because he is paid to do so.'"[8]

In all cases when Ribhu seems to negate the Absolute, declaring the nonexistence of Liberation, Knowledge, the Self, Brahman, and so forth and so on, it is not actually the existence of the Absolute that is negated, but rather notions regarding these. The Absolute can never be an object of thought. Indeed, it is in freedom from thought entirely that one truly knows the Absolute as it truly is. In Self-Realization, which is the Realization of the Absolute, Consciousness knows itself, by itself, in itself. The Self can never be a thought, and thought can never know the Self. The thought of "the Self" is certainly not the Self itself. Here, knowing is Being. Relinquishing the idea of "the Self," the Self knows itself. This Knowledge is continuous, and that which is continuous is eternal. No thought is continuous or eternal; Being-Consciousness is never interrupted, is indestructible, and is ever existent. Whatever thought may appear, be it gross or subtle, very deluded or lofty, it fails as a definition for the Self or as Knowledge of Reality. To abide free of misidentification with any thought, having ceased the projection of the sense of reality, of identity, and of happiness upon any of them, is to realize true Knowledge. It is this non-conceptual, real state of pure Being that is referred to by "the Self," "Realization," "Brahman," "Siva," and such other terms indicative of the Absolute.

The abandonment of the idea of "liberation" presupposes the previous complete elimination of all ideas of ignorance. The release of any thought of "nonduality" presupposes the previous utter destruction of dualism without a trace of it remaining. The relinquishment of the thought of "Brahman" assumes the previous attainment of the understanding that all that is not Brahman is utterly unreal.

What has just been stated regarding references to terms applicable to the Absolute is also true regarding all the negations in *Ribhu Gita* of various spiritual practices. Only the one who abides in perpetual meditation and who has attained that steadiness of abidance in which there is no possibility of non-meditation is capable of relinquishing "meditation" and every notion of differentiation regarding it in the way that Ribhu intends. Similarly, it is the one who has deeply inquired into the nature of the Self or who has utterly surrendered, reaching the apex of devotion, or who has thoroughly renounced all worldliness who can release all of these. One liberates oneself from duality prior to releasing an idea concerning nonduality, abandoning that which is lower, before passing beyond that which is higher. In a similar way, to truly stand free of the mind, one first stands free of the body, which is but an appearance in the mind; or the freedom from the mind must include freedom from the body. The Reality of the Absolute transcends even the subtlest and loftiest of ideas. Therefore, silence is most eloquent in teaching about it. Ribhu employs his instruction by negation to cause one to abide in transcendent Silence.

The declarations affirming the reality of "the Self," "Brahman," "Siva," and such, also serve the same purpose for those who truly listen and comprehend. Abidance in the Silence of the Self is being as you really are.

Spiritual practice is the endeavor to be as you really are. The essence is true and forever beyond notions and their negation. Thus, the negation of that which is spiritual in the *Ribhu Gita* is always entirely the destruction of notions regarding such and not the discarding of the essential experience, be it of practice or Realization.

The supreme Knowledge contained herein is also called Siva-Knowledge. Ribhu declares that Siva himself is his Guru and that the instruction he bestows upon his disciple, Nidagha, is the very same that Lord Siva gave him. In the final chapters, symbols, forms of worship of Siva—such as the wearing of the sacred ash—and Siva's Grace are extolled. Every chapter of this holy scripture concludes with a verse or verses that serve to recapitulate in very brief form some salient points of the chapter and to praise Siva. These verses, though some of them may not be uttered by Ribhu but by someone else who is difficult to identify with Ribhu, are expressive of the same supreme Truth and the glorification of

Siva. Siva is the supreme. Siva is all in all, yet transcendent of all. Siva is the one who liberates, and Siva is the source of grace. Siva it is who is realized by them who are devoted to the Supreme. With Siva they merge. In Siva they are absorbed. Their individuality is utterly effaced, and Siva alone remains. Siva is the infinite Consciousness. Siva is pure Being. Siva is the supreme Bliss. Siva is the Good, the Auspicious One. Siva is Consciousness, inherent in which is the power to destroy all ignorance and illusion, and which remains by itself as nondual, undifferentiated, absolute Being. The Guru is Siva. Being enlightened by Ribhu, Nidagha says, "There is no doubt that whoever expounds this treatise is, indeed, the Guru. The expounder of this treatise is, indeed, the Supreme Brahman. There is no doubt of this. The expounder of this treatise is Siva himself and none else," and also, "This Knowledge of Siva is pure and destructive of the pairs of opposites." The Guru abides as the Self, the Absolute Brahman. He is called a "knower of the Self" or a "knower of Brahman," yet the Self alone knows the Self, Brahman alone knows Brahman. The Guru is the Self, replete with full, perfect Knowledge of the Self. For the disciple, the Guru is Grace incarnate, yet the Guru, in his Grace, completely obliterates all dualism and even the very notions of form and incarnation, revealing the bodiless, unborn, undying reality of the Self. The disciple is absorbed, and the Guru alone remains. The highest Truth, which the Guru is and reveals, forms the content of the *Ribhu Gita*.

Again and again, the great sage, Ribhu, explains the true nature of the Self, the real significance of "I." Again and again, Ribhu explains the truth about Brahman. The descriptions are of identical meaning. The real meaning of the mahavakya-s such as "That you are," "Consciousness (or Supreme Knowledge) is Brahman," "This Self is Brahman," and "I am Brahman" is brought forth in this *Ribhu Gita* again and again. The meaning is to be experientially realized by the removal of every concept about Brahman, or That, and by liberating oneself of every misidentification and sankalpa about oneself. If the Self is realized as it is, it, itself, is that which is called Brahman, and this entire *Ribhu Gita* is then

xxvi

seen as a description of one's own Self. The purpose of this Gita is the removal of all false notions—the awakening from the dream-like illusions of all that is unreal—and the Realization of That, which alone is, always.

As is proclaimed in Chapter 38, this *Ribhu Gita* is the quintessence of all essences. The reading, as a meditation, is a kind of sadhana, or spiritual practice, as the Maharshi has indicated and as the Gita itself declares. One should not simply read, but feel beyond all feeling the Truth of what is stated herein. Dive within and realize how true the Truth truly is. Even with the eyes open reading this sacred text, inwardly inquire into the Self and understand this exquisite description of your own ineffable nature. Regardless of one's initial comprehension, even the simple seeing or hearing, again and again, of this precious spiritual instruction will bring about great spiritual benefit. "Once Sri Bhagavan presented her [Sampurnamma] a copy of *Ribhu Gita* and asked her to study the book. When she wanted to be excused on the ground that she did not understand a word of it, Sri Bhagavan persisted and asked her to read it all the same. 'It does not matter that you do not understand,' He said. 'Still, it will be of benefit to you.'"[9]

Let there be the inquiry into the nature of the Self, and there will be abidance in the lasting happiness and peace of Self-Realization. Let there be the heart's pure devotion, and there will be absorption in the ocean of Grace. Let there be meditation upon the nondual Truth, Advaita Vedanta, and there will be the Knowledge of Brahman, the Knowledge of the Self. May they who read this sacred scripture, *Ribhu Gita*, realize the nondual Truth and, being free from even the least trace of delusion, blissfully abide as the one Self.

May Siva be pleased with all that is written here.
May Ribhu be pleased with all that is written here.
May the Maharshi be pleased with all that is written here.
May all wise sages everywhere rejoice in this eternal Truth.

REFERENCES:

1. Annamalai Swami, *Mountain Path,* June, 1993, pp. 52-53.
2. Arthur Osborne, *Ramana Maharshi and the Path of Self-Knowledge,* First Edition (London: Rider. 1954), p. 81.
3. Sri V. Ganesan, *Moments Remembered,* First Edition (Tiruvannamalai: Sri Ramanasramam, 1990), p. 79.
4. *Talks with Sri Ramana Maharshi,* Fourth Edition (Tiruvannamalai: Sri Ramanasramam, 1968), p. 269.
5. *Letters from Sri Ramanasramam,* First Combined Volume Edition (Tiruvannamalai: Sri Ramanasramam, 1970), p. 75.
6. *Day by Day with Bhagavan,* Second Reprint (Tiruvannamalai: Sri Ramanasramam, 1970), pp. 172-173.
7. *Talks with Sri Ramana Maharshi,* p. 178.
8. *Day by Day with Bhagavan,* pp. 173-174.
9. *Mountain Path,* June, 1993, p. 103.

ṛbhu-nidāgha-saṁvādaḥ
RIBHU-NIDAGHA DIALOGUE

Skanda:
The Rishi-s spoke thus to Ribhu, the devotee of Sambhu, the desireless, the best among sages, decked with ashes and rudraksha-s (seeds of holy berries), who was at Kedara on the Himalayan peak worshipping the Lord of Kedara.

2, 3. Rishi-s:
Worthy son of Brahma, the lotus born! For our Liberation, please enlighten us with the Knowledge, the wisdom of the Vedas and mahavakya-s (great aphorisms), which you obtained on Mount Kailasa by worshipping Lord Isvara, by means of which we shall be enabled to cross the shoreless ocean of samsara (the repetitious cycle of birth and death).

4. Suta:
Gladdened by the words of the sages and looking around, he (Ribhu) addressed the wise assembly, who were established in the contemplation of the feet of the Lord of the octonary form.

5. Ribhu:
There is nothing secret from you, great souls, the noble devotees of Sambhu. Looking at you from the mansion of love of the three-eyed Lord, I shall communicate to you this:[1]

---

[1]*That*

1

6. the aphoristic Knowledge of Sankara, a great emanation from the head of the Vedas. Hear this, best of men, seekers after the Knowledge of Brahman! Hear this: the Ocean of Siva-Knowledge,

7. by which you shall, conquering your [attachment to the] senses by devotion to Siva, cross that sea of samsara. Offering obeisance to Mahadeva, I shall expound to you the knowledge of Isvara.

8. Ribhu:
The cause of the universe is the divine Consort of Uma alone, the shining illuminator, the one cause of the sentient and the insentient world, and the one cause of joy. For Him, the great Isvara (Mahesvara), there is no need for any action. He, Hara, alone is the cause of all.

9. The charioteer born of the arrow, and the horses from the faces of the charioteer, the pair of eyes of you, the rider, as the pair of chariot wheels, the chariot fitted and yoked for the hunt, seated in the chariot with a crown on the head and bows and arrows in front, and steering the chariot—may the dust of this Sthanu (the immovable, motionless One, Siva) protect us!

10. Then, addressing Nidagha, Ribhu said:
I shall tell you about the definition of the Self, which is not available in all the triad of time (past, present, and future)—

11. ever the most secret of the secret, by summarizing what has been expounded by Siva. There is nothing that can be talked of as non-Self, neither the mind as the non-Self nor the world[1] as the non-Self. Be of the certitude that there is nothing that is non-Self.

[1] jagat, universe

12. By the absence of all sankalpa-s, by the elimination of all forms, by the conviction of there being only Brahman, be of the certitude that there is not anything that is non-Self.

13. In the absence[1] of mind, there is no thinking; in the absence[1] of the body, there is no aging. With the conviction of there being only Brahman, be of the certitude that there is no non-Self.

[1]*nonexistence*

14. Because of the absence[1] of feet, there is no walking; because of the absence[1] of hands, there is no work. There being only Brahman alone, be of the certitude that there is no non-Self.

[1]*nonexistence*

15. Because of the absence[1] of Brahma (the Creator), there is no world, and, in the absence[1] thereof, there is no Hari (the Sustainer). There being only Brahman alone, be of the certitude that there is no non-Self.

[1]*nonexistence*

16. In the absence of aging, there is no death; nor is there the world or the Vedas or the gods. There being only Brahman alone, be of the certitude that there is no non-Self.

17. There is no dharma (righteous conduct), there is no purity, there is no [concept of] truth, and no fear. There being only Brahman alone, be of the certitude that there is no non-Self.

18. Because there is no decay, there is no movement. Because there is no decay, there is no insentience. There being only Brahman alone, be of the certitude that there is no non-Self.

19. The guru, also, indeed, does not exist; truly, there is no disciple. There being only Brahman alone, be of the certitude that there is no non-Self.

20. There being nothing that is the first, there is nothing that is the second; there being no second, there is nothing as the first. If there is the [concept of] truth,[1] something as untruth[2] will also arise.

[1] *truthfulness*   [2] *untruthfulness*

21. If there be any [concept of] untruth, a [concept of] truth will also arise with it. If there is inauspiciousness, know that there is a notion of auspiciousness. Likewise, if there is auspiciousness, there will be inauspiciousness.

22. If you think of fearlessness, fear is postulated; fear is concomitant with fearlessness. There being only Brahman alone, be of the certitude that there is no non-Self.

23. If there is bondage, there is liberation; in the absence[1] of bondage, there is no liberation. If there is death, there is birth; in the absence of birth, there is no death either.

[1] *nonexistence*

24. If there is "you," there is "I"; if there is no "you," there is no "I." If there is "this," there is "that;" in the absence[1] of "that," there is no "this" either.

[1] *nonexistence*

25. "If it is there" implies something not being there; "it is not there" implies something being there. If there is an effect, there is some cause; in the absence[1] of effect, there is no cause.

[1] *nonexistence*

26. If there is duality, there is [a concept of] nonduality; in the absence[1] of duality, there is no [concept of] nonduality either. If there is something to be seen, a seer is also there; in the absence[1] of anything to see, there is no seer at all either.

[1] *nonexistence*

27. If there is an interior, there surely is an exterior; if there be no interior, there is also no exterior. If there be [a concept of] completeness,[1] it implies, consequently, something of incompleteness.[2]

[1]*fullness;* [2]*non-fullness*

28. If there is a little that can be thought of, it becomes all in no time; if there is not a little—nothing whatsoever of anything at anytime—nothing arises.[1]

[1]*follows*

29. Therefore, all this does not exist in the least at any time: neither you nor I, neither this nor that. There being only Brahman alone, be of the certitude that there is no non-Self.

30. There is nothing by way of example in this world, nor is there anything for which an example is to be given. There being only Brahman alone, be of the certitude that there is no non-Self.

31. There is no mind to think, "I am the Supreme Brahman," "This universe is only Brahman alone," "You are also only Brahman."

32. I am just Consciousness alone, and there is no non-Self. Be of this certitude. Thus, in brief, the definition of the Self has been told to you.

33. By hearing this well once, one, indeed, becomes Brahman oneself.

34. Nidagha:
Who are you? Who indeed? Tell me, best among speakers, that upon hearing which one is released instantaneously from the great hardship[1] of samsara.

[1]*difficulty, danger*

35. Ribhu:
I, indeed, am the Supreme Brahman. I, indeed, am the supreme happiness. I, indeed, am myself.[1] I, indeed, am. I am Brahman alone.

[1] I

36. I am Consciousness alone. I am possessed of divine Knowledge. I am without any words[1] to express myself. I am Brahman alone.

[1] all letters

37. I have no meaning. This is without meaning. I am devoid of[1] the meaning of all.[2] I am Brahman alone.

[1] free from [2] all meanings

38. I am ever pure, enlightened, eternal, totally blemishless. I am of the nature of the ever-blissful. I am Brahman alone.

39. I am of the nature of the eternal perfection. I am Existence-Consciousness-Bliss. I am of the nature of nonduality alone. I am Brahman alone.

40. I am of the nature that cannot be described. I am without beginning and without end. I am not of the nature of insentient matter. I am Brahman alone.

41. I am without any sankalpa of my own. I am devoid of all nescience. I am all. I am That itself. I am Brahman alone.

42. I am devoid of all names and such. I am devoid of all forms. I am devoid of all attachments. I am Brahman alone.

43. I am the creator of all speech. I am beyond the end of all the Vedas (Vedanta). I am the end of all times. I am Brahman alone.

44. I am the end of all forms. I am the joy that is the end of all names. I am the end of all the eons of time. I am Brahman alone.

45. I, myself, am joy and nothing else. I, myself, am change-less Consciousness. I myself am everywhere. I am Brahman alone.

46. I am the Self, which is Brahman alone. I am solely a mass of pure Consciousness. I am the sole-existent, undivided Essence. I am Brahman alone.

47. I am solely of the nature of Knowledge. I am of the nature that exists by itself. I am the sole-existent, complete Essence. I am Brahman alone.

48. I am of the nature of Existence. I, indeed, am of the nature of beatitude.[1] I am beyond meaning or absence of meaning. I am Brahman alone.

[1] *kaivalya*

49. I am of the nature that is immeasurable. I am of the nature that cannot be discussed. I am of the nature that cannot be comprehended. I am Brahman alone.

50. I am of the nature that is not woven together. I am without sorrow. I shine uninterruptedly. I am Brahman alone.

51. I am devoid of all activity. I am devoid of all differences. I am devoid of all doubts. I am Brahman alone.

52. I am without an ego.[1] I am without a master.[2] I am ever of the nature of Brahman. I am Brahman alone.

[1] *"I" bhāva* [2] *I am without "I am without"*

53. I am devoid of Brahma or the characteristics of Brahma and others, devoid of the characteristics of Kesava (Vishnu) and others. I am without the characteristics of Sankara and others. I am Brahman alone.

54. I am silently luminous. I am Brahman alone. I am[1] nothing. I am[1] not the highest. I am a small thing. I am also the Supreme.

[1]*there is*

55. I do not have a lustrous body; nor am I the illuminator of the universe. I am a mass of Consciousness. I am of the nature of Consciousness. I am ever of the nature of Existence.

56. I am joyous. I am the embodiment[1] of joy. I am Brahman alone. I am neither a boy nor am I a youth, nor an old man. I am higher than the highest.

[1]*nature*

57. I am not of the nature that is manifold. I am Brahman alone. This, my own experience, has thus been told, the supreme Essence of all the Upanishads.

58. Whoever hears this becomes himself Brahman.

59. Those deluded by the intellect with ideas of little of learning and omniscience and the like, arising out of [conceptual interpretations of] the Vedas, scriptures, treatises, aphorisms, and the like, cannot, even by the study of hundreds of scriptures, know Sankara as being neither the gross nor the atomic, nor fire, wind, space, water, or earth, but as merely the shining Heart-space inside the sheaths within all beings.

Chapter Two

sivena kumāropadeśa-varṇanam
DESCRIPTION OF SIVA'S TEACHING TO KUMARA (THE SAME TEACHING GIVEN BY SIVA TO RIBHU)

Nidagha:
Revered Ribhu! In this state of affairs, who qualifies for Brahman-hood? Please tell me especially that Knowledge which has come out of the words of Sankara.

2. Ribhu:
You, indeed, are Brahman. You, indeed, are the Supreme Guru. You, indeed, are of the nature of space. You are Brahman. There is no doubt of this.

3. You, indeed, are of all [manner of] being. You, indeed, are the meaning of all this. You are changeless. You are devoid of all. You are the Witness. You are ever without a witness.

4. You are time. You are devoid of all. You are ever without a witness. You are devoid of time. You are time. You are ever Brahman, the mass of Consciousness. You are the nature of all Truth. You are Brahman. Of this there is no doubt.

5. You are the Truth. You are the accomplished. You are the ancient One. You are the liberated; you are Liberation. You are ever immortal. You are God. You are peaceful. You are without afflictions. You are Brahman. You are purnam (the perfect fullness). You exist on all sides.

6. You are equable. You are also the Truth. You are ancient. You are set forth by the word "truth" and these other words. You are devoid of all limbs. You are ever firm. You are Brahman. You are full and perfect. You are the high and the low.

7. You are free from the perplexing misconception of all the phenomenal world. You arise in all the beings that ever are. You are ever without sankalpa. You are Brahman. You are fullness. You exist on all sides.

8. You are ever joyous and happily established,[1] ever without enmity,[2] ever without action and such. You are Brahman, full and existing on all sides.
[1]abiding; [2]hatred

9. You are of the nature of the space[1] of Consciousness. You are Consciousness alone. You are unfettered. You abide only in yourself.[2] You are Brahman. There is no doubt of this.
[1]the true nature of the form; [2]the Self

10. You are Bliss. You are the Supreme. You are devoid of all, [and you are] attributeless. You are the One alone, without a second. You are Brahman. There is no doubt of this.

11. You are of the nature of a mass of Consciousness-Bliss. You are ever Consciousness-Bliss. You are of the nature of the all-complete. You are Brahman. There is no doubt of this.

12. You are That. You are yourself. You are the enlightened.[1] You are He. You know, you see, you are Consciousness. You are born of Brahman; you are Brahman. There is no doubt of this.
[1]wise

13. You are immortal. You are all-pervasive.[1] You are God. You are great. You are speech (lit., the mark of the moving lips). You are Brahman. There is no doubt of this.
[1]omnipresent

14. You are all. You are devoid of all. You are peaceful. You are, indeed, the Supreme. You are the cause. You are serene. You are Brahman. There is no doubt of this.

15. You are of the nature of Existence only. You are, indeed, natural[1] Existence. You are of the nature of the ever-pure. You are Brahman. There is no doubt of this.

[1]*universal*

16. You are devoid of even a little of anything. You are without even an atom. You are devoid of [objective] existence. You are devoid of nonexistence and such.

17. Whoever you are, you are He. You are all those who are great. You are Brahman. There is no doubt of this.

18. You are devoid of indications and qualities. You are just Consciousness. You are afflictionless. You are ever[1] the one undivided Essence. You are Brahman. There is no doubt of this.

[1]*eternally*

19. You are of the nature of the substratum of all. You are of the nature of the light of all. You are devoid of all differences of meaning. You are Brahman. There is no doubt of this.

20. Indeed, you are Brahman, devoid of differences and devoid of disturbance and such. You are peaceful.[1] You are devoid of differences. You are Brahman. There is no doubt of this.

[1]*śiva, Siva*

21. You are devoid of the term "exalted knowledge."[1] You perceive your own nature. You abide in your own nature. You are Brahman. There is no doubt of this.

[1]*prajñāna*

11

22. You are left with[1] your nature. You recognize only your nature. You are immersed in the waters of your own joy. You are Brahman. There is no doubt of this.

[1] *remain as*

23. You alone exist in the kingdom of your Self. You bow only to your own Self. You are of the nature that is full.[1] You are Brahman. There is no doubt of this.

[1] *is your own perfect fullness*

24. Rooted in your own joy, you are yourself. You do not perceive anything outside yourself. In your Self you shine and are like space. You are Brahman. There is no doubt of this.

25. You do not swerve from your nature. You do not perceive anything outside your nature. You, in your own nature, are nectar. You are Brahman. There is no doubt of this.

26. You shine with your own nature. You blossom with your own nature. You are no different from[1] your own nature. You are Brahman. There is no doubt of this.

[1] *not other than*

27. You are ever yourself. You see yourself everywhere. You enjoy yourself in yourself. You are Brahman. There is no doubt of this.

28. Suta:
Then, pleased with the words of Nidagha, Ribhu, beloved son of the lotus-born Brahma, looking at him, a fit person (vessel) fully qualified for the essence of the love of Siva, continued to instruct him.

29. Ribhu:
Once, on Mount Kailasa, Sankara instructed his son. I shall tell you the same. Listen with an attentive mind.

30. This phenomenal world does not exist, indeed. It never was created; nor does it ever exist by itself. This has been called the world-picture; it is ever unreal.

31. The phenomenal world never exists; nor do thought and such; nor does the ego or an individual soul exist. There being only Brahman alone, these are unreal—ever unreal.

32. There are no effects of delusion[1] and such. There is no fear of the effects of delusion.[1] There being only Brahman, these are unreal, indeed, ever unreal.

[1]*māyā*

33. There is no doer; there is no action; there is nothing to be done, son! There being only Brahman, these are unreal, indeed, ever unreal.

34. There is no "one"; there is no "two." There is no mantra, no tantra or anything else like these. There being only Brahman, these are unreal, unreal, ever unreal.

35. There is no sravana (listening) or manana (reflection); nidhidyasana (profound meditation) is a misapprehension. There being only Brahman, all these are unreal, indeed, ever unreal.

36. The two types of samadhi (absorption in meditation; savikalpa and nirvikalpa) do not exist. The measure and the measurement do not exist. There being only Brahman, all these are unreal, indeed, ever unreal.

37. Indeed, ignorance does not exist. Lack of discrimination also does not exist. There being only Brahman, all these are unreal, indeed, ever unreal.

38. The tetrad of related adjuncts that follow does not exist, and, indeed, the triad of connections does not exist. There being only Brahman, all these are unreal, indeed, ever unreal.

39. There are no such things as the past and the future any-where. Indeed, there is no such thing as the present any-where. There being only Brahman, all these are unreal, indeed, ever unreal.

40. The words indicating[1] the Ganga (a holy river), Gaya (a holy center) and, likewise, for Sethu (land's end in the south of India), or anything else do not exist. There being only Brahman, these are unreal, indeed, ever unreal.

[1] The vows and religious observances pertaining to

41. There is no earth, no water, no fire, no air, no space any-where. There being only Brahman, these are unreal, indeed, ever unreal.

42. There are, indeed, no gods, no guardians of the directions, no father, and no guru at any time. There being only Brah-man, these are all unreal, indeed, ever unreal

43. There is nothing afar or near, no end, no middle, nor is there any other state at any time. There is no nonduality, no duality, no truth, no untruth, nor is there anything [to be pointed out] as "this."

44. There is no liberation, and there is no bondage. Indeed, there is no word[1] or time,[2] at any time, in the least. There is no reality and no unreality, nor is there a [state of] happiness.[3]

[1] account [2] favorable moment; [3] nor are there joys

45. There are no pairs of opposites, nor is there any non-Self[1] at any time. There are no duties relating to holy waters and such, no growth, no generation, no death, nor the mis-apprehension of coming and going.

[1] "Self and non-Self"

46. There is no here, nor is there hereafter.[1] There is no guru, no disciple, no reality, no unreality, no existence, no action to perform, and no action performed.

[1]*beyond*

47. There is no community,[1] no refuge, no caste, and nothing customary. Indeed, there is no sextet of sama and others, no niyama (physical and mental regulations), and no yama (ethical restraints) either.

[1]*birth, position*

48. There is no such thing as "All is illusion" or "All is [as] Brahman." Indeed, there is nothing "as Consciousness." There is no such thing to be spoken of as "I am Consciousness."

49. Indeed, nothing as "I" exists; there is never anything as "I am eternal." There being only Brahman, all these are unreal, indeed, ever[1] unreal.

[1]*entirely*

50. Whatever is spoken through words, whatever is thought of by the mind or determined by the intellect, and whatever is known by thought,

51. what is united by yoga, what is done by the senses and others, and the waking, dream, and deep sleep states, and the fourth state—

52. all these do not exist. It is to be known that all these are determined by conditionings.[1] Never is purity achieved by ablutions, never is purity achieved by contemplation.[2]

[1]*upādhi* [2]*dhyānāt, by meditation*

53. The triad of guna-s (qualities) does not exist in the least; nor is there anything beyond the three guna-s. Words such as "one" and "two" do not exist. Great misapprehensions and delusions do not exist.

54. Fear[1] and absence of fear[1] are, indeed, not there. Be of the certitude that nothing in the least is there. There being only[2] Brahman, nothing else remains.

[1]*bhrānti, wandering, perplexity, error* [2]*kevalaṁ*

55. Whoever hears [and understands] this well becomes Brahman himself.

56. Isvara:
Like bubbles arising on the waters of the ocean, gods and men and beasts of the phenomenal world arose, and will arise again and again, on the waters of the mass of solid Bliss (ghana ananda) in the Consort of Uma (Siva). There is no worldly misery for those who, through their experience, perceive all this arising out of the waves of delusion clearly as myself.

57. Because of delusion, people do not realize Hara to be known as the cause of every little thing and as the cause of every being and also as the boundless cause of even greater dissolution. When the presence of the Consort of Uma (Siva) shines in the reflecting pool of the recesses of the space of the heart, like the revered of birds (garuda), the destruction of the serpent of mundane misery results.

Chapter Three

prapañcasya saccinmayatva-kathanam
DESCRIPTION OF THE PHENOMENAL WORLD
BEING EXISTENCE-CONSCIOUSNESS

Isvara:
Religious vows are illusory. The worlds are illusory. Various states are illusory. Abodes are illusory. Fear, also, is illusory. Supports and such are illusory. Enjoyment is illusory. The multitude of relationships is illusory.

2. The Vedas, also, are illusory. Speech is illusory. Sentences are illusory. The manifold is illusory. Wealth[1] is illusory. Sky and other such [elements] are illusory. The moon is illusory. All things are illusory.

[1]*vittāni, great quantity, variety*

3. The guru, also, is illusory. Good qualities and defects, as well, are both illusory. What is secret is illusory. Counting is illusory. To speak articulately is illusory. Going is illusory. What is traversed is illusory. All are illusory.

4. The Vedas, scriptures, legendary lore,[1] and, likewise, cause and effect, Isvara, the world, the elements, sentient beings, people, and all, indeed, are illusory. There is no doubt of this.

[1]*purāṇam*

5. Bondage, liberation, happiness, sorrow, meditation, thought, gods and demons, the secondary, the principal, the highest, and the separate[1] are all illusory. There is no doubt of this.

[1]*other*

6. Whatever is uttered by words is entirely illusory. There is no doubt of this. So, also, is whatever is imagined by sankalpa or thought of by the mind.

7. What little is decided by the intellect, what little is led along by thought, and whatever there is in this quintuplicated world are all illusory. This is certain.

8. Whatever is heard by the ears and observed by the eyes, the eyes themselves, the ears, and the body are all illusory, indeed. There is no doubt of this.

9. Whatever is pointed out as "this" or imagined as "this"— whatever object is thus known—all is illusory. There is no doubt of this.

10. "Who am I?" "What is that or this?" "I am He." These and other such sentences are unreal. Whatever happens in this world is all illusory. There is no doubt of this.

11. All that is to be practiced, all that is to be kept secret, and all causes are illusory. The term "all beings" is also illusory. There is no doubt of this.

12. All differences and differentiations and all sankalpa-s are illusory. All defects and their differentiation are entirely illusory. There is no doubt of this.

13. "The protector is Vishnu," "Brahma is the cause of creation," "Siva is the destroyer," and other such statements— all these [concepts] are illusory. There is no doubt of this.

14. Ablutions, prayer, penance,[1] fire oblations, daily studies, worship of deities, incantations, lineage, and good company,[2] are all illusory. There is no doubt of this.

[1]*japastapo* [2]*satsaṅgaḥ*

15. All is illusory. The world[1] is illusory. Likewise are the past, present, and future illusory. Any particular attitude of mind is unreal, utterly unreal. All is illusory. There is no doubt of this.

[1]*jagat, universe*

16. Differentiation in thought and differentiation of the world[1] are entirely effects of ignorance. The several millions of universes are all Brahman. Be of this certitude.

[1]*jagat, universe*

17. All the good in all three worlds, the development of good and bad qualities, and the wise words[1] of all the gurus[2] are all Brahman. Be of this certitude.

[1]*sayings* [2]*deśika, spiritual guide, spiritual teacher*

18. The sublime and the vile, the best and the mediocre, the sacred Omkara (the letters or sound of Om), and "a" the first letter, as well, are all Brahman. Be of this certitude.

19. Whatever appears in this world, whatever is observed in this world, and whatever exists in this world are all Brahman. Be of this certitude.

20. Whatever is said by whatever word, whatever is connected with whichever thing, and whatever is led by anybody—all that is Brahman. Be of this certitude.

21. Whatever is traversed by whomever, whatever is enjoyed by whomever, and whatever is told by whomever—all that is Brahman. Be of this certitude.

22. Whatever is given by whomever, whatever is done by whomever, and wherever there is a bath in holy water—all are Brahman. Be of this certitude.

23. Wherever there are good actions, wherever there are evil actions, and whatever you do sincerely—all that is illusory. Be of this certitude.

24. All this and all of myself are entirely Brahman. Be of this certitude. Whatever little is understood—all that is illusory. Be of this certitude.

25. Ribhu:
I shall tell you again the most secret of secrets, that which is extremely wonderful, which was told by Sankara to His son[1] on Mount Kailasa.

[1]kumāra, Kumāra

26. All the subtle senses (sight, sound, touch, taste, and smell) are all only Consciousness, ever the one undivided Essence. They are just Consciousness, which cannot be enumerated. All is only Consciousness, indeed.

27. All this, also, is only Consciousness. All is full of Consciousness. The reflection of oneself is, also, only Consciousness. All is full of Consciousness, indeed.

28. All the world, also, is only Consciousness. All is full of Consciousness only. Yours and mine, also, are only Consciousness. There is nothing besides Consciousness alone.

29. Space, earth, water, air, fire, Brahma, Hari, Siva, whatever little of these and whatever little of anything else there is are all but Consciousness.

30. All is the one undivided essence, which is only Consciousness. The past and the future are only Consciousness. All is full of Consciousness alone.

31. Substances and time are only Consciousness. Knowledge is full of Consciousness. The knowable and knowledge are, also, only Consciousness. All is full of Consciousness alone.

32. Conversation is only Consciousness. Indeed, words, also, are only Consciousness. The true and the false are only Consciousness. All is full of Consciousness.

33. The beginning and the end are only Consciousness. If a thing exists, it is always full of Consciousness alone. If there is Brahma, he is only Consciousness. Vishnu is only Consciousness, indeed.

34. Rudra and the deities, also, are only Consciousness. Likewise, men and beasts and the gods and demons, Guru and sishya (disciple), and conscious knowledge[1] are all only Consciousness, indeed.

[1]*Knowledge of Truth, Knowledge of only Being*

35. The seer and the seen are only Consciousness, as are the knower and the knowable and what is fixed and what is not fixed. All things wondrous are only Consciousness. The body is only Consciousness, indeed.

36. A linga is also only Consciousness. So, also, are cause and effect. Form and formlessness are also only Consciousness. So, also, are papa (demerit) and punya (merit).

37. Duality and nonduality are also only Consciousness. So, also, indeed, are the Vedas and Vedanta. The directions and the directionless are also only Consciousness. So, also, are the guardians of the directions.

38. All worldly interactions are only Consciousness. So, likewise, are the past, future, and present. Name and form are only Consciousness. So, also, are the beings and the worlds.

39. Prana (vital breath) is only Consciousness. All the senses are only Consciousness. The five sheaths and such are only Consciousness. Only Consciousness is spoken of as Bliss.

40. The eternal[1] and the ephemeral[2] are only Consciousness. All is only Consciousness, indeed. There is nothing eternal, save Consciousness. There is nothing real, save Consciousness.

[1]*nitya* [2]*anitya*

41. Dispassion, too, is only Consciousness. "This," indeed, is only Consciousness. All support is only Consciousness; likewise, all that is supported, O Rishi![1]

[1]*munīśvara*

42. Whatever and however much, whatever and whenever seen, is Consciousness. Whatever and however much is far out of reach is entirely only Consciousness.

43. Whatever beings there may be and however many of them there may be, whatever is spoken, whenever, and whatever and however much is said by the Vedas—all are only Consciousness, indeed.

44. There is no bondage, but only Consciousness. There is, then, no liberation, but only Consciousness. Just Consciousness is the only Reality. This is the Truth, the Truth, I say in the name of[1] Siva.

[1]*spṛśe, I touch, hold, attain to, describe*

45. All that is said by the three Vedas is only Consciousness, indeed. This was said to Kumara (Skanda) by Siva, and this has been told to you. Whoever hears this even once, he himself becomes Brahman.

46. Suta:
Internally I shall perform worship to the One whose body is space by "Isavasya" and other mantras, by offering a seat and garments and praise, offering worship to the Isana linga for the Supreme One, the Great, who is established in the midst of the primal cosmos, anointing one who cannot be wetted, offering garments to one who is clothed in space, offering sweet smelling flowers to the One who is without nose or smell or form or appearance,

47. offering lamps to One who is self-illumined, offering naivedya (consecrated cooked food) to one who is the ever-satisfied all-devourer, with circumambulations and prostrations to the One who strides over the worlds. In this, my authority is, indeed, the crest of the Vedas.

48. Those who know not offer worship by means of an endless parade of symbolism and with a mind set on rituals. Those who know, however, worship inwardly, in abstract meditation, their minds attuned to the prescribed injunctions. Yet, Isvara, though continuing to confuse the world, takes into His abode all who worship with various bhava-s and makes them transcendent in Knowledge.

svātma-nirūpaṇam
DEFINITION OF ONE'S SELF

Ribhu:
I shall tell you that which is most wondrous, that which is the rarest in all the worlds. It is the quintessence of the Vedas and other scriptures. Rare, rare, indeed, ever.

2. Mantra is one undivided Essence. Its result is one undivided Essence. The individual soul is one undivided Essence. Religious rite is one undivided Essence.

3. Earth is one undivided Essence. Water is one undivided Essence. Scent is one undivided Essence. The sky[1] is one undivided Essence.

[1]air

4. Scriptures are one undivided Essence. The Vedas are one undivided Essence. Brahman is one undivided Essence. Religious vows are one undivided Essence.

5. Vishnu is one undivided Essence. Siva is one undivided Essence. Brahma is one undivided Essence. The gods are one undivided Essence.

6. All is one undivided Essence. Oneself is one undivided Essence. The Self, also, is one undivided Essence. The guru is one undivided Essence.

7. Whatever can be spoken of is one undivided Essence. Light is one undivided Essence. The body is one undivided Essence. The mind is one undivided Essence.

8. Thought is one undivided Essence. Joy is one undivided Essence. Knowledge is one undivided Essence. The changeless is one undivided Essence.

9. Eternality is one undivided Essence. The Supreme is one undivided Essence. The trivial is from one undivided Essence. I am from one undivided Essence.

10. Either the one undivided Essence exists, or the one undivided Essence does not exist, and whatever is separate is from the one undivided Essence. The highest is from the one undivided Essence.

11. The gross is from the one undivided Essence. People are the one undivided Essence. The subtle is the one undivided Essence. The dyad is one undivided Essence.

12. What is nonexistent is one undivided Essence. Strength is one undivided Essence. Vishnu is from one undivided Essence. The atom is from one undivided Essence.

13. What is nonexistent is one undivided Essence. You are from one undivided Essence. Indeed, there is only one undivided Essence. All this is from the one undivided Essence.

14. Knowledge is from the one undivided Essence. Existence[1] is from one undivided Essence. Dissolution is one undivided Essence. The father is one undivided Essence.

[1]*sthitam*

15. Devotees are one undivided Essence. The husband[1] is one undivided Essence. The mother is one undivided Essence. Virat is one undivided Essence.

[1]*patih, Lord*

16. The body is one undivided Essence. The head is one undivided Essence. The nose is one undivided Essence. The exterior is one undivided Essence.

17. The perfectly full is one undivided Essence. The immortal is one undivided Essence. The ear is one undivided Essence. The home is one undivided Essence.

18. What is to be kept secret is one undivided Essence. Siva is one undivided Essence. Name is one undivided Essence. The sun is one undivided Essence.

19. The moon is one undivided Essence. The guru is one undivided Essence. The witness is one undivided Essence. The friend[1] is one undivided Essence.

[1] *suhṛt, good-hearted*

20. The relative is one undivided Essence. I am one undivided Essence. The king is one undivided Essence. The city is one undivided Essence.

21. Lordship[1] is one undivided Essence. The Lord[2] is one undivided Essence. Mantra is one undivided Essence. Japa is one undivided Essence.

[1] *aiśvaryaṁ* [2] *prabhuḥ*

22. Contemplation[1] is one undivided Essence. An abode[2] is one undivided Essence. What is to be grasped is one undivided Essence. What is great is one undivided Essence.

[1] *dhyānam, meditation* [2] *padam*

23. Light is one undivided Essence. The transcendental[1] is one undivided Essence. The consumable is one undivided Essence. The oblation is one undivided Essence.

[1] *param, absolute*

24. The homa (oblation by pouring clarified butter and such into a consecrated fire) is one undivided Essence. Victory is one undivided Essence. Heaven is one undivided Essence. Oneself is one undivided Essence.

25. There is nothing apart from the nature of the one undivided Essence—ever, at any time. Hear again the wondrous treasure[1] of the eternal Experience,[2]

[1]*great wonder* [2]*anubhava-sampadam, attainment, perfection, Being, complete*

26. so very rare—so rare to come by in all the worlds, the rarest, indeed. I am. I am the transcendent.[1] I am the luminous; I am the illuminator.

[1]*param̐*

27. I am the guru of all forms; I am [of] all forms. Such a one am I.[1] I am myself. I am pure. I am the magnificent. I am the Supreme.

[1]*so'smyaham̐, That am I*

28. I am. I am ever the knower. I am the Truth. I am blemishless. I am the empirical knowledge.[1] I am special. I am the common.[2] I am all.

[1]*vijñāna, awareness* [2]*equal, the same*

29. I am pure. I am without sorrow. I am Consciousness. I am equanimous. I am devoid of honor and dishonor. I am without attributes. I am Siva.

30. I am without [the concepts of] duality or nonduality. I am without the pairs of opposites. Such a one am I.[1] I am without existence or absence of existence. I am without language. Such a one am I.[1]

[1]*so'smyaham̐, That am I*

31. I am of the nature of[1] the void and the absence of the void. I am the auspicious. I am the mind. I am without equality or inequality. I am, and I am not of the nature of the trivial.

[1] *the power over, excelling, the origin of*

32. I am ever devoid of all. I am the amiable.[1] I ever am. I am devoid of numbers like one; nor have I a number like two or a second.[2] I am not.

[1] *sātvikaḥ, endowed with sattva, genuine, natural* [2] *The number two is not*

33. I am without differences of reality and unreality. I am without volition.[1] I am without the difference of multiple selves. What is nonexistent in the least, that am I.[2]

[1] *saṅkalpa, concept* [2] *I am without the difference of multiple selves, which does not exist in the least. That am I*

34. I am not myself;[1] nor am I another. I am without the body and such. I am without a refuge or a substratum. I am without support.

[1] *"I"*

35. I am without bondage, liberation, or any other [state]. I am He, the pure Brahman, and such. I am without a mind and all. I am the highest. I am the Supreme.

36. I am ever of the nature of inquiry. I am without anything into which to inquire. Such a one am I.[1] I am of the nature of the letter "a"; I am the letter "u" and the others.[2] I am joyous.

[1] *so'smyaham, That am I.* [2] *I am of the nature of the letter "a" and such; I am the letter "u."*

37. I am without contemplation[1] and without the absence of contemplation.[1] I am without anything upon which to contemplate. Such a one am I.[2] I am fuller than the full. I am perfectly full. I am all fullness. Such a one am I.[2]

[1]dhyāna, meditation [2]so'smyaham, That am I.

38. I am of the nature of that which transcends all. I am the Supreme Brahman. Such a one am I.[1] I have no objectivity or characteristics to perceive. I do not merge with anything.[2] Such a one am I.[1]

[1]so'smyaham, That am I. [2]I am without dissolution (laya).

39. I am without a measurement, and there is nothing that can measure me. There is nothing for me to measure. Such a one am I.[1] I am also the seer of the world.[2] I am without eyes or any other means [of perception].

[1]so'smyaham, That am I. [2]the entire universe

40. I am the fully-developed. I am the awakened. I am the ever-present.[1] I am the Supreme. I am bereft of all organs.[2] I am amenable to all actions.[3]

[1]prasanna, clear, bright, pure, gracious, favorable [2]senses [3]I am all wholesome, beneficial actions.

41. I am satisfied with all the Vedanta. I am ever easy of approach. I am joyous and joyless. I am the fruit of all silence.

42. I am ever of the nature of Consciousness alone. I am the real and the unreal and full of Consciousness. Of whatever I am devoid, nothing in the least has been grasped by me.

43. I am without the knot of the heart. From the Heart, I am all-pervasive; I am devoid of the six changes. I am without the six sheaths.

44. I am liberated from the group of six enemies. I am the inmost of the interior. I am without space or time. I am with the directions as my apparel (clothed in space).[1]

[1]*digambara-mukha.*

45. I am free from "is" and "is not." I am without the negative syllable "na" (in any attributes). I am of the nature of all that is only Consciousness. I am Existence-Consciousness-Bliss.

46. I am of the nature of the undivided; I am the undivided nature. I am the mind of the world of beings.[1] I am without any world of beings.[2]

[1]*prapañca-citta-rūpa* [2]*prapañca*

47. I am of the nature of all manner of forms. I am not without the nature of Existence. I am devoid of the triad of time (past, present, and future). I am without desire and other such [undesirable qualities].

48. I am liberated from the body and from being the possessor of the body. I am attributeless. I am without liberation; I am liberated; I am without [a concept of] liberation forever.

49. I am devoid of [the concepts of] reality and unreality. I am ever Reality alone. I am without any place to which to go. I am without movement.[1]

[1]*going*

50. I am ever of the nature of remembrance. I am peaceful. I am entirely acceptable and good. Thus, my own experience has been explained. This explanation is a superb one.[1]

[1]*mahat*

51. Whoever hears this even once becomes himself Brahman. Lord! With stout arms rivalling the trunk of an elephant, arisen to destroy the world born out of the microcosm! Wrencher of the head of Brahma! Glory to the Undivided, bearing in his arms the arrows and bow and serpents!

52. They reach the Realization of the Self, whose minds are merged with the Self of the universe, the Nondual, the Lord, Consort of Uma, of the nature of Light, of the nature of the formless, of the nature of the infinite. Others, with thoughts of differentiation, wearied by the burden of the idea of castes and asrama-s (stages of life), and other such things mentioned in the scriptures, devoid of peace, and lost in worldly matters, experience sorrow day after day.

Chapter Five

prapañca-śūnyatva-sarvanāstitva-nirūpaṇam
DETERMINATION OF THE PHENOMENAL WORLD BEING VOID AND THE NONEXISTENCE OF ALL

Ribhu:
I shall tell you about the world being void. It has been equated to the horns of a hare. This knowledge is rare in all the worlds. Listen with an attentive mind.

2. This phenomenal world, whatever little one hears or sees of it, the form that is seen, and the form of the seer are all like the horns of a hare.

3. Earth, water, fire, air, space, mind, intellect, ego, and light are all like the horns of a hare.

4. Destruction, creation, existence, the world, the galaxies, merit, demerit, victory, and delusion are all like the horns of a hare.

5. Desire, anger, greed, infatuation, pride, delusion, love, steadfastness, and guru, disciple, instruction, and such are all like the horns of a hare.

6. "I," "you," "the world," and all other such notions, the beginning, the end, and the middle, the past, the future, and the present are all like the horns of a hare.

7. The gross body, the subtle body, the cause and the effect, and what little there is of the seen and the seeing are all like the horns of a hare.

8. The enjoyer, the enjoyable, and the enjoyment, the primary and secondary meanings of a word,[1] nondifference[2] among these, tranquility, inquiry, and happiness[3] are all like the horns of a hare.

[1]indicated with characteristics, the aim and the indication
[2]advayam [3]santoṣaḥ

9. Yama (self-control), niyama (observances), pranayama (breath control) and other such terms, forward movement, oscillation,[1] and thinking are all like the horns of a hare.

[1]calanaṁ

10. The ears, eyes, body, lineage, what is to be kept secret, inertia, Hari, Siva, the beginning, the end, and the urge for liberation are all like the horns of a hare.

11. The organs of knowledge, the senses,[1] the group of organs of action, waking, dream, deep sleep, and any other such state are all like the horns of a hare.

[1]subtle elements

12. The tattva-s (twenty-four verities), the four means, similar categories, and dissimilar categories are all like the horns of a hare.

13. All the worlds, all the beings, all dharma-s with their philosophies, all learning,[1] and all ignorance[2] are all like the horns of a hare.

[1]vidyā [2]avidyā

14. All the castes, all the communities, all holy shrines and waters, all Vedas, and all scriptures are all like the horns of a hare.

15. All bondage, all liberation, all knowledge,[1] Isvara, all time, and all instruction[2] are all like the horns of a hare.

[1]vijñānam [2]bodha

16. All existence, all actions, all meetings with the wise (lit., great), and all duality are of the nature of unreality; all are like the horns of a hare.

17. All Vedanta, all determined conclusions,[1] all the definitions of scriptural meanings, and "the reality of all life"[2] are all like the horns of a hare.

[1] *siddhāntaḥ* [2] *all existence of individuality (jīvatva)*

18. Whatever little is known, whatever is seen in this world, and whatever you hear from the guru are all like the horns of a hare.

19. Whatever you contemplate upon in your thoughts, whatever is your sankalpa at any time, and whatever is decided upon by the intellect—all that is like the horns of a hare.

20. Whatever is brought out by words, whatever is explained by words, and whatever is sensed by all the sense organs are all like the horns of a hare.

21. Whatever object is renounced, whatever is heard or seen, and one's own or others are all like the horns of a hare.

22. Whatever manifests as an existence, whatever manifests as an object with an essence, and whatever is imagined in the mind are all like the horns of a hare.

23. Whatever is determined as the Self, whatever words are (considered to be) eternal, and whatever is inquired into in the mind are all like the horns of a hare.

24. Siva ever destroys, Vishnu protects the triad of worlds, and Brahma creates the worlds—all these concepts are like the horns of a hare.

25. What is said to be the soul,[1] whatever words are spoken, what the word transmigration[2] signifies—all are like the horns of a hare.

[1]*jīva* [2]*saṁsāra*

26. Whatever is in the Purana-s, whatever is defined in the Vedas, the stand of all the Upanishads—all are like the horns of a hare.

27. This explanation—"like the horns of a hare"—has been told to you. Whoever hears this secret becomes himself Brahman, indeed.

28. Hear further, Nidagha! It is certain that all is Brahman, good soul! This (Knowledge) is rare to come by for men and even for gods.

29. Whatever form is called "this," whatever, again, is "I," and what is seen as "this"—all is Brahman alone.

30. The sankalpa that I am the body—that itself is said to be fear. In all the triad of time, it is not so. All is Brahman alone.

31 . The sankalpa that I am the body—that is said[1] to be the inner senses[2] (mind, ego, and such). In all the triad of time, it is not so. All is Brahman alone.

[1]*smṛtam, thought* [2]*antaḥkaraṇaṁ*

32. The sankalpa that I am the body—that is said to be the cycle of birth and death.[1] In all the triad of time, it is not so. All is Brahman alone.

[1]*saṁsāra*

33. The sankalpa that I am the body—that is said, here, to be bondage. In all the triad of time, it is not so. All is Brahman alone.

34. The [false] understanding that I am the body—that is said[1] to be hell. In all the triad of time, it is not so. All is Brahman alone.

[1]*thought*

35. The sankalpa that I am the body—that is said to be all the phenomenal world.[1] In all the triad of time, it is not so. All is Brahman alone.

[1]*jagat*

36. The sankalpa that I am the body—that is said to be "the knot in the heart." In all the triad of time, it is not so. All is Brahman alone.

37. The sankalpa[1] of being the triad of bodies—that is said to be the knowledge of the body. In all the triad of time, it is not so. All is Brahman alone.

[1]*bhāvaṁ*

38. In all the triad of time, the sankalpa[1] that I am the body and, also, the idea of "reality and unreality" are not so. All is Brahman alone.

[1]*bhāvaṁ*

39. The sankalpa that I am the body—that is said, here, to be the manifest world. In all the triad of time, it is not so. All is Brahman alone.

40. The sankalpa that I am the body—that itself is said to be ignorance. In all the triad of time, it is not so. All is Brahman alone.

41. The intellectual conclusion that I am the body—that is said to be the tainted past impressions.[1] In all the triad of time, it is not so. All is Brahman alone.

[1]*vāsano, tendency*

42. The intellectual conclusion that I am the body—that is truly the individual soul,[1] indeed. In all the triad of time, it is not so. All is Brahman alone.

[1]*jīvaḥ*

43. The sankalpa that I am the body is spoken of as the great hell. In all the triad of time, it is not so. All is Brahman alone.

44. The intellectual conclusion that I am the body—that is certainly the mind only. In all the triad of time, it is not so. All is Brahman alone.

45. The intellectual conclusion that I am the body—that is spoken of as delimitation. In all the triad of time, it is not so. All is Brahman alone.

46. The [false] understanding that I am the body—that is spoken of as all sorrow. In all the triad of time, it is not so. All is Brahman alone.

47. The [false] understanding that I am the body—that is said to be the conflict.[1] In all the triad of time, it is not so. All is Brahman alone.

[1]*toil of saṁsāra*

48. The intellectual conclusion that I am the body—that itself is understood to be death. In all the triad of time, it is not so. All is Brahman alone.

49. The intellectual conclusion that I am the body—that itself is understood to be the inauspicious. In all the triad of time, it is not so. All is Brahman alone.

50. The intellectual conclusion that I am the body—that itself is understood to be a great sin. In all the triad of time, it is not so. All is Brahman alone.

51. The intellectual conclusion that I am the body—that itself is said to be a great prejudiced conception.[1] In all the triad of time, it is not so. All is Brahman alone.

[1] *tuṣṭā (satisfaction), perhaps an error for duṣṭa, wrong, fault, corruption*

52. The sankalpa that I am the body—that itself is understood to be all defects. In all the triad of time, it is not so. All is Brahman alone.

53. The sankalpa that I am the body—that itself is said to be the blemish. In all the triad of time, it is not so. All is Brahman alone.

54. The sankalpa that I am the body—that itself is said to be the great uncertainty.[1] In all the triad of time, it is not so. All is Brahman alone.

[1] *doubt*

55. Whatever little there is of thought is sorrow. Whatever little there is of thought is the world. Whatever little there is of thought is desire. Whatever little there is of thought is a blemish.

56. Whatever little there is of remembrance of sin, whatever little of thought there is about the mind, what little sankalpa there is, is said to be the great disease.

57. What little sankalpa there is, is said to be the great delusion. What little sankalpa there is, is given as the example of the triad of afflictions.

58. What little sankalpa there is, is said to be craving and anger. What little sankalpa there is, is said to be[1] attachment, nothing else.

[1] *is*

59. What little sankalpa there is, is all sorrow, nothing else. What little sankalpa there is, is a misapprehension about the reality of the world.

60. What little sankalpa there is, is a great defect, nothing else. What little sankalpa there is, is said to be the triad of time.

61. What little sankalpa there is, is said to be the multiplicity of forms. Wherever there is sankalpa, there is the great world.[1]
[1]*jagat, universe*

62. Wherever there is sankalpa, there is unreality, indeed. What little sankalpa is there is the phenomenal world.[1] There is no doubt of this.
[1]*jagat*

63. What little sankalpa is there, all that does not exist. There is no doubt of this. The mind only is all the world. The mind itself is the great enemy.

64. The mind only is itself transmigration.[1] The mind, itself, is the triad of worlds. The mind, itself, is the great sorrow. The mind, itself, is old age and others.
[1]*saṁsāra*

65. The mind only is itself time. The mind only is itself the blemish, ever. The mind, itself, is sankalpa. The mind, itself, is the basis of the individual soul.[1]
[1]*jīvakaḥ, living being*

66. The mind only is itself the pollution, always. The mind, itself, is marvelous magic.[1] The mind, itself, is the great illusion.[2] The mind is like the son of a barren woman.
[1]*Indra's net* [2]*sadā mithyā, ever false*

67. The mind, itself, does not exist, ever. The mind, itself, is ever inert. The mind, itself, is thought, and the mind, itself, is the ego.

68. The mind, itself, is the great bondage. Sometimes, the mind, itself, is antahkarana (the inner faculty). The mind, itself, is the earth, also. The mind, itself, is water.

69. The mind, itself, is fire. The mind, itself, is the great air. The mind, itself, is space, also. The mind, itself, is what produces sound.[1]

[1] śabdakaḥ

70. The mind, itself, is of the nature of touch. The mind, itself, is what creates forms.[1] The mind, itself, is of the nature of taste. The mind, itself, is said to be smell.

[1] rūpakam

71. The sheath of food (the physical body) is of the nature of the mind. The sheath of prana-s (vital airs) is of the nature of the mind. The sheath of mind is of the nature of the mind. Empirical knowledge[1] also is of the nature of the mind.

[1] vijñānam, intellect, awareness

72. The mind, itself, is the sheath of bliss. The mind is the waking state, the mind, itself, is the dream state, and the mind, itself, is the deep sleep state.

73. The mind is the gods and the others. The mind is Yama (god of death) and others. The mind, itself, is what little there is. The mind, itself, is pervaded by[1] the mind.

[1] composed of

74. This universe is filled with the mind. This body is filled with the mind. Whatever has happened and whatever seems to exist is filled with the mind.[1] This duality is filled with the mind.

[1] manomayam

75. This identification as a category is filled with the mind. This attribute is filled with the mind. This which is seen is filled with the mind. This insentience[1] is filled with the mind.

[1] jadam

76. Whatever is, is filled with the mind. The mind appears[1] as the individual soul.[2] Ignorance is due only to sankalpa. Difference is due only to sankalpa, certainly.

[1]sthitam, stands [2]jīva

77. Empirical knowledge[1] is only sankalpa. The pairs of opposites are only sankalpa, indeed. Time, also, is only sankalpa. Space[2] is only sankalpa.

[1]vijñānam, intellect, awareness [2]place

78. The body is only a sankalpa and prana (the life force) is only sankalpa. Reflection is only sankalpa. Listening is ever only sankalpa.

79. Hell is only a sankalpa. Heaven, also, is only a sankalpa. "Only Consciousness" is only a sankalpa, indeed. The thought of the Self is also only a sankalpa.

80. Whether it is the sankalpa of trivial entities or the sankalpa about Brahman, what little of sankalpa there is, is nonexistent at any time.

81. Sankalpa is unreal, unreal, indeed. The triad of worlds is unreal, unreal. The guru is unreal, unreal. The sishya is unreal, also, in fact.

82. The body also is unreal, unreal. The mind does not exist, does not exist, ever. The trivial does not exist, does not exist either. The entire world[1] does not exist, does not exist.

[1]jagat, universe

83. Beings do not exist, do not exist, either. All is nonexistent; there is no doubt about this. Nidagha! That all is nonexistent has been said by me in this discussion. Whoever hears this even once, he himself becomes Brahman, indeed.[1]

[1]alone

84. The peace, which the mind can attain by Vedanta, by the love of the lotus feet of the Lord with the crest of the crescent moon, by the liberation of oneself from the forest of (attachment to) the beloved wife and sons and others by renunciation, and by meditation just once on the feet of Siva, cannot be obtained by vociferous disputation and sophistry.

85. For the seers who have become liberated from the endlessly appearing objects that are seen, who are ever established without any sankalpa, there are no states of waking, dream, and deep sleep and no life and no death.

Chapter Six

ahaṁ-brahmāsmi-prakaraṇa-nirūpaṇam
THE CHAPTER OF THE DETERMINATION OF "I AM BRAHMAN"

Nidagha:
Exalted Guru! Where do you have your ablution? What is the mantra for ablution? What is the appropriate time for ablution and for tarpana? Please tell me.

2. Ribhu:
The bath in the Self is the great ablution, the daily[1] ablution. None other is so. This, indeed, is the great ablution: the certitude that I am Brahman.

[1]*nitya, eternal*

3. I am of the nature[1] of the Supreme Brahman. I am the supreme Bliss. This, indeed, is the great ablution: the certitude that I am Brahman.

[1]*svarūpaḥ*

4. I am just[1] of the nature of Knowledge. I am only the Supreme alone. I am of the nature of peace alone. I am the immaculate.

[1]*kevalaṁ, alone*

5. I am only[1] of the nature of the eternal. I am the permanent alone. [All] this, indeed, is the Supreme Brahman. I am Brahman alone.

[1]*kevalaṁ*

43

6. I am simply[1] of the nature of all. I am the released.[2] I am. [All] this, indeed, is the Supreme Brahman. I am Brahman alone.

[1]kevalaṁ [2]tyaktaḥ

7. I am of the nature devoid of all. I am the space of Consciousness. I am. [All] this is, indeed, the Supreme Brahman. I am Brahman alone.

8. I am of the nature of [only] the fourth state alone. I am [only] of the nature that transcends the fourth state alone. [All] this is, indeed, the Supreme Brahman. I am Brahman alone.

9. I am ever of the nature of Consciousness. I am Existence-Consciousness-Bliss. [All] this is, indeed, the Supreme Brahman. I am Brahman alone.

10. I am of the nature of Kaivalya[1] (That which alone exists). I am ever of the nature of the pure. [All] this is, indeed, the Supreme Brahman. I am Brahman alone.

[1]kevalākāra

11. I am pure Knowledge alone. I am Kaivalya.[1] I am the Beloved. [All] this is, indeed, the Supreme Brahman. I am Brahman alone.

[1]kevalaḥ

12. I am only agitation-less.[1] I am. I am, indeed, of my own nature.[2] [All] this is, indeed, the Supreme Brahman. I am Brahman alone.

[1]nirvikalpaḥ, undifferentiated [2]svasvarūpaḥ, my own true nature

13. I am ever of the nature of satsang. I am ever the Supreme. [All] this is, indeed, the Supreme Brahman. I am Brahman alone.

14. I am ever certainly of one nature. I am ever happiness itself, nothing else. [All] this is, indeed, the Supreme Brahman. I am Brahman alone.

15. I am of the nature that has no limitations. I am endless Bliss. [All] this is, indeed, the Supreme Brahman. I am Brahman alone.

16. I am of the nature of true Bliss. I am the Supreme Consciousness-Bliss. [All] this is, indeed, the Supreme Brahman. I am Brahman alone.

17. I am of the nature of endless Bliss, beyond the range of speech and mind. [All] this is, indeed, the Supreme Brahman. I am Brahman alone.

18. I am of the nature of Brahman-Bliss. I am ever of the nature of Existence-Bliss, the real Bliss.[1] [All] this is, indeed, the Supreme Brahman. I am Brahman alone.

[1]*satyānandaḥ*

19. I am of the nature of the Self alone. I am full of the Bliss of the Self. [All] this is, indeed, the Supreme Brahman. I am Brahman alone.

20. I am of the nature of the radiance[1] of the Self. I am the essence of the light[2] of the Self. [All] this is, indeed, the Supreme Brahman. I am Brahman alone.

[1]*prakāśa, illumination* [2]*jyotiḥ*

21. I am without beginning, middle, or end. I am like the sky.[1] [All] this is, indeed, the Supreme Brahman. I am Brahman alone.

[1]*ākārasadṛśo, resemble form, perhaps should be ākāśasadṛśo, resemble space*

22. I am of the nature of eternal Existence. I am eternally liberated. This is ever so. [All] this is, indeed, the Supreme Brahman. I am Brahman alone.

23. I am of the nature that is ever complete. I am ever without a mind. [All] this is, indeed, the Supreme Brahman. I am Brahman alone.

24. I am of the nature of eternal Existence. I am eternal Liberation.[1] This is ever so. [All] this is, indeed, the Supreme Brahman. I am Brahman alone.

[1]*muktaḥ, liberated one*

25. I am ever of the nature of authoritative Knowledge.[1] I transcend everything, always. [All] this is, indeed, the Supreme Brahman. I am Brahman alone.

[1]*śabda, sound, correct expression, Om*

26. I am of the nature that transcends form. I am ever of the nature that is space-like. [All] this is, indeed, the Supreme Brahman. I am Brahman alone.

27. I am of the nature of the joy[1] of beings. I am the joy of language. [All] this is, indeed, the Supreme Brahman. I am Brahman alone.

[1]*ānanda*

28. I am of the nature that is the substratum of all. I am ever the mass of Consciousness. [All] this is, indeed, the Supreme Brahman. I am Brahman alone.

29. I am devoid of the attitude of having a body. I am, indeed, devoid of a mind. [All] this is, indeed, the Supreme Brahman. I am Brahman alone.

30. I am without any activities of the body. I am, indeed, the mantra, I, ever. [All] this is, indeed, the Supreme Brahman. I am Brahman alone.

31. I am devoid of all things to see. I am, indeed, of the nature that is [to be] seen. [All] this is, indeed, the Supreme Brahman. I am Brahman alone.

32. I am ever of the nature of the complete.[1] I am ever satisfied. [All] this is, indeed, the Supreme Brahman. I am Brahman alone.

[1] *pūrṇa, perfectly full*

33. This Brahman, is, indeed, all. I am Consciousness alone, indeed. [All] this is, indeed, the Supreme Brahman. I am Brahman alone.

34. I am, indeed, only myself.[1] Nothing else exists. [All] this is, indeed, the Supreme Brahman. I am Brahman alone.

[1] *I*

35. I am, indeed, the great Self. I am, indeed, the ultimate goal.[1] [All] this is, indeed, the Supreme Brahman. I am Brahman alone.

[1] *final end*

36. "I am, indeed, the great Void." This is the best mantra of all. [All] this is, indeed, the Supreme Brahman. I am Brahman alone.

37. I, indeed, manifest as if another. I, indeed, [manifest] as if the body. [All] this is, indeed, the Supreme Brahman. I am Brahman alone.

38. I also [manifest] as if the disciple. I [manifest] as if the triad of worlds. [All] this is, indeed, the Supreme Brahman. I am Brahman alone.

39. I transcend the triad of times. I am meditated upon[1] by the Vedas. [All] this is, indeed, the Supreme Brahman. I am Brahman alone.

[1] *honored, worshiped*

40. I have been implied[1] in the scriptures. I reside in the mind. [All] this is, indeed, the Supreme Brahman. I am Brahman alone.

[1] *ascertained*

41. Excluding me, there is nothing else. Excluding me, the earth does not exist. [All] this is, indeed, the Supreme Brahman. I am Brahman alone.

42. Excluding me, there is no water. This is the best mantra of all. [All] this is, indeed, the Supreme Brahman. I am Brahman alone.

43. I am Brahman. I am pure. I am always pure, ever. I am without qualities. I am without desires,[1] thus indeed. This is the best mantra of all.
[1]*motionless, indifferent*

44. I am of the nature of Hari, Brahma, and the others. I am also not any of these differentiations.[1] I am just Brahman alone. I am Kaivalya.[1] I am the unsurpassed.[2]
[1]*kevalaḥ* [2]*ajayaḥ, invincible*

45. I, myself, shine by myself, by myself alone, and not by anything else. I abide in myself. This is the best mantra of all. I, myself, enjoy myself. I, myself, revel in myself. I, myself, am my own Light. I, myself, revel in myself.

46. I, myself, revel in my own Self. I see only my own Self. I am happy in my own Self. This mantra, thus, is the best. I remain in my own Consciousness. I revel in joy in the realm of my Self. I am seated on the throne of my own Self. This is, thus, the best mantra.

47. Ever seeing the mantra of one's Self, ever exercising[1] the Knowledge of one's Self, the mantra "I-am-Brahman-I-am" will destroy [all] sins relating to oneself.
[1]*practicing*

48. The mantra "I-am-Brahman-I-am" will destroy the defect of duality. "I-am-Brahman-I-am" will destroy the sorrow of differentiation.

49. The mantra "I-am-Brahman-I-am" will destroy the disease of thought. The mantra "I-am-Brahman-I-am" will destroy the disease of intellect.

50. The mantra "I-am-Brahman-I-am" will destroy the disease of mental agony. The mantra "I-am-Brahman-I-am" will destroy all the worlds.[1]

[1]*world*

51. The mantra "I-am-Brahman-I-am" will destroy the defect of desire. The mantra "I-am-Brahman-I-am" will destroy the defect of anger.

52. The mantra "I-am-Brahman-I-am" will destroy the defect of conceptualizing.[1] The mantra "I-am-Brahman-I-am" will also destroy sankalpa.

[1]*cintā*

53. The mantra "I-am-Brahman-I-am" will destroy the sorrow pertaining to [all] this. The mantra "I-am-Brahman-I-am" will burn up the blemish of lack of discrimination.

54. The mantra "I-am-Brahman-I-am" will utterly destroy ignorance. The mantra "I-am-Brahman-I-am" will destroy millions of defects.

55. The mantra "I-am-Brahman-I-am" will do away with all rituals.[1] The mantra "I-am-Brahman-I-am" will destroy mistaken[2] [notions of] the body.

[1]*tantraṁ* [2]*defective*

56. The mantra "I-am-Brahman-I-am" will efface [the distinction of] the seen and the unseen. The mantra "I-am-Brahman-I-am" will reveal the Knowledge of the Self.

57. The mantra "I-am-Brahman-I-am" bestows success[1] in the realm of the Self. The mantra "I-am-Brahman-I-am" will destroy the unreality and such.

[1]*victory*

58. The mantra "I-am-Brahman-I-am" will destroy all else. The mantra "I-am-Brahman-I-am" will confer indescribable[1] joy.

[1]incomprehensible by logic

59. The mantra "I-am-Brahman-I-am" will remove the idea[1] of non-Self. The mantra "I-am-Brahman-I-am" confers the bliss of Knowledge.[1]

[1]jñāna

60. Completely abandoning all mantras, renouncing the seven million great mantras, which can only confer hundreds of millions of births, one should resort to[1] the japa [of this one mantra].

[1]completely practice

61. Immediately, one attains Liberation. There is no doubt of this for me. Thus, the explanation of the mantra has been told, the secret in all the millions of Vedas. Whoever hears this even once, becomes Brahman oneself.

62. That mind is fit for the supreme Liberation that is aware that He alone is the One who is the ever-blissful, the source of supreme joy, the permanent, from whom there is nothing apart, from whom have been born all the worlds,[1] who cannot be comprehended by words or the mind or the assemblage of senses or the body, who is indivisible, who is the physician for [the ills of] the world, and who is Isvara.

[1]jagat

Chapter Seven

brahma-tarpaṇātma-homākhya
prakaraṇa-dvaya-varṇanam
DESCRIPTION OF THE TWIN TOPICS OF TARPANA
TO BRAHMAN AND HOMA TO THE SELF

Nidagha! Listen to my words. I shall now explain to you the daily[1] tarpana (libation of water). This explanation is very difficult for men to come by[2] in all the scriptures.[3]

[1]nitya, eternal [2]rare [3]vedaśāstreṣu

2. The manifold universe does not, indeed, exist, ever; nor is there anything to be pointed out as "this." There is only Brahman, which is ever complete.[1] This is the tarpana to Brahman.

[1]pūrṇaṁ

3. I am Brahman with form, indeed. I am also Existence-Consciousness-Bliss. I am only a mass of Bliss. This is the tarpana to Brahman.

4. I am ever the complete[1] Void. I am ever full of the Bliss of the Self. I am of the nature[2] of the permanent and the impermanent. This is the tarpana to Brahman.

[1]entire [2]svarūpa

5. I am the space of Consciousness alone. I am ever the space of the Self. I am satisfied in the Self.[1] This is the tarpana to Brahman.

[1]ātmanā'tmani, by the Self in the Self

51

6. I cannot be counted by numbers such as one and so forth. I am formless. I am nondual. I am of the nature of the eternally pure. This is the tarpana to Brahman.

7. I am subtler than space. I am the absolutely nonexistent. I am of the nature of the all-illumined. This is the tarpana to Brahman.

8. I am of the nature of the Supreme Brahman. I am happiness—higher, lower, and all-inclusive.[1] I alone am of the nature of oblations.[2] I am devoid of the seer and the seen and the like.

[1]parāvara [2]satra: a type of yagna

9. I am not anything at all. I am, here, complete Silence.[1] I am of the nature of pure Liberation. This is the tarpana to Brahman.

[1]the silence of silence

10. I am of the nature of the all-blissful. I am ever of the nature of the Bliss of Knowledge. I alone am of the nature of empirical knowledge.[1] This is the tarpana to Brahman.

[1]vijñāna, awareness

11. All this is only Brahman. Nothing else exists anywhere, I affirm.[1] I am That, indeed; there is no doubt. This is the tarpana to Brahman.

[1]te śape, swear to you

12. A thing like "you," a thing like "that"—never, never is there any such thing. I am only pure Consciousness.[1] This is the tarpana to Brahman.

[1]caitanya

13. I am of the nature of Absolute[1] Nonexistence. I am, indeed, the highest of the high. I am myself happiness and nothing else. This is the tarpana to Brahman.

[1]total

14. "This is of the nature of gold"—there is no such thing at all, none whatsoever, I affirm.[1] I am of the nature of the Bliss without attributes. This is the tarpana to Brahman.

[1]*swear to you*

15. There being nothing for me to witness, I am never a witness, being only[1] of the nature of Brahman. This is the tarpana to Brahman.

[1]*kevalaṁ*

16. I am without distinguishing attributes, yet I am myself the one with name. I am myself non-delusion. This is the tarpana to Brahman.

17. I am of the nature devoid[1] of the senses. I am of the nature devoid[1] of all. I am devoid of bondage and liberation. This is the tarpana to Brahman.

[1]*of the nonexistence*

18. I am of the nature of the all-blissful. I am a mass of the all-blissful. I am eternal Consciousness alone. This is the tarpana to Brahman.

19. I am also beyond the range of words; words or the mind do not exist in the least. I am also Consciousness-Bliss. This is the tarpana to Brahman.

20. I am of the nature of fullness,[1] always. I am happiness, always. Always, I am of the nature that cannot be conceived. This is the tarpana to Brahman.

[1]*pūrṇa*

21. I am of the nature of satisfaction at all times. I am only all-bliss. I am of the nature of the complete Void. This is the tarpana to Brahman.

22. I am ever of the nature of myself. I am one who is supremely blissful. I, myself, am only one.[1] This is the tarpana to Brahman.

[1]*eka evāham-evāham*

23. I am free.[1] I am of the nature of Liberation.[2] I am the supreme, complete Silence. I am of the nature of complete Liberation.[3] This is the tarpana to Brahman.

[1]*muktaḥ* [2]*mokṣa* [3]*nirvāṇa*

24. I am ever of the nature of the Truth.[1] I am ever one who is of the turiya (the fourth state beyond waking, dream, and deep sleep). I am of the nature of turiyatita (transcending the fourth state). This is the tarpana to Brahman.

[1]*sat*

25. I am only Truth and Knowledge.[1] I am one who is only Truth[2] and Bliss. I am of the nature that is indeterminate.[3] This is the tarpana to Brahman.

[1]*true Knowledge* [2]*sat* [3]*nirvikalpa, undifferentiated*

26. I am, indeed, ever of the nature of the unborn. I am without desire.[1] I am untainted. I am of the nature of Brahman-Knowledge. This is the tarpana to Brahman.

[1]*motionless*

27. Tarpana to Brahman has thus been so told; this is my explanation. Whoever hears this even once, he himself becomes Brahman.

28. I shall now speak of the daily[1] homa. This is rare to come by in all the Vedas. This is nonduality, the meaning of all scriptures. Listen attentively.

[1]*nitya, eternal*

29. I am Brahman. I am pure. I am eternal. I am the Lord. I am of the nature of the meaning of the syllable Om. This is the very rare homa.

30. I am of the nature of the Supreme Self. I am full of the Supreme Bliss. I am of the nature of Consciousness-Bliss. This is the very rare homa.

31. I am of the nature of eternal Bliss. I am of the nature of the undefiled.[1] I am of the nature of Consciousness. This is the very rare homa.

[1]*stainless*

32. I am not, indeed, of the nature of anything, in the least. I am not myself,[1] nor am I he. I am of the nature that has no interaction.[2] This is the very rare homa.

[1]*I* [2]*is at leisure, is unoccupied*

33. I have no parts. I have no image.[1] I am neither the mind nor the senses, neither the intellect nor any misapprehension.[2] This is the very rare homa.

[1]*ābhāsaḥ, mere appearance* [2]*vikalpaḥ*

34. I am not of the nature of the body and such. I am free of the triads and such. I am not of the nature of wakefulness or dream. This is the very rare homa.

35. I have no listening, reflection, or one-pointed profound meditation;[1] nor do I have anything self-inspired.[2] This is the very rare homa.

[1]*Listening, reflection, or one-pointed profound meditation is not* [2]*svagataṁ, of own self*

36. The mind-stuff[1] is unreal. Intelligence[2] is unreal. Know the ego to be unreal. The triad of time is ever unreal.

[1]*manaḥsattā* [2]*buddhi*

37. Know the triad of guṇa-s to be unreal. This is the very rare homa.

38. Look upon[1] all that is heard as unreal. Look upon all the Veda-s as ever unreal. Look upon all philosophies[2] as unreal. This is the very rare homa.

[1]*Know* [2]*tatva*

39. Look upon the various forms as unreal. Look upon the variety of colors to be ever unreal. Look upon the variety of categories[1] to be unreal. This is the very rare homa.

[1]*jāti, births, castes*

40. Look upon all scriptural knowledge as unreal and all the Vedic knowledge and tapas (religious austerities) also as unreal. Look upon all holy waters as unreal. This is the very rare homa.

41. Look upon the Guru and the disciple as unreal; then look upon the teachings[1] of the Guru also as unreal. Look upon as unreal whatever[2] is an object of perception. This is the very rare homa.

[1]*mantra* [2]*that which*

42. Look upon all enjoyment as unreal. Whatever can be thought of is ever unreal. Look upon as unreal whatever is an object of perception. This is the very rare homa.

43. Look upon all the senses as unreal and also all mantras as unreal. Look upon all the prana-s as unreal. This is the very rare homa.

44. Look upon life[1] and the body as unreal. Certainly, there is nothing as such existing in the Supreme Brahman. Know all in me as unreal. This is the very rare homa.

[1]*jīva, the individual*

45. Look upon what is seen and heard as unreal. The warp and woof in me are unreal. All action and inaction are unreal. This is the very rare homa.

46. Look upon the power to see as unreal. So, too, is happiness[1] unreal. Look upon all actions as unreal. This is the very rare homa.

[1] being pleased, contented, satisfied

47. Look upon all and the absence of all as unreal. Look upon completeness[1] and incompleteness in the Supreme as unreal. Look upon happiness and misery as unreal. This is the very rare homa.

[1] pūrṇa

48. Look upon adherence to dharma as unreal. Look upon punya (merit due to good action) and the negation of it[1] as unreal. Look upon gain and loss as unreal. The body is ever unreal, ever.

[1] apuṇyam

49. Ever look upon success as ever unreal and the sense of pride as ever unreal. Look upon all that pertains to the mind as unreal. Likewise should you view doubt and certitude.

50. Look upon all sound as unreal and all touch as ever unreal. Look upon all forms as unreal and all taste as ever unreal.

51. Look upon all smell as unreal. Look upon all knowledge as ever unreal. Look upon past and future as unreal. Prakriti is said to be unreal.

52. All is ever unreal, indeed. Existence and creation[1] are unreal. All the guna-s are unreal. This is the very rare homa.

[1] udbhavam

53. You are like the horns of a hare, indeed. I am like the horns of a hare. [All] this is like the horns of a hare, indeed. The innermost is like the horns of a hare.

54. Thus the explanation of the homa of the Self has been told by me. Whoever hears this even once will himself become Brahman.

55. Skanda:
The universe, a happy aspect of Siva, wherein arises and dissolves all in entirety, wherein shine the sun and the moon, lightning, fire, the gods of wind, and water, worshipping Isvara with awe, wherein manifest the gods and demons and men and all that is imperceptible—none of these truly exist here. Nothing at all is here. Nothing is desirable but the contemplation of God.

56. That Siva who, though in the midst of the beings of the world, cannot be perceived in His subtlety and cannot be perceived by the variations of the breath of inhalation and exhalation (breath control), by thought, by reflection and intellect, by the fivefold concentrations of the mind and such, or by the hundreds of Vedic words provided by the intellect, can be better perceived from one wise word of the Guru by those filled with yoga and devotion, not otherwise.

Chapter Eight

jīvanmukta-prakaraṇam
TOPIC OF THE LIBERATED WHILE ALIVE

Ribhu:
I shall now explain the knowledge of Brahman and the characteristics of a jivanmukta. One who abides solely in the Self is called a jivanmukta.

2. I am the same as Brahman; I am the Self. There is no doubt of this. One who is firm in the conviction that I am Caitanya-Atma (the Consciousness-Self) is called a jivanmukta.

3. I am the Self, [which is] Consciousness.[1] I am Paramatman (the Supreme Self). I am attributeless. I am higher than the highest. One who has this certitude is called a jivanmukta.

[1]Cit

4. I am beyond the triad of bodies. I am Brahman, Consciousness. One whose final conclusion is that I am Brahman is called a jivanmukta.

5. I am of the nature of a mass of Bliss. I am higher than the highest Bliss. One whose mind[1] is thus all[2] bliss is called a jivanmukta.

[1]cid, Consciousness [2]para, supreme

6. He who has no body or such, who is certain that he is Brahman, and who is filled[1] with the highest Bliss is called a jivanmukta.

[1]*full*

7. He who has no trace of ego,[1] who abides only in Consciousness, who has the highest Bliss, and who revels in Bliss is called a jivanmukta.

[1]*ahaṁ, "I"*

8. He who is definite of being only Consciousness, who is of the nature of Consciousness alone, and who does not remember anything else is called a jivanmukta.

9. He who is ever satisfied[1] everywhere, who abides in the Self, comprehending the Self everywhere, and who is ever complete in the Self everywhere is called a jivanmukta.

[1]*perfectly full*

10. One ever absorbed in the Supreme Self, certain of being the Supreme Self, of the nature of Bliss, and unmanifest is called a jivanmukta.

11. One living in this pure beatitude alone, bereft of all attachments, as the Self ever present in Bliss is called a jivanmukta.

12. Of just one nature, the Self in peace, devoid of thoughts of anything being separate, such a one who does not, in the least, have anything, is called a jivanmukta.

13. I have no mind. I have no intelligence.[1] I have no ego. Nor do I have senses. One who is Brahman alone is called a jivanmukta.

[1]*buddhi*

14. I have no defects. I have no body. I have no prana. I have nothing, ever. Whoever firmly abides in this certitude within is called a jivanmukta.

15. I have no delusion. I have no desire. I have no anger. I am beyond [all] these. There is nothing here of mine. Such a one [who knows this] is called a jivanmukta.

16. Faults have I none. Characteristics have I none. Attachments[1] have I none. There is no world[2] for me. Such a one [who has realized this and] who eternally dwells in permanent Bliss is called a jivanmukta.

[1]bandha, bondage [2]jagat, universe

17. Ears I do not have; nose I do not have; eyes I do not have; tongue I do not have; a mind I do not have. He who is definite in this is called a jivanmukta.

18. I have no body. I have no distinguishing marks. I have no cause. I have no fourth state. He who is established in himself thus is called a jivanmukta.

19. All this is none of mine; all that is none of mine. One who is established thus in Brahman alone is called a jivanmukta.

20. There is not even a little of mine; there is nothing of mine. There is no world[1] for me—not a bit of it, ever. I am myself.[2] One who is thus established is called a jivanmukta.

[1]jagat [2]eva

21. I have no time. I have no space. I have no objects. I have no being.[1] There is no ablution or renunciation for me. Such a one is called a jivanmukta.

[1]sthitiḥ

22. For me there is no holy river, no god, no service (to a god), and no shrine. I am without the least difference. He who is so is called a jivanmukta.

23. I have no attachment.[1] I have no birth. I have no knowledge. I have no position.[2] I have no speech. He who so abides in himself is called a jivanmukta.
[1]*bandham* [2]*padam*

24. I have no punya (merit). I have no papa (sin). I have no body. I have nothing auspicious. I have nothing to see. Such a seer[1] is called a jivanmukta.
[1]*jñānī, knower*

25. I have no sound. I have no touch. I have no sight.[1] I have no taste.[2] I have no life.[3] One who realizes thus is called a jivanmukta.
[1]*rūpam, form* [2]*rasaḥ, essence* [3]*jīva, individual*

26. I have none of it all.[1] I have not the least of it. I have no life.[2] I have no [place] anywhere. I have no attitudes.[3] I have no possessions.[4] One who has realized thus is a jivanmukta.
[1]*I have none at all* [2]*jīvaṁ, individual* [3]*bhāvaṁ* [4]*vastu*

27. There is nothing in liberation for me. There is no duality for me, no Vedas for me, no scriptural injunctions for me, and no distance for me. One who thus abides in himself is a jivanmukta.

28. There is no guru for me, no disciple for me, no teaching for me, nothing higher for me, and no object is exalted[1] for me. Such a one is called a jivanmukta.
[1]*splendid*

29. For me there is no Brahma, no Vishnu, no Rudra, no Ravi (Sun). There are no actions[1] for me. There is nothing for me. One who has realized thus is called a jivanmukta.
[1]*karmaṁ*

30. For me there is no earth, no water, no light,[1] and no space.[2] There is no action for me. One who abides in himself thus is called a jivanmukta.
[1]*tejo* [2]*viyat, air*

31. There are no words for me, no sentences for me, no lineage for me, no race[1] for me, and no knowledge for me. One who abides in himself thus is called a jivanmukta.

[1]kulam, family

32. There is no audible sound for me, no inaudible sound (sabda and nada) for me, no ideal[1] for me, no future or worldly life for me, and no contemplation.[2] One who abides in himself thus is called a jivanmukta.

[1]lakśyam, aim, indirectly expressed [2]dhyānam, meditation

33. There is no cold for me, no heat for me, no delusion for me, no recitation of mantras[1] for me, and no dawn or dusk[2] for me. One who abides in himself thus is called a jivanmukta.

[1]japa [2]sandhya

34. There is no muttering of mantras[1] for me, no mantras at all for me, no homa-s for me, no night for me—none of all [this] for me. One who abides in himself thus is called a jivanmukta.

[1]japa

35. There is no fear for me, also no food for me, no thirst for me, and no hunger for me. There is also no self for me. One who abides in himself thus is called a jivanmukta.

36. There is no front for me, no rear for me, and there is nothing above me. There are no directions for me. There is no mind of mine.[1] One who abides in himself thus is called a jivanmukta.

[1]for me

37. There is nothing in the least that I have to say. There is not a whisper that I have to hear. There is nothing ever so little to be thought of by me. One who is thus is called a jivanmukta.

38. There is nothing in the least to be experienced by me. There is not even an atom to be contemplated upon by me, nor is there anything to be remembered by me. One who is thus is called a jivanmukta.

39. There is no enjoyment for me. There is no sickness for me. There is no yoga for me. There is no dissolution for me. There are none at all for me. One who abides in himself thus is called a jivanmukta.

40. There is no existence[1] for me. There is no birth for me; there is no aging for me; there is no decay for me. There is no superimposition for me. One who abides in himself thus is called a jivanmukta.

[1]*astitvaṁ*

41. Superimposing is not at all for me. Refutation is not at all for me. There is nothing at all of "I"[1] for me. One who is thus is called a jivanmukta.

[1]*ahaṁ*

42. There is no purity for me. There is no shining for me, nor is there one or many for me. There is no past for me, nor any actions. One who is thus is called a jivanmukta.

43. "Who am I?" is not for me. "This" is not for me. "Not another" is not for me. "Oneself" is not for me. There is nothing at all for me—none at all. One who abides in himself thus is called a jivanmukta.

44. Neither flesh, nor blood, nor marrow, nor excrement, nor bone exist for me. One who abides in himself thus is called a jivanmukta.

45. There is nothing of all for me. There is neither white nor blue, nor is there anything separate for me. One who abides in himself, by himself, thus is called a jivanmukta.

46. There is no longing[1] for me, no covetousness for me, no indirect or metaphorical meaning for me, no fame for me, and no philosophy[2] for me. One who abides in himself thus is called a jivanmukta.

[1] tāpaṁ [2] tattva

47. There is no mistaken notion for me, no knowledge for me, nothing to be kept secret for me, no lineage for me—nothing at all for me. Contemplating[1] thus, one is called a jivanmukta.

[1] Meditating

48. There is nothing I have to relinquish, nothing I have to grasp. There is nothing I have to laugh at for me. There is no dissolution, nor is there any god for me. One who abides in himself thus is called a jivanmukta.

49. There is no vow for me, no fatigue for me, no sorrow for me, and no happiness for me. Surely, there is nothing for me. Such a one is called a jivanmukta.

50. There is neither knower nor knowledge nor anything to be known for me. There is nothing of mine for me. There is nothing at all.[1] Such a sage[2] is called a jivanmukta.

[1] There is no all for me [2] jñānī

51. For me there is no such thing as "to you" or "to me" or "from you" or "from me." There is no guru for me—not for me. Such a one is called a jivanmukta.

52. There is no lassitude[1] for me. There is no delirium[2] for me. There is no fatigue[3] for me. There is nothing good for me, either. One who is established in "not for me, not for me" is called a jivanmukta.

[1] jaḍam, inert [2] caityaṁ, individual soul [3] exhaustion

53. There is no lineage for me. There is no aphorism[1] for me. There is no status[2] for me. There is no compassion for me. There is nothing at all for me. One who contemplates[3] thus is called a jivanmukta.

[1]sūtram [2]competent person, master [3]meditates

54. There is no self for me, no non-Self for me. There is no heaven for me, no fruit for me, and there is nothing to be condemned[1] by me. Such a one is called a jivanmukta.

[1]dṛṣyam, visible for me, worth seeing by me

55. There is no practice for me. There is no learning[1] for me. There is no peace for me, no self-restraint for me, and no body for me. Such a sage[2] is called a jivanmukta.

[1]vidyā, knowledge [2]jñānī

56. There is no distress for me, no doubt[1] for me, no sleep for me, no mind for me, and no uncertainty[2] for me. One who has this conviction is called a jivanmukta.

[1]fear [2]vikalpa

57. No old age exists for me. No childhood exists for me. Not an atom of youthfulness exists for me. No death exists for me. No darkness exists for me. Such a one is called a jivanmukta.

58. Remembering that the world is not for me, nor its experiences—nothing of all this—such a one who has found that silence, also, is not for me is called a jivanmukta.

59. I am, indeed, Brahman. I am, indeed, Brahman. I am, indeed, Brahman. It is certain. I am Consciousness. I am Consciousness. One who is thus is called a jivanmukta.

60. I am Brahman. I am Consciousness. I am the highest, there is no doubt. I am myself the self-luminous. One who is thus is called a jivanmukta.

61. One who sees only himself in himself, who abides only in himself, and who exists only in his own Self is called a jivanmukta.

62. One who enjoys himself in the Bliss of his own Self, who resides in the domain of his own Self, and who sees himself in the domain of his own Self is called a jivanmukta.

63. I am myself the one-pointed. I am myself the Lord of myself. I perceive myself as of the nature of myself. One who is thus is called a jivanmukta.

64. The explanation of the jivanmukta is difficult[1] to come by in all the Vedas. Whoever hears this even once, himself becomes Brahman.

[1]*rare*

65. Those who, by the ideas of differentiation engendered by the arguments and injunctions of the Veda-s, emaciate themselves with their minds set on acquiring punya (merit) and inflict untold hardship on their bodies will at no time attain the happiness that flows from your feet, O Lord!

66. Who can cross this ocean of samsara (worldly existence) of the nature of successive waves of birth and death? One who is imbued with the meditation on Siva, well instructed in the modes of worship of Isvara, can alone make the crossing by the boat of the difference-less Knowledge.

Chapter Nine

videhamukti-prakaraṇa-varṇanam
DESCRIPTION OF THE TOPIC OF LIBERATION OUT OF THE BODY

Ribhu:
Hear, Nidagha, the rare explanation of the Liberation from the body. He is the videhamukta, indeed, who does not re-member whatever he has discarded and not discarded.

2. Of the nature of Brahman, the peaceful Self, without any form, ever blissful and abiding in himself in utter[1] Silence is the videhamukta.

[1]*great*

3. The Self of all, the Self of all beings, the Self in peace, with-out [a concept of] liberation, without "being the single Self, the witness [of all]" is the videhamukta.

4. The ideal Self, the beloved Self, am I—the Self which plays, just my own Self, fully the natural Self, the silent Self. He who is thus is the videhamukta.

5. I am myself the Self, the shining Self, the Self of all, just my own Self, the unborn Self, and the immortal Self. He who is thus is the videhamukta.

6. The blissful Self, one's own dear Self, the liberated Self,[1] and the settled[2] and thus one-pointed[3] is the videhamukta.

[1]*ko'pi, whoever is* [2]*certain* [3]*absorbed in meditation*

7. The one who does not think "I, indeed, am Brahman," "I, indeed, am Consciousness," or "I, indeed, am the One," and who remains purely as Consciousness is the videhamukta.

8. Leaving aside[1] even the certitude—the certitude that I am Brahman—and full of Bliss is the videhamukta.

[1]*completely abandoning*

9. Leaving aside any certainty that all is there or nothing is there and being established in "I am Brahman and I am none else"—such is the videhamukta.

10. He does not remember himself in the least, anywhere at any time. He who remains in his natural state is the videhamukta.

11. He has no thoughts of "I am the Self; another is the Self," or "I am the Self, which is Consciousness." He abides in the Knowledge that I alone remain. Such is the videhamukta.

12. Remaining silent, silent in all ways, silent in whatever, I am bereft of any purpose. Such is the videhamukta.

13. The Supreme Self, transcending the guna-s, not accepting even "the Self of all," and he who is the great Self in all ways is the videhamukta.

14. He who has no differences of time, of place, of object, and of oneself—no differences of whatever kind—is the videhamukta.

15. I, you, that, this, he, this [person]—none of this exists. I am only intense[1] Bliss. Such is the videhamukta.

[1]*complete*

16. Ever ascertained as the Self without qualities, the selfless, the eternal Self, the Self that is void, the subtle nature—he who is thus is the videhamukta.

17. The Self of all, the Self devoid of all, the Self of time, the cause of time, the Self of God, devoid of God—he who is thus is the videhamukta.

18. The Self that is a measure, the Self with nothing to measure, devoid of the ignorant self and non-Self, the Self alone, the Absolute Self—such is the videhamukta.

19. The Self, ever without insentience,[1] the inner Self of all and which is said to belong to all is the videhamukta.
[1]the inert

20. Bereft of all sankalpa and being just Existence-Consciousness-Bliss, he who does not conclude that he exists[1] is the videhamukta.
[1] "I abide"

21. All do not exist. Only That exists. Just Consciousness exists, ever. The enlightened one does not exist. He who is of this conclusion is the videhamukta.

22. Whoever is the Supreme Self alone, who is just an embodiment of Knowledge, and who is of the nature of Existence alone is the videhamukta.

23. Whoever has no conclusions regarding the individual soul,[1] Isvara, the universe,[2] the Vedas, the scriptures, you and me, and Brahman, indeed, is the videhamukta.
[1]jīva [2]caitya, sacred place, individual soul

24. I am Brahman alone. I am, indeed, all. Nothing else of the world exists. One who has this certitude is the videhamukta.

25. All this is Consciousness alone; I am only Consciousness, indeed. One who has such certitude is the videhamukta. (A variant manuscript reads: All this is Consciousness; I am only Consciousness. One who has no[1] such certitude is the videhamukta.)
[1]*is devoid of*
_____

26. Merged in[1] Consciousness alone, reposing in himself, and being established in happiness with only Bliss as his inner core is the videhamukta.
[1]*with*
_____

Alternative translation of verse 26:
Completely established as Consciousness alone, delighting in his own Self, seated in happiness, happiness alone the interior essence, is the videhamukta.

27. Of the nature of the limitless Self, spotless to the finest degree, transcending the fourth state, and in the highest Bliss is the videhamukta.

28. Without even a name, the Self of all, without form, not an atheist either, and existing as the Self of the nature of the Supreme Brahman—such is the videhamukta.

29. Transcending the fourth state, transcending himself, and transcending bondage, he is of the nature of Truth.[1] He is equanimous in[2] both the bad and the good. Such is the videhamukta.
[1]*sanmayaḥ,* [2]*at peace [with]*
_____

30. The Self that is utterly peaceful in bondage and liberation, the Self of all, the inner Self, the Self of the phenomenal universe, the Self of That is certainly the highest—such a one is the videhamukta.

31. The Self that is perfectly full everywhere, ever higher than the highest, the inner Self, the endless[1] Self—he who is thus is the videhamukta.

[1] *infinite*

32. The Self devoid of being ignorant or knowledgeable, without being sentient or insentient, and [without the concepts of] truth and untruth[1] is the videhamukta.

[1] *the Self of all the truth and untruth*

33. Immersed in meditation[1] and non-meditation,[2] devoid of being with a goal or being without a goal, the Self alone that is existent and nonexistent[3] is the videhamukta.

[1] *within samādhi* [2] *non-samādhi* [3] *full and not full*

34. The Self full of [all] Consciousness—the expanse[1] of Consciousness, the Bliss of Consciousness, clothed in Consciousness[2]—and the Self of the nature of Consciousness alone is the videhamukta.

[1] *space* [2] *cidambaraḥ*

35. The Self of the nature of Existence-Consciousness-Bliss, the embodiment[1] of Existence-Consciousness-Bliss, the Self full of Existence-Consciousness-Bliss is the videhamukta.

[1] *beautiful, fine form*

36. Ever of the nature of Brahman, ever remaining[1] in himself, and ever the one undivided Self is the videhamukta.

[1] *eternal, abiding*

37. The Self that is, indeed, a mass of Knowledge,[1] the embodiment[2] of a mass of Knowledge, ever supremely blissful in Knowledge is the videhamukta.

[1] *prajñāna* [2] *beautiful, fine form*

38. One who never has a body, for whom there is no remembrance of anything, the Sadatma (true Self) who is established in himself is the videhamukta.

39. He for whom the mind has been banished,[1] for whom the natural state[2] is the Self of Brahman, who is the Self of yoga, and who is the Self merged with yoga is the videha-mukta.

[1] *without the imaginings of the mind*   [2] *abidance*

40. He for whom all thought is cast aside, there being only Consciousness, and who is the end of the modification of qualities and absence of qualities is the videhamukta.

41. One who ultimately[1] has no time or place and such, nothing to be grasped, nothing else to be remembered, and who has also cast aside[2] all certitude is the videhamukta.

[1] *finally*   [2] *completely abandoned*

42. One who is devoid of worldly happiness, the bliss of the highest, and the happiness of enjoyment, who is the witness, and who is also without a witness is the videha-mukta.

43. He is also someone,[1] though he is not anyone. He is a little, a little; he is nothing. He is the Self, the non-Self, and the Self of Consciousness. He is Consciousness, and non-Consciousness, and also the "I."

[1] *anyone*

44. He for whom the phenomenal universe is non-Self, for whom even the nature of Brahman is not here, who is of his own nature, and who is self-illumined is the videhamukta.

45. In the Bliss beyond the range of words, devoid of all senses, and transcending the transcendent is the videha-mukta.

46. He who transcends the activities[1] of the mind, who is not the illuminator of the activities[1] of the mind, and who is de-void of all activities[1] is the videhamukta.

[1] *vṛtti-s*

47. He who has no remembrance of the body—neither the gross nor the subtle (body)—at the time of leaving the body is the videhamukta.

48. Ever devoid of everything, he who remains as the ever so little, who remains as Brahman alone, is the videhamukta.

49. The Supreme Brahman, the Supreme Bliss, the Supreme Self, higher than the highest, and with his interior or exterior unseen by others is the videhamukta.

50. He is the pure essence of Vedanta. He abides in the pure, true Self. He has discarded[1] that difference also. Such a one is the videhamukta.

[1]abandoned

51. Relishing the nectarean essence of Brahman, the immortal elixir of Brahman, and immersed in the nectarean essence of Brahman is the videhamukta.

52. With the nectarean essence of Brahman as his support, himself the nectarean essence of Brahman, and satisfied in the nectarean essence of Brahman is the videhamukta.

53. Blissful in the great[1] Bliss of Brahman, shining in the Bliss of Brahman, the great luminary[2] of the Bliss of Brahman is the videhamukta.

[1]supreme [2]Light

54. Blissful in the essence of the Bliss of Brahman, ever in the pause-less nectar of Brahman, blissful in Brahman, and always in Bliss is the videhamukta.

55. He who is the experience of Brahman-Bliss, who is the Bliss of the worship of Siva, and who is the Brahman nectar, which relishes the essence of Brahman-Bliss, is the videhamukta.

56. Elated in[1] the Bliss of Brahman, belonging to the "family of Brahman-nectar," and surrounded by[2] people in the Bliss of Brahman is the videhamukta.

[1]Married to [2]joined to, united with

57. Residing in the delectable Brahman-nectar, remaining in the temple of the Bliss of Brahman, and reciting constantly the mantra[1] of Brahman-Bliss is the videhamukta.

[1]japa

58. The end of whose body is the Bliss of Brahman, whose senses are the Bliss of Brahman, and whose Knowledge is that of the nectar of Brahman is the videhamukta.

59. Intoxicated in the Bliss of Brahman, brimming with the nectarean essence of Brahman, and ever established[1] in Brahman-Self is the videhamukta.

[1]self-abiding

60. This exposition of the Liberation from the body, rare in all the scriptures, has been told by me to you, great rishi![1] Liberation from the body will be [attained] by hearing this.

[1]mahāyogin

61. Skanda:
Lord of the helpless! I worship your feet. Be the Lord of my meditation. Lord of the night! Destroyer of Manmatha (Kama) by a spark of fire emanating from your forehead, which wears the moon as a crown! Lord of the Pramatha-s, be my savior!

62. Lord, with the body adorned with ashes! May the lotus of my mind ever attain the friendliness of the triad of your eyes by a momentary glance therefrom. Even the crest of the Vedas does not know the escape from the current of sorrow for the multitude of people confused by constant bondage.

Chapter Ten

sarvam-ātma-prakaraṇam

DESCRIPTION OF THE SELF BEING ALL

Ribhu:
Hear about the nature of the Self, rare to come by in [all] the world, the highest,[1] the essence of the essence. All this is of the nature of the Self. All is of the Self. Nothing else exists.

[1]*supreme*

2. All is the Self, the Supreme, the Supreme Self, of the nature of the highest, the Self of the nature of eternal Bliss. Certainly, nothing exists besides the Self.

3. The Self is great and of the nature of fullness. The Self is pure. It is of the nature of the eternal. The Self is changeless and blemishless. It is of the nature of the selfless.

4. The Self is of the nature of the peaceful and the peaceless. Certainly, nothing exists besides the Self. The individual self is the Supreme Self, indeed. It is of the nature of the mind[1] and no-mind. It is filled with[2] Consciousness. It is the One Self. It is the Self of a single nature. It is the manifold self. It is without a self.

[1]*citta* [2]*full of*

5. The Self is of the nature of the liberated and the unliberated. It is without liberation and non-liberation. The Self is of the nature of Liberation. Nothing exists besides the Self.

6. The Self is of the nature of the dual and the nondual, yet it is devoid of duality and nonduality. The Self of all is devoid of all. Nothing exists besides the Self.

7. The Self is of the nature of joy and joylessness. The Self is [of the nature of] Liberation. The Self is of the nature of the divine. The Self is of the essence of the sankalpa-less. Nothing exists besides the Self.

8. The Self is partless. The Self is blemishless. The Self is intelligence.[1] The Self is of the nature of Purusha. The Self is Bliss. Certainly, the Self is without origin.[2] Nothing exists besides the Self.

[1]*buddhi* [2]*also unborn*

9. The Self is beyond count. The Self is a multitude, also. The Self is immortal. The Self is the core of immortality. The Self is the past, present, and future. Nothing exists besides the Self.

10. The Self is all. The Self is independent. The Self is the respected.[1] The Self is of the nature[2] of Existence. The Self is of the nature of the presence of Turiya, the fourth state. Nothing exists besides the Self.

[1]*venerable, honored* [2]*ascertainment*

11. The Self is of the nature that is ever directly present.[1] It is ascertained by its eternal presence.[1] The Self is of the nature devoid of anything else. Nothing exists besides the Self.

[1]*pratyakṣa*

12. The Self is of the nature devoid of nonexistence. It is devoid of anything else, itself being Supreme. The Self is pure and beyond knowledge and ignorance. It is without proof or absence of proof.

13. The Self is devoid of permanence and impermanence. It is beyond the fruits of the "here" or the "there" (the next world). The Self is devoid of the sextet of sama and others.[1] Nothing exists besides the Self.

[1]see glossary: Four Requisites For Realization of Brahman

14. The Self is without the desire for Liberation also. The Vedas[1] are the Self. Dama is of the nature of the Self. Uparati is ever of the nature of the Self. Nothing exists besides the Self.

[1]śabda

15. Titiksa is at all times of the nature of the Self. Samadhana ever abides in the Self. The Self is pure. The Self[1] abides in itself. Certainly, nothing exists besides the Self.

[1]svātmā, one's own self

16. The Self is without the anna kosa. It is without the prana kosa. It is without the mano kosa. Certainly, nothing exists besides the Self.

17. The Self is without the vijnana kosa. It is without the ananda kosa and any other (sheath). The Self is without the pentad of sheaths. Certainly, nothing exists besides the Self.

18. The Self is of the nature of nirvikalpa. The Self is devoid of savikalpa. The Self is devoid of compliance with the scriptures. Certainly, nothing exists besides the Self.

19. The Self is without the gross body; the Self is without the subtle body; the Self is without the causal [body] or any other body. Nothing exists besides the Self.

20. The Self is the Void,[1] which is endowed with seeing. The Self is devoid of mixing with (being affected by) the seen (seeing). It is without beginning, middle, or end. It is peaceful. The Self is without[2] samadhi. Nothing exists besides the Self.

[1]śūnyātmā [2]devoid of

21. The Self is without the aphorisms of wisdom. It is without [aphorisms like] aham brahmasmi (I am Brahman). Aphorisms like tattvamasi (That you are) and others are the Self. Nothing exists besides the Self.

22. The Self is without such aphorisms as ayam atma (This is the Self), "All is Self," and others. The syllable Om is the Self. The guna-s are the Self. Nothing exists besides the Self.

23. The Self is of the nature devoid of the waking state. It is without the state of dreams. The Self is of the nature of bliss and is perfectly full. Nothing else exists besides the Self.

24. The Self is the past. The Self is also the future. The Self is imperishable. Consciousness is of the nature of the Self. The Self is of the nature of the beginning-less and middle-less. Nothing exists besides the Self.

25. The Self is devoid of all sankalpa. It is just shining Consciousness alone. It is undecaying. The Self is devoid of the knower and the knowable and such. Nothing exists besides the Self.

26. The Self is One; the Self is devoid of oneness. It is devoid of duality and [a concept of] nonduality. The Self is itself. The Self is natural.[1] Nothing exists besides the Self.

[1] *its own existence*

27. The fourth state is the Self. Eternality is the Self. Whatever is here, in the least, is of the nature of the Self. The Self is the measure; the Self is without a measure. Nothing exists besides the Self.

28. The Self is the limit of the many words. It is the joy that is spoken about. It revels in itself. The Self is devoid of everything. The Self is, indeed, all. Nothing exists besides the Self.

79

29. Look at[1] the Self alone. Consider yourself to be the Self. Be in your Self. Experience the Self yourself. Nothing exists besides the Self.

[1] *See*

30. Being happy only in one's own Self, [considering] oneself as the Self, indeed, one should perceive oneself as the Self, understanding[1] oneself as the Self.

[1] *śrutam, heard, learned*

31. Oneself satisfied in one's own Self, oneself filled up by one's own Self, one should reduce oneself to ashes. Nothing exists besides the Self.

32. Enjoying, oneself, one's Self, oneself full of love for one's Self, one should reflect only on one's Self. Nothing exists besides the Self.

33. Only the Self is to be heard; let the Self be the only thing you hear. The Self alone should be desired, ever. Ever worship the Self.

34. The Self should ever be praised. Attend to the Self [always]. The Self should ever be desired. Nothing else exists besides the Self.

35. This earth is only the Self. This water is only the Self. This light[1] is only the Self. Nothing exists besides the Self.

[1] *jyothir*

36. This air is only the Self. This space is only the Self. This ego is only the Self. Nothing exists besides the Self.

37. This thought[1] is only the Self. This mind[2] is only the Self. This intellect[3] is only the Self. Nothing exists besides the Self.

[1] *cittaṁ* [2] *manaḥ* [3] *buddhir*

38. This body is only the Self. This guna is only the Self. This truth is only the Self. Nothing exists besides the Self.

39. This mantra is only the Self. This japa is only the Self. This world is only the Self. Nothing exists besides the Self.

40. This sound is only the Self. This taste is only the Self. This touch is only the Self. Nothing exists besides the Self.

41. This smell is only the Self. This tranquility is only the Self. This sorrow is only the Self. This happiness is only the Self.

42. All this phenomenal world[1] is only of the Self. The dream is only of the Self. The deep sleep state is also of the Self. Nothing exists besides the Self.

[1]*jagat*

43. Activity is only the Self. Plenitude is only the Self (alternative translation: "In all probability" is only the Self). The one without a second is the Self. Nonduality is of the Self. Nothing exists besides the Self.

44. Whoever is, is of the Self. Whatever is, is of the Self. This world is of the Self. Nothing exists besides the Self.

45. All this that is to be seen is only the Self. These people are only the Self. All this is only the Self. Nothing exists besides the Self.

46. This God, Sambhu, is only the Self. This world of movement[1] is only the Self. This Brahma is only the Self. Nothing exists besides the Self.

[1]*jagat, universe*

47. This sun is only the Self. This which is insentient[1] is only the Self. This meditation is only the Self. This result is only the Self.

[1]*inert*

81

48. This yoga is only the Self. All this world[1] is pervaded by the Self. All that exists is of the Self. Nothing exists besides the Self.

[1]*jagat*

49. Consider all as of the nature of the Self. The Guru is entirely of the nature of the Self. The shishya is entirely of the nature of the Self. Nothing exists besides the Self.

50. A god is entirely of the nature of the Self. The fruits are entirely of the nature of the Self. All goals are of the nature of the Self. Nothing exists besides the Self.

51. Holy waters are all of the nature of the Self. Oneself is entirely of the nature of the Self. Liberation is entirely of the nature of the Self. Nothing exists besides the Self.

52. Desire is entirely of the nature of the Self. Action is entirely of the nature of the Self. Anger is entirely of the nature of the Self. Nothing exists besides the Self.

53. Knowledge is entirely of the nature of the Self. The directions are entirely of the nature of the Self. Covetousness is entirely of the nature of the Self. Nothing exists besides the Self.

54. Infatuation[1] is entirely of the nature of the Self. Fear is entirely of the nature of the Self. Thinking[2] is entirely of the nature of the Self. Nothing exists besides the Self.

[1]*mohaḥ* [2]*cintā*

55. Courage is entirely of the nature of the Self. Determination is entirely of the nature of the Self. Truth is entirely of the nature of the Self. Nothing exists besides the Self.

56. Knowledge is entirely of the nature of the Self. Steadfastness is entirely of the nature of the Self. The measureable is entirely of the nature of the Self. Nothing exists besides the Self.

57. The mysterious[1] is entirely of the nature of the Self. The auspicious is entirely of the nature of the Self. The pure is entirely of the nature of the Self. Nothing exists besides the Self.

[1] *guhyaṁ, secret*

58. All is entirely of the nature of the Self. The Self is Truth. Truth is the Self, ever of the Self. Fullness is the Self. Decay is also the Self. The highest[1] is the Self. It is higher than the highest.

[1] *supreme*

59. "Hence" is also the Self; "thence" is also the Self. "From then on" is also the Self, only the Self. Truly, all is pervaded by[1] the Self. Nothing exists besides the Self.

[1] *of the nature of*

60. All is of the nature of the Self alone—the seen and the unseen, the moving and the unmoving. Understanding that all is the Self, man attains Liberation.

61. He only, Bhagavan (the Lord), the Consort of Uma, changeless, with His own power, with His own maya, is the efficient cause of this wondrous waking world of bodies and succession of activities.

Chapter Eleven

ātmānanda-prakaraṇa-varṇanam
DESCRIPTION OF THE TOPIC OF THE BLISS
OF THE SELF

Ribhu:
Listen! All is only Brahman. I say, in the name of Siva, this is
the truth, this is the truth. O Master of yoga![1] There is nothing
else whatsoever.

[1] *yogīndra*

2. The unreal is not even an atom. All this, surely, is not even
an atom. The body, too, is not even an atom. There is nothing
else whatsoever.

3. All is only the Self, the pure Self. All is only Consciousness
without a second. The Self is eternal, spotless, and pure.
There is nothing else whatsoever.

4. If the Self is considered as merely atomic in dimension,
all is not even an atom. Absence of sankalpa, too, is a mere
atom. There is nothing else whatsoever.

5. Sankalpa is only Consciousness. Consciousness is the
highest state. Bliss is the supreme measure. All this that is
seen is nothing.

6. The syllable Om is only Consciousness. Consciousness itself is all. Bliss is the supreme measure. All this that is seen
is nothing.

7. I, myself, am also Bliss. I, myself, am changeless Consciousness. Bliss is the supreme measure. All this that is seen is nothing.

8. I, myself, am the mysterious Self. I, myself, am the interstice-less. Bliss is the supreme measure. All this that is seen is nothing.

9. I, myself, am the Supreme Brahman. I, myself, am the teacher of teachers.[1] Bliss is the supreme measure. All this that is seen is nothing.

[1] *guru of gurus*

10. I, myself, am the support of all. I, myself, am happiness beyond happiness. Bliss is the supreme measure. All this that is seen is nothing.

11. I, myself, am the great Light. I am of the Self of all. Bliss is the supreme measure. All this that is seen is nothing.

12. I, myself, am the satisfied Self. I, myself, am the attribute-less. Bliss is the supreme measure. All this that is seen is nothing.

13. I, myself, am the perfectly full Self. I, myself, am the ancient. Bliss is the supreme measure. All this that is seen is nothing.

14. I, myself, am the peaceful Self. I, myself, am permanent. Bliss is the supreme measure. All this that is seen is nothing.

15. I, myself, am everywhere. I, myself, am the well-established. Bliss is the supreme measure. All this that is seen is nothing.

16. I, myself, am the jiva (individual soul). I, myself, am higher than the highest. Bliss is the supreme measure. All this that is seen is nothing.

17. I, myself, am the meaning of the great aphorisms. I, myself, am Sankara. Bliss is the supreme measure. All this that is seen is nothing.

18. I, myself, am the hard-to-see. I, myself, am the illuminator. Bliss is the supreme measure. All this that is seen is nothing.

19. I, myself, am myself—only myself; I, myself, am my Self. I, myself, am the great[1] Bliss. I, myself, am full of Consciousness.

[1] *supreme, absolute*

20. I, myself, am the pure Self. I, myself, am the Truth alone. I, myself, am the Self of the Void. I, myself, am the all-reaching.[1]

[1] *sarvagaḥ*

21. I, myself, am the Vedanta. I, myself, am the highest— Supreme Consciousness.

22. I, myself, am Consciousness alone. I, myself, am filled with Consciousness. I am nothing else. I am of the nature of Consciousness. I am devoid of anything exterior.

23. I am nothing. I am the Self of Brahman. I am not anything else. I am the Supreme. I am ever pure and liberated. I am ever satisfied and untainted.

24. Bliss, the great[1] Bliss! There is nothing else whatever. There is nothing; there is nothing; there is nothing beyond the highest of the high.

[1] *supreme*

25. All this world[1] is only the Self. All this arising out of the mind is only the Self. All this happiness is only the Self. This world[1] is only the Self.

[1] *jagat*

26. Brahman is all, Consciousness alone. I am Brahman alone. Bliss is the greatest measure. All this that is seen is nothing.

27. All that is seen is the Supreme Brahman. Whatever is seen is, indeed, ever nonexistent. This is ever so. All sankalpa is only Brahman. Brahman—nothing else—is the greatest, [ever]. Bliss is the supreme measure. All this that is seen is nothing.

28. Brahman, indeed, is Brahman, of the nature of Consciousness and Consciousness itself.[1] The world[2] is pervaded by Consciousness. All this world of movement[2] is unreal. The entire phenomenal world is unreal.

[1]*alone* [2]*jagat*

29. "I alone am" is also unreal; "you alone exist" is also unreal. All modes of activities[1] of the mind are, indeed, unreal. Qualities and absence of qualities are, indeed, unreal.

[1]*vṛttiḥ*

30. All earth is unreal, indeed. Water is ever unreal, indeed. This mine[1] of a world is unreal, indeed. Light also is unreal, indeed.

[1]*khāni, space*

31. Wind (air) is ever unreal, indeed. "This" also is unreal, indeed. Ego is unreal, so also the intellect, Brahma, and the beings of the world.

32. Thought is ever unreal, indeed; it is only the Self. There is no doubt. All the demons are unreal, indeed. The form of Isvara is unreal, indeed.

33. The universe is ever unreal. Hari is ever unreal, indeed. Brahma is ever unreal, indeed. All his creations are, indeed, unreal.

34. Mahadeva is unreal, indeed. The Lord of the retinue[1] is unreal, indeed. Uma, also, is ever unreal. Skanda and the chiefs of the retinues are unreal.

[1] *gaṇeśvara*

35. The individual soul[1] is unreal, indeed. The body is unreal, indeed. The Veda-s are ever unreal, indeed. The demise[2] of the body, too, is unreal.

[1] *jīva* [2] *end*

36. The dharmasastra-s (codes of conduct) and purana-s (legends) are all distortions of the truth and are unreal. All is, indeed, only unreal. Genealogy[1] is unreal.

[1] *paraṁparā, lineage*

37. All this, from beginning to end, is unreal. The elite of sages are unreal. The worlds are ever unreal, indeed. What is to be seen in the world, also, is unreal.

38. Happiness and sorrow are, indeed, unreal. Success and failure are unreal, indeed. The greatest bondage is unreal, indeed. Liberation, indeed, is surely unreal.

39. Death and birth are unreal, indeed. Sentience and insentience are unreal, indeed. The entire world is, indeed, unreal. The concept[1] of oneself[2] is unreal, indeed.

[1] *bhāvanā* [2] *the self*

40. Forms are all unreal, indeed. [The idea of] an auspicious state is unreal, indeed. "I" ever is unreal, indeed. "You" is also unreal, indeed.

41. Everywhere there is unreality. The moving and unmoving are unreal, indeed. All beings are unreal. All results [of action] are unreal.

42. All the universe is unreal. All attributes are unreal. All the rest is unreal. All that is dual is unreal.

43. All sin is unreal. The triad of sravana and others (listening, reflection, and one-pointed profound meditation) is unreal. Single categories and multiple categories are ever unreal.

44. All power[1] is unreal. All things[2] are ever impermanent. Gods and others are unreal. All purpose is unreal.

[1]authority [2]sense objects

45. Sama is always unreal; sama is ever unreal. The doubtful is unreal. The fight between gods and demons is unreal.

46. The concept of Isvara is unreal. Worship[1] is unreal. Time and space and such are unreal. The concept of holy shrines[2] and such is unreal.

[1]worshipful meditation [2]kṣetra

47. Dharma and adharma arising therefrom, as also their definitions, are unreal. All activities are unreal. The misapprehension as oneself and another is unreal.

48. The concept of the existence of the mind is, also, unreal. The gross body is unreal. The subtle body is also unreal. I say, in the name of Siva, all I say is truth, the truth.

49. Heaven and hell are unreal; happiness arising therefrom (from heaven) is unreal. All grasping is unreal; all that is of the form of the graspable is unreal.

50. "Shining like truth" is unreal. I say, in the name of Siva, it is all unreal. All that is said to be of the nature of the present is unreal. All that is of the nature of the past is unreal.

51. What is said to be the future is unreal, too. This is the truth, the truth, I say in the name of Siva. Of this world, the beginning is unreal, the middle is unreal, and the end is unreal.

52. The probable is always unreal. Ever, there is no doubt that it is unreal. Knowledge, ignorance, and what is to be known are ever unreal.

53. The universe is ever unreal. The inert is ever unreal. The seen is ever unreal. These are like the horns of a horse.

54. Thought[1] is ever unreal. The existence of sheaths is unreal. All mantras are unreal. There is no doubt that this is the truth. This is the truth.

[1]*bhāvaḥ*

55. There is no world[1] apart from the Self. There is nothing of this non-Self, ever. Anything apart from the Self is unreal. This is the truth, the truth. There is no doubt of this.

[1]*universe*

56. There is no happiness apart from the Self. There is nothing else apart from the Self. There is nowhere to go apart from the Self. One should remain forever in the Self.

57. There is nothing anywhere apart from the Self. There is not a blade of grass apart from the Self. There is nothing whatever apart from the Self. There is nothing apart from the Self at any time.

58. This explanation of the Bliss of the Self has been expounded to you by me. Whichever wise man hears this once, himself becomes Brahman.

59. This gives instant Liberation from bondage by being heard even once. By understanding the meaning of this treatise, one is liberated from everything.

60. Suta:

Worship with a committed heart the full, the true, the great Isvara. One who does so uninterruptedly becomes, here in this world, ever Brahman, with the divine Truth of the Self, eternal and without agitation of the mind. He exists, with knots cut asunder, in Isvara, at the pure feet of Siva, and shines inwardly. He becomes restful inside and surely becomes, after death, the entire universe.

brahmaiva sarvaṁ prakaraṇa-nirūpaṇam
DEFINITION OF THE TOPIC OF
"BRAHMAN, INDEED, IS ALL"

I shall reveal the great secret, more mysterious than the most mysterious, the most difficult to come by in this world: all is only Brahman alone.

2. All this is only just Brahman. Brahman, indeed, is the only thing that is not unreal. All that is heard is Brahman. All is only Brahman alone.

3. The great yantra-s (mystic diagrams) are only Brahman. Action and result are only Brahman. The great aphorisms are only Brahman. All is only Brahman alone.

4. The entire world[1] is only Brahman. The sentient and insentient[2] are only Brahman. The body that is considered separate[3] is only Brahman. All is only Brahman alone.
[1]*jagat* [2]*inert* [3]*paraṁ*

5. Qualities are said to be only Brahman. This vast creation[1] is only Brahman. The great Brahma[2] is only Brahman. All is only Brahman alone.
[1]*mahat* [2]*paraṁ brahma*

6. This thing is only Brahman. That man, also, is only Brahman. Whatever is there, also, is only Brahman. All is only Brahman alone.

7. The limitless Self is only Brahman. The greatest happiness is only Brahman. The highest[1] Knowledge is only Brahman. All is only Brahman alone.

[1]*supreme*

8. The shore beyond is only Brahman. The triad of bodies is only Brahman. Plurality is only Brahman. All is only Brahman alone.

9. Brahman alone is smell. Brahman only is the highest[1] state. Brahman alone is the nose. All is only Brahman alone.

[1]*supreme*

10. Brahman alone is touch. Brahman alone is sound. Brahman alone is form. All is only Brahman alone.

11. Brahman alone is the world. Brahman alone is taste. Brahman alone is the mind.[1] All is only Brahman alone.

[1]*cittaṁ*

12. The word "That" is ever Brahman; the word "you" is, indeed, only Brahman; the word "are" is only Brahman (in the aphorism "That you are," tat tvam asi). All is ever one with Brahman.

13. Brahman alone is the mysterious.[1] Brahman alone is the exterior. Brahman alone is the eternal. All is only Brahman alone.

[1]*secret*

14. Brahman alone is the principle of all creation[1] from That, the state of the beginning and the end of the world.[2] Brahman alone is the beginning and the end of the world. All is only Brahman alone.

[1]*tajjalāni, sprung from That* [2]*jagat*

15. "Is" and "is not" are only Brahman. I am only Brahman. There is no doubt of this. Whatever in the least there is is only Brahman. All is only Brahman alone.

16. Brahman alone is all wakefulness. "I" and "another"[1] are only Brahman. Brahman alone is truly existence. Brahman alone is said to be the fourth state.

[1]*param*

17. Brahman alone is the substratum[1]—only Brahman. Only Brahman is to be regarded as the Guru. The state of being a good disciple is only Brahman. Liberation is only Brahman alone.

[1]*sattā, existence*

18. The anterior and the posterior, the prior and the subsequent, are only Brahman. Brahman is the complete[1] and ancient.[2] Brahman alone is the immediate presence.[3] All is only Brahman alone.

[1]*pūrṇaṁ, perfectly full* [2]*sanātanam, eternal* [3]*sākṣāt*

19. Brahman alone is Existence-Consciousness-Happiness. Brahman is the full. Brahman is the ancient.[1] Brahman alone is the immediate presence.[2] All is only Brahman alone.

[1]*sanātanam* [2]*sākṣāt*

20. Brahman alone is the sole Existence-Consciousness. Happiness is only Brahman. Brahman is the bliss that exists everywhere in a nature that is lovable.

21. By good proclivities,[1] the jiva shines ever, like Siva. By sinful proclivities, the jiva remains as the experiencer of hell.

[1]*vāsanayā*

22. Only Brahman shines as the senses. Only Brahman is the worldly[1] objects. Only Brahman is all worldly transactions. All is only Brahman alone.

[1]*sense*

DEFINITION OF THE TOPIC OF "BRAHMAN, INDEED, IS ALL"   12:31

23. Only Brahman is all the Bliss. Only Brahman is the embodiment of Knowledge. Brahman is said to be the action of illusion. All is only Brahman alone.

24. Brahman alone is the invocation of sacrifice. Brahman alone is the space of the heart. Brahman alone is said to be the essence of Liberation. All is only Brahman alone.

25. Brahman alone is purity and impurity. Brahman alone is the cause of all. Brahman alone is all the action on earth. All is only Brahman alone.

26. Brahman alone is the ever-satisfied Self. Brahman alone is all the days. Brahman alone is the silent Self. All is only Brahman alone.

27. Brahman alone is the meaning of the essence of the Vedas. Brahman alone is the range of meditation. Brahman alone is said to be the yoga of the yogas. All is only Brahman alone.

28. Brahman is seen in various forms because of conditionings. When this conditioning is known to be an illusion, it truly ceases to exist.

29. Brahman alone appears as the world and, likewise, as the people. Brahman alone appears as forms. In Reality, there is nothing whatever.

30. Brahman alone is the godly forms. Brahman only is the assembly of sages. Brahman alone is of the nature of meditation. All is only Brahman alone.

31. Brahman alone is worldly and spiritual knowledge.[1] Brahman alone is the Supreme Isvara. Brahman alone is the pure, enlightened Self. All is only Brahman alone.

[1] *jñānavijñānam*

95

32. Brahman alone is the great[1] Bliss. Brahman alone pervades the vastness. Brahman alone is the Absolute Truth. All is only Brahman alone.

[1]*supreme*

33. Brahman is of the nature of yajna (oblation). Brahman alone is also the oblation. Brahman alone is the Self that has become a living entity. All is only Brahman alone.

34. Brahman alone is the entire world. Brahman alone is the duo of Guru and shishya. Brahman alone is the end[1] of all. All is only Brahman alone.

[1]*accomplishment*

35. Brahman alone is all the mantras. Brahman alone is all the japa. Brahman alone is all action.[1] All is only Brahman alone.

[1]*kāryaṁ, religious action*

36. Brahman alone is all peacefulness. Brahman alone is the core of the heart. Brahman alone is all the beatitude.[1] All is only Brahman alone.

[1]*kaivalyaṁ*

37. Brahman alone is of the nature[1] of the imperishable. Brahman alone is the characteristic of the imperishable. Brahman alone is of the nature[2] of Brahman. All is only Brahman alone.

[1]*existence* [2]*form*

38. Brahman alone is the abode of Truth. I am only Brahman. There is no doubt about this. Brahman is also the meaning of the word "tat" (That). All is only Brahman alone.

39. Brahman alone is also the meaning of the word "aham" (I). Brahman alone is the Supreme Lord. Brahman alone is also the meaning of the word "tvam" (you). All is only Brahman alone.

40. Brahman alone is whatever is great.[1] Brahman alone is the ultimate goal. Brahman alone is the state of understanding.[2] All is only Brahman alone.

[1]*paramaṁ* [2]*nonexistence of causing or doing*

41. Brahman is all. There is no doubt of this. You are only Brahman, ever beatific.[1] All of this world[2] is only Brahman. All is only Brahman alone.

[1]*sadāśivaḥ, ever Siva* [2]*jagat, universe*

42. Brahman alone is the all-easy. Brahman alone is itself the Self itself. Brahman alone is Bliss.[1] All is only Brahman alone.

[1]*sukhamātratvāt*

43. Brahman alone is all, only Brahman. All, apart from Brahman, is ever unreal. Brahman alone is the Self that is just Brahman. All is only Brahman alone.

44. Brahman is the meaning of all the great aphorisms. Brahman is the highest abode. Brahman alone is truth and untruth. All is only Brahman alone.

45. Brahman alone is the One, without beginning and end. Brahman alone is the only One. There is no doubt of this. Brahman only is the one Consciousness-Bliss. All is only Brahman alone.

46. Brahman alone is the one eternal joy. Brahman is the only one to be sought. Brahman alone is the one Supreme Brahman. All is only Brahman alone.

47. Brahman only is Consciousness itself, abiding in itself. Brahman alone is without attributes. Brahman alone is all that is nearest. All is only Brahman alone.

48. Brahman alone is all that is spotless. Brahman alone is ever easy of access. Brahman alone is the Reality of realities. All is only Brahman alone.

49. Brahman alone is happiness; happiness is Brahman alone. I am, indeed, Brahman, the Self of happiness. Brahman alone is ever to be spoken of. All is only Brahman alone.

50. Brahman alone is all Brahman. Brahman is the one witness of all. Brahman alone is the abode of prosperity.[1] All is only Brahman alone.

[1]*abundance, importance*

51. Brahman alone is the fully satisfied Self. Brahman is the immutable essence. Brahman alone is the root cause. Brahman is the one goal.

52. Brahman alone is the Self of all beings. Brahman is the vigraha (embodiment) of joy. Brahman alone is the ever satisfied Self. All is only Brahman alone.

53. Brahman alone is the Self of just nonduality. Brahman only is lordly like space. Brahman alone is the Bliss of the Heart. All is only Brahman alone.

54. There is nothing higher than Brahman. There is no world[1] apart from Brahman. Apart from Brahman, I am not I. All is only Brahman alone.

[1]*jagat*

55. There is no joy other than Brahman. There is no fruit other than Brahman. Other than Brahman, there is not a blade of grass. All is only Brahman alone.

56. All states other than Brahman are illusory. There is nothing in the least other than Brahman. Other than Brahman, the world is an illusion. All is only Brahman alone.

57. Apart from Brahman, I am illusory. I am myself, indeed, just Brahman, Brahman alone. Other than Brahman, there is no guru. All is only Brahman alone.

58. Other than Brahman, all action is unreal. Other than Brahman, all bodies are unreal. Other than Brahman, there is no mind. All is only Brahman alone.

59. Other than Brahman, the world is an illusion. There is nothing else other than Brahman. Other than Brahman, there is no ego. All is only Brahman alone.

60. This explanation, which has been given[1] by me, is that Brahman alone is all. One who reads or listens to this immediately becomes Brahman himself.

[1]declared

---

61. He knows who knows all is only Brahman, who knows the truth that the real and the unreal, the world, and likewise the words of the Vedas, and all arising therefrom are only Brahman. One who loses this knowledge in delusion suffers in this world, bereft of knowledge. Brahman, indeed, is the only one, ever.

Chapter Thirteen

cideva-tvam-prakaraṇa-varṇanam
DESCRIPTION OF THE TOPIC OF
"YOU, INDEED, ARE CONSCIOUSNESS"

Ribhu:
I shall speak of that which is extremely difficult to find in the Vedas, sastras, and agamas. Listen attentively. All is simply unreal.

2. Whatever in the least is seen in this world, whatever in the least is spoken of in this world ever, whatever in the least is experienced in this world, wherever, all that is only unreal.

3. Whatever little japa or purification bath or holy water there is, and whatever is apart from the Self is entirely unreal. This is doubtless.

4. The action of the mind, the action of the intellect, and, likewise, the action of delusion,[1] and whatever little there is apart from the Self—all that is only unreal.

[1] *māyā*

5. The nature of difference of the ego, "this," "you," "the truth," and whatever is apart from the Self is only unreal.

6. Multiplicity and, likewise, forms, here and there, interactions, and whatever there is, are of the Self only; all of that (apart from the Self) is unreal.

7. The differences of philosophy,[1] the differences of the world—all differences—are of the unreal. Differences of desire and differences of the world—all are only unreal.

[1]*tatva*

8. Differences of duality, differences of the phenomenal,[1] and differences of wakefulness are of the nature of the mind. Differences as "I" and differences as "this"—all are simply unreal.

[1]*manifold, variegated*

9. Differences of dreams, differences of deep sleep, and differences of the fourth state are not of the nature of difference. Differences of the doer, differences of action, differences of qualities of the nature of taste, differences of characteristics—all this difference is simply unreal.

10. Differences of the self, differences of the nonexistent, and differences of the existent—even an atom thereof—are unreal. Differences of the totally nonexistent and existent are, also, simply unreal.

11. The differences of "is" and the differences of "is not," nondifference, the misapprehension of differences, the differences due to misapprehensions, and the differences of existence are simply unreal.

12. The differences of "again" and "elsewhere," the fear of "this" and "something else," differences of punya, and the differences of papa—all are simply unreal.

13. Differences as sankalpa, differences as "That," all differences ever, wherever, due to knowledge or ignorance—all, are simply unreal.

14. The difference as Brahma, the difference as a king, differences as past and future, and differences as "this" and as "I"—all are simply unreal.

15. Difference as Vedas, difference as gods, and, likewise, the differences of the qualities of the world, and the pancaksara mantra (five-lettered mantra: namah sivaya) are ever unreal—all are simply unreal.

16. The sensory organs are ever unreal. The organs of action are always unreal. What are called sound and such are, indeed, unreal. Their results are, likewise, unreal.

17. What is called the pentad of elements is unreal. The pentad of deities is unreal. What is called the pentad of sheaths is unreal. All are simply unreal.

18. The sextet of modifications is unreal. Unreal is the sextet of anxieties. Unreal is the sextet of enemies. The sextet of seasons is, likewise, unreal.

19. The twelve months are unreal; the year is likewise unreal. Also, what is called the sextet of states is unreal. The sextet of times is only unreal.

20. The sextet of philosophical systems is, indeed, unreal, simply unreal. Knowledge is ever unreal. The state of "Being alone" is, indeed, unreal.

21. What should not be said, what is said, and what is not said are simply unreal. I have explained the definition of the unreal, hard to come by in all the Vedas.

22. Listen again, master of yoga![1] I shall tell you what is immediate Liberation. I only am the Real, the Self, Existence-Consciousness-Bliss alone.

[1]yogīndra

23. The Self is only Bliss that is just Existence, a mass of Bliss that is just Consciousness, a mass of Bliss filled with Consciousness, Consciousness-Bliss alone,

24. Bliss that is the Light of Consciousness alone, the vigraha of Light that is just Consciousness. Isvara[1] is the Light of Consciousness, ever Bliss alone.

[1]*īśāna*

25. All is the Light of just Consciousness. I am only the Light of Consciousness. I am entirely only Consciousness. All is only Consciousness.

26. Thought is only Consciousness. Liberation is only Consciousness. Manana is only Consciousness. Sravana is only Consciousness.

27. I am myself only Consciousness. All is only Consciousness. The attributeless Brahman is only Consciousness. The Supreme with attributes is only Consciousness.

28. I am only Consciousness. You and all are only Consciousness. The Heart is only Consciousness, just Consciousness, full of Consciousness always.

29. You are only Consciousness; I am only Consciousness; all is Consciousness alone. Peacefulness is only Consciousness; the characteristics of peacefulness are Consciousness alone.

30. Higher Knowledge[1] is only Consciousness alone. Brahman is only Consciousness. Sankalpa is only Consciousness. [All] the three worlds are only Consciousness.

[1]*vijñānaṁ*

31. Everywhere is only Consciousness. The Guru is pervaded by Consciousness alone. Purity is only Consciousness. Brahman is only Consciousness alone.

32. Awareness[1] is only Consciousness. The sun and such are only Consciousness. Existence alone is only Consciousness. The universe, indeed, is only Consciousness.

[1]*caitanyaṁ*

33. Good action is only Consciousness. Perpetual auspiciousness is just Consciousness. Brahma is only Consciousness alone. Hari is Consciousness alone.

34. The silent Self is only Consciousness. All siddhi-s are only Consciousness. Birth is only Consciousness. Happiness is, indeed, only Consciousness.

35. The sky is only Consciousness. The mountains and waters are only Consciousness. The stars are only Consciousness. The clouds are only Consciousness.

36. The forms of gods are only Consciousness. The worship of Siva is only Consciousness. Hardness is only Consciousness. Coldness[1] is only Consciousness.

[1]*cold water*

37. What is to be thought of is Consciousness. What is to be seen is Consciousness. All is only Consciousness. This world and the father are only Consciousness.

38. The mother is only Consciousness. There is nothing apart from Consciousness. The eye is only Consciousness. Listening and happiness are only Consciousness.

39. Action to be performed is only Consciousness. The work[1] of Isvara is only Consciousness. Truth is just Consciousness, full of Consciousness. There never is any non-existence of Consciousness.

[1]*activity*

40. Vedanta is only Consciousness. The certitude about Brahman is only Consciousness. The awareness of Existence is only Consciousness. Consciousness alone shines ever.

41. Consciousness alone is the universe with form. Consciousness alone is the Supreme State. Consciousness alone is of the nature[1] of Consciousness. Consciousness alone, indeed, is the immutability of Consciousness.

[1]*form*

42. Consciousness alone is the nature[1] of Siva. Consciousness alone is the embodiment of Siva. All this is only of the nature[1] of Consciousness. Happiness and sorrow are only of the nature of Consciousness.

[1]*form*

43. The nature of insentience[1] is only Consciousness. The interstice-less is only Consciousness. Understanding is only Consciousness. The concept of individual soul[2] is only Consciousness.

[1]*jaḍākāram* [2]*jīvākāram*

44. The forms of gods are only Consciousness. The worship of Siva is only Consciousness. You are only Consciousness. I am only Consciousness. All is, indeed, only Consciousness.

45. The nature of the Supreme is only Consciousness. Afflictionless-ness is only Consciousness always. The permanent is only Consciousness. The goal is only Consciousness.

46. Dispassion is only Consciousness. Attributeless-ness is only Consciousness always. Moving about is only Consciousness. Mantra and tantra are only Consciousness.

47. This universe is of the nature of Consciousness. All the three worlds are only of the nature of Consciousness. The ego is of the nature of Consciousness. The highest of the high is of the nature of Consciousness.

48. All this difference is an aspect[1] of Consciousness. Even a blade of grass and such are aspects[1] of Consciousness. The space of Consciousness is of the nature of Consciousness. Formlessness is of the nature of Consciousness.

[1]of the nature

49. Great joy[1] is of the nature of Consciousness. The joy of joys is of the nature of Consciousness. Happiness is of the nature of Consciousness. What is to be enjoyed is of the nature of Consciousness. The supreme Guru is of the nature of Consciousness.

[1]bliss

50. This universe is of the nature of Consciousness. This man is of the nature of Consciousness. The originless[1] peace is of the nature of Consciousness. Being without afflictions is an aspect[2] of Consciousness.

[1]ajaṁ, unborn [2]of the nature

51. Transcending all others is an aspect[1] of Consciousness. The nature of Consciousness is only of the nature of Consciousness. The space of Consciousness is of the nature of Consciousness. Consciousness-space yields Siva-hood.

[1]of the nature

52. Thought is ever an aspect[1] of Consciousness. Immortality is ever an aspect[1] of Consciousness. The space of Consciousness is of the nature of Consciousness; likewise is the inmost of the interior of all.

[1]of the nature

53. This fullness is of the nature of Consciousness. This love is of the nature of Consciousness. All this is of the nature of Consciousness. I am ever of the nature of Consciousness.

54. This place is of the nature of Consciousness. The space of the Heart is of the nature of Consciousness. The Knowledge of Consciousness is an aspect[1] of Consciousness. Pervasiveness, likewise, is an aspect[2] of Consciousness.

[1] *of the nature* [2] *likewise, ever is the space*

55. Being ever full is an aspect[1] of Consciousness. Great results are an aspect[1] of Consciousness. The supreme Truth is an aspect[1] of Consciousness. The Supreme and you[2] are an aspect[1] of Consciousness.

[1] *of the nature* [2] *you present (a respectful term)*

56. Joy is ever an aspect[1] of Consciousness. Death is ever an aspect[1] of Consciousness. The Supreme Brahman is an aspect[1] of Consciousness. I am Consciousness; ever, I am Consciousness.

[1] *of the nature*

57. I am Consciousness. I am Consciousness; so also is thought, one's own thought. There is no doubt of this. The world[1]-form is only Consciousness. Sivasankara is only Consciousness.

[1] *universe*

58. The form of space is only Consciousness. The Lord of the gana-s (retinue) is only Consciousness. The world-form is only Consciousness. The transmigration aspect[1] is only Consciousness.

[1] *conception of worldly existence*

59. The nature of the heart is only Consciousness; the Lord of the heart is only Consciousness. The nature of immortality is only Consciousness. The cause for movement is only Consciousness.

60. I am only Consciousness. I am only Consciousness—all Consciousness, all Consciousness, ever. True belief is only Consciousness. The conviction of being Brahman is only Consciousness.

61. The Supreme God is only Consciousness. The temple of the heart is only Consciousness. All aspects are only Consciousness. The multitude of people is only Consciousness.

62. All bliss is only Consciousness. Loving, endearing talk is only Consciousness. You are only Consciousness. I am only Consciousness. All is Consciousness alone.

63. The supreme meditation is only Consciousness. Supreme veneration is only Consciousness. You are only Consciousness. I am only Consciousness. All is entirely Consciousness.

64. This exposition that you are only Consciousness is rare in all the Vedas. By hearing this once, one surely becomes Brahman.

65. He becomes forever rid of misapprehensions in this world, his inner Self becoming Brahman forever—he, by whose yoga of meditation freedom is gained from birth and death, by whose changeless mode the knots of the heart, born of fear, are rent asunder by virtue of being rid of the infatuation of delusion, and whose world becomes the essence transcending the world—by the fulfillment of his desire of obtaining a vision of Yourself.

Chapter Fourteen

sarva-siddhānta-saṁgraha-prakaraṇam
TOPIC OF THE SUMMARY OF ALL SETTLED CONCLUSIONS

Ribhu:

Nidagha! Listen to me; listen to the most secret, which is the summary of the settled conclusion of all. This duality and nonduality are void. There is only the peaceful Brahman, ever.

2. I alone am the Supreme Brahman. I alone am the highest of the high. This duality and nonduality are void. There is only the peaceful Brahman alone.

3. I alone am the peaceful Self. I alone am the one that reaches everywhere. I alone am the pure Self. I alone am the eternal.

4. I alone am the Self in variety. I alone am the attributeless. I alone am the eternal Self. I alone am the cause.

5. I alone am all the world.[1] I alone am this also. I alone am the joyous Self. I alone am the liberator.

[1]*jagat, universe*

6. I alone am Consciousness.[1] I alone am pervaded by Consciousness.[2] I alone am Consciousness. I am ever the innermost of all.

[1]*caitanyaṁ* [2]*cinmayaḥ*

109

7. I alone am the Self of the elements. I alone am the Self of all that is composed of elements. I alone, indeed, am you. I, indeed, am alone myself[1] also.

[1]*I*

8. I alone am the jivatma (individual soul). I alone, I alone, am the Supreme Isvara. I alone am ever the glorious. I alone am myself, ever.

9. I alone am really[1] the imperishable. I alone am what I desire.[2] I alone am ever Brahman. I alone am ever immutable.

[1]*sākṣād* [2]*what is dear to me*

10. I alone, I alone, am in the front. I alone am in the inmost of the recesses.[1] I alone am the space of Consciousness. I alone am the illuminator.

[1]*inner*

11. I alone am ever the creator. I alone am the protector. I alone am the playful Self. I alone am the certainty.

12. I alone am ever the witness. You, yourself, alone are the ancient. You alone are the Supreme Brahman. You alone are the continuous.

13. I alone, I alone, am myself.[1] I alone am you alone. I alone am of the nature of the nondual. I alone am the bodiless.

[1]*I*

14. I alone am my support. I alone am ever of the Self. I alone am the quiescent Self. I only am the spirit of titiksa (endurance).

15. I alone am samadhana (tranquility). I alone am sraddha (sincere attention, faith). I alone am the great space. I alone am possessed of parts.

16. I alone am the end of desire. I alone am ever the interior. I alone am ever the front. I alone am the posterior. I ever am.

17. I alone am the universal Self. I alone am the solitary One.[1] I alone am the Supreme Brahman. I alone am higher than the highest.

[1]*kevalam*

18. I alone am Consciousness-Bliss. I alone am happiness and unhappiness. I alone am Gurutvam (Guru-hood). I alone am ever the imperishable.

19. I alone am Vedanta. I alone am thinking. I am the body and the pure Consciousness. I am without a doubt.

20. I alone am the Supreme Light. I alone am the Supreme Abode. I alone am the indestructible Self. I alone am the ancient.

21. I am Brahman; there is no doubt. I alone am the partless. I am the Fourth State; there is no doubt. I am the Self; there is no doubt.

22. I am not even "I." I am without attitudes. I alone am the limit[1] of attitudes. I alone am the resplendent.

[1]*end*

23. I transcend even a moment of time. I alone am the auspicious. I am the imperishable joy.[1] I am the pause-less continuity.

[1]*bliss*

24. I alone am the inscrutable Self. I am without sankalpa. I am the enlightened, the Supreme Abode. I am devoid of intellect.

25. I alone am ever the Truth. I alone am ever happiness. I alone am ever attainable. I am the cause that is easily accessible.

26. I am the Knowledge that is easily obtainable. I am the Knowledge that is ever rare even for the wise. I am the Self of Consciousness alone. I am the mass of Consciousness.

27. I alone am you alone. I am Brahman, I am. There is no doubt of this. I am the Self. There is no doubt of this. I am all-pervasive. There is no doubt of this.

28. I am the Self, the desirable.[1] This is the truth. This is the truth. This is the truth, again and again. I am the ageless Self, the pervasive. I alone am my own Guru.

[1]*dear, loved*

29. I alone am the immortal, the liberated. I alone am the undisturbed. I alone am the eternal Self. I am liberated. There is no doubt of this.

30. I am the ever pure. I am the attributeless. I am devoid of the phenomenal world. I am without a body.

31. I am the Self without desire. I am devoid of delusion.[1] I am the Self that enters mistaken propensities.[2] I am without samsara.

[1]*māyā* [2]*faults*

32. I am without sankalpa and without vikalpa. [I am] peaceful.[1] I alone am the Self of the Fourth State. I alone am the blemishless.

[1]*śiva*

33. I alone am ever the Light. I alone am ever the Lord. I alone am ever Brahman. I alone am ever the Supreme.

34. I alone am ever Knowledge. I alone am ever the gentle.[1] I alone am also thought. I am devoid of pride.[2]

[1]*gracious, compassionate* [2]*opinion*

35. Egoism is the wheel of birth and death.[1] Egoism is ever unreal. I alone am just Consciousness. There is nothing apart from me, nothing, indeed.

[1] saṁsāra

36. I alone am my own, truly. There is nothing apart from me. There is no word as "That" apart from me. There is no word as "you" apart from me.

37. There is never anything as punya, nor is there anything as papa, nor differences as "this thing," nor differences as "this person," nor differences as unreal and real.

38. There is nothing because of you, nothing. This is the truth; this is the truth; this is the truth, again and again. It is certain that nothing ever is, nothing. All is ever nonexistent.

39. This alone is the Supreme Brahman. I am Brahman. You alone are Brahman. Time is Brahman. A division of time (kala, which is a duration of one minute, forty-eight seconds or eight seconds) is Brahman. Action is Brahman. Likewise is a fleeting moment.

40. All is Brahman, and I am Brahman. There is no doubt that I am Brahman. Thought is Brahman. The mind is Brahman. Truth is Brahman. Truly, I ever am Brahman.

41. I am the Supreme, the attributeless Brahman, the eternal, the pause-less. I alone am Brahman from beginning to end. Never, indeed, has there been a beginning or end.

42. There is no such word as "I" or its remembrance or utterance. All is Brahman, indeed. There is no doubt of this. There never is anything such as "you."

43. This teaching[1] is rare. There is no doubt of this. There are none to expound this. This is capable of conferring Liberation immediately. It confers Liberation immediately.

[1] gītā

44. Immediately, one reaches the abode of Brahman. There is no doubt of this. By hearing this once, it immediately confers Liberation.

45. This is rare to come by in this world, rare in all the three worlds. I am Brahman. There is no doubt of this. You should steadfastly have this conviction. Then, renouncing everything, abide in Silence, at ease.[1]

¹happy

46. Suta:
Meditating on the connection between heaven and earth, immersed in the limbs of yoga and the practices such as yama, niyama, and others, and smeared with holy ashes, rid of the bondage of sheaths, with their intent fully turned toward Bliss and their hearts joyous with the desire for the Supreme, the devotees of Siva become Siva themselves.

Chapter Fifteen

ṛbhu-nidāgha-saṁvādaḥ
RIBHU-NIDAGHA DIALOGUE

Ribhu:
Hear again the supreme Truth that confers Liberation at once. All is ever Brahman; all is peace. There is no doubt of this.

2. This imperishable Brahman is all. There is no other nature of "this." Saying "this" is a mistake, as is also saying "we."

3. Whatever, in the least, is remembrance and whatever, in the least, is even meditation is nonexistent. Whatever, in the least, is of the nature of Knowledge alone—all that is only Brahman.

4. Whatever, in the least, is spoken about Brahman, whatever, in the least, is the word of the Vedas, whatever, in the least, is the word of the Guru—all that is only Brahman.

5. What little there is of evil[1] or truth, what little there is of loving talk, what little there is of the existence of reflection—all that is only Brahman.

[1] *darkness, sin*

6. What little there is of daily listening, what little of meditation is practiced, what little there is of certitude and sincerity[1]—all that is only Brahman.

[1] *faith*

115

7. What little there is of the teaching of the Guru, what little there is of thinking about the Guru, or what little there is of different yogas—all that is only Brahman.

8. Renouncing all, renouncing the guru, and renouncing everything ever, sit in Silence. Brahman-Bliss alone exists.

9. Renouncing all is happiness forever. Renouncing all is great joy. Renouncing all is the supreme bliss. Renouncing all is the supreme happiness.

10. Renouncing all is renouncing the mind. Renouncing all is renouncing the ego. Renouncing all is the great yaga. Renouncing all is the supreme happiness.

11. Renouncing all is the great Liberation. Renouncing thought is also the same, for thought is, indeed, ever the world,[1] and thought, indeed, is, ever, transmigration.

[1]*jagat*

12. Thought, indeed, is the great delusion.[1] Thought, indeed, is all that pertains to the body. Thought is the fear of the body. Thought alone is what pervades the mind.[2]

[1]*māyā* [2]*manomayam*

13. Thought, indeed, is known as the phenomenal world. Thought, indeed, is the pollution.[1] Thought, indeed, is all insentience.[2] Thought, indeed, is the senses and others.

[1]*darkness* [2]*jaḍaṁ*

14. Thought, indeed, is ever the Truth. Thought, indeed, is ever nonexistent. Thought, indeed, is the great scripture.[1] Thought, indeed, begets the mind.

[1]*śāstram*

15. Thought, indeed, is ever sin. Thought, indeed, is ever religion.[1] Thought, indeed, is said to be all. Always, conquer thought itself.

[1]*mataṁ, doctrine, respected idea*

16. If there is the mind that there is no mind, the Self only is manifested.[1] If there is the thought that thought is present, the state of thinking is only yourself.

[1]shines

17. Only oneself is said to be thought. Oneself is Brahman. There is no doubt of this. Thought alone is said to be all. Thought alone is regarded[1] as all.

[1]thought

18. I am Brahman alone, the self-luminous. I am Brahman alone. There is no doubt of this. All is Brahman. There is no doubt of this. All is only the Light of Consciousness.

19. I am Brahman alone, the eternal Self, ever fuller than the fullest. I am with earth and such. I am also without any distinguishing characteristics.

20. I am the interior of the subtle body. I, myself, am the ancient. I myself am the Self that is the measure. All is Brahman alone.

21. I am fully of the nature of Consciousness. This world[1] is of the nature of complete Consciousness. The space of Consciousness is of the nature of Consciousness. I am ever this Consciousness-space.

[1]jagat

22. You yourself are the space of Consciousness. I am ever the space of Consciousness. The space of Consciousness is alone this Consciousness. There is nothing apart from Consciousness-space.

23. All is pervaded by the space of Consciousness. Consciousness-space is the illuminator. The nature of the mind is Consciousness-space. Consciousness-space alone is the mass of Consciousness.

24. Consciousness-space is the Supreme Brahman. Consciousness-space is all Consciousness.[1] Consciousness-space is auspiciousness itself.[2] I am ever Consciousness-space.

[1]*cinmayaḥ* [2]*śivaṁ sākṣāt*

25. I am of the nature of Existence-Consciousness-Bliss, ever Existence-Consciousness-Bliss, ever the Reality of Existence-Consciousness-Bliss alone, ever of the conviction of Existence-Consciousness-Bliss.

26. I am filled with[1] Existence-Consciousness-Bliss. I am the cause of Existence-Consciousness-Bliss. I am the mass of Existence-Consciousness-Bliss. I am the Lord of Existence-Consciousness-Bliss.

[1]*perfectly full*

27. I am ever[1] Existence-Consciousness-Bliss, the characteristic of[2] Existence-Consciousness-Bliss. I am Existence-Consciousness-Bliss alone. I am of the nature of Existence-Consciousness-Bliss.

[1]*eternal* [2]*characterized by*

28. The Self alone is all this. The Self alone is myself.[1] There is no doubt of this. I alone am the Self, the Supreme Truth. The Self is the Supreme Abode.

[1]*I*

29. The Self alone is the form of the world. The Self alone is the triad of worlds. The Self alone is the best of the world. Whatever is filled with the mind is, indeed, the Self.

30. The Self, indeed, is the protector of the world. The Self is the Guru of the Self. The Self manifests in[1] multiplicity. The Self, indeed, is One. The highest is of the Self.

[1]*alone shines as*

31. The Self alone is the Supreme Brahman. I, indeed, am the Self. There is no doubt of this. The Self alone is the supreme world. The Self alone is greater than the Self.[1]

[1]*is from the Supreme Self*

32. The Self, indeed, is the Self of the nature[1] of the jiva (individual soul). The Self, indeed, is the nature[1] of Isvara. The Self, indeed, is Hari and Bliss. The Self, indeed, is oneself.

[1]*form*

33. The Self, indeed, is a mass of Bliss. This Self, indeed, is this everlasting happiness. The Self, indeed, is the eternally pure Self. The Self, indeed, is supreme in[1] the universe.

[1]*the absolute of*

34. The Self, indeed, is the Self of the five elements. The Self, indeed, is the Light of the Self. The Self, indeed, ever is. Nothing else ever is. The Self, indeed, is the immutable Supreme.

35. The Self, indeed, is the Self that illumines the Self. The Self alone is the changeless glory. The Self alone is Brahman-Knowledge. The Self alone is "I" and "you," indeed.

36. The Self alone is the Supreme Bliss. I am, indeed, the Self, which pervades this universe. I am, indeed, the Self, which is the illuminator of the world. I am but the Self, nothing else.

37. The Self alone is the ablution of the Self. The Self alone is the japa of the Self. The Self alone is the joy of the Self. The Self alone is the beloved of the Self, ever.

38. The Self is ever of the Self. The Self is the manifester[1] of the guna-s. The Self, indeed, is the Self of the nature of the fourth state. The Self is transcendent beyond that (beyond the fourth). It is, then, the Supreme.

[1]*cause of the appearance*

39. The Self alone is the ever-full Self. I am the Self alone. There is no doubt of this. The Self, indeed, is you. I, also, am the Self. All, indeed, is only the Self alone.

40. I am eternal. I am eternally full. I am eternal, always and forever. I am the Self alone. The world[1] is not something different. The Self is immortal and ancient.

[1] *universe*

41. I am ancient. I am the Purusha. I am Isvara. I am higher than the highest. I am the Supreme Isvara. I bestow worldly existence, and I destroy worldly existence. I bestow happiness. I am of the nature of happiness. I am nondual.

42. I am Bliss. I am the endless.[1] I am immortal. There is no doubt of this. I am unborn. I am of the nature of the Self and nothing else. I am always full of love.

[1] *entirety*

43. I am only Brahman. This is Brahman. All is Brahman, the ever changeless. There is never such a word as "all"; "all" is never there.

44. I am without qualities. [I am] without support. "I" am ever nonexistent. There is no root for the meaningless. There is no effect of delusion[1] at all.

[1] *māyā*

45. There never is any power of ignorance. I am Brahman. There is no doubt of this. All is Brahman, the space of Consciousness. I am only That. There is no doubt of this.

46. I am only That. I am also myself. I am also another.[1] I am the Supreme Isvara. I am the substratum of Knowledge alone here. There is really nothing such as knowledge and ignorance.

[1] *param, the Supreme*

47. I am Consciousness. I am Consciousness, eternally. I am the Fourth State. I am, besides, the experiencer of the Fourth State. Brahman alone is all. Brahman alone is all. I am ever Brahman.

48. There is nothing in the least apart from me. There is no Brahman apart from me at any time. There is no Supreme apart from me. There is no word "Consciousness" apart from me.

49. There is no denotation as "reality" apart from me. Apart from me, there is no denotation as "Consciousness" for me. Apart from me, there is no abode. There is no Brahman, indeed, apart from me.

50. Apart from me, there is no cause. Apart from me, there is not the least atom. There is no sattva guna[1] apart from me, nor is there any purity apart from me.

[1] *rūpam, form, nature*

51. Apart from me, there is nothing sanctified. Apart from me, there is no word as "That." Nor is there any form of dharma apart from me—nor anything of all.

52. Apart from me, there is only unreality here. Apart from me, there is only illusion.[1] All who manifest themselves apart from me and all that are apart from me are like the horns of a hare.

[1] *mithyā*

53. If anything manifests itself apart from me, it is illusion. All apart from me is as magic. There is nothing uncertain apart from me, nor is there any cause and effect apart from me.

54. "All this is Brahman; I am He" should be the meditation. All this has been said by the Lord. Be of the certitude that this is so.

55. What of repetitious sayings, Yogi! Be of this certitude, ever. Having this certitude, one, indeed, becomes Brahman oneself.

56. This world of forests and mountains is not apart from Sankara. This universe of demons and others is only that God of gods. It is He, the Supreme Siva, that is perceived by the subtle mind in the form of sheaths that are the body, mind, and others.

57. The eye, the ear, the mind, and others illumined well in the heart from deep inside, in the course of time, dissolve themselves therein only, with the scent of the vasana-s (acquired tendencies). What has been indicated by the Consort of the Mountain-born Himself is only the nectar of Brahman, which animates thought and is far beyond the reach of the heart and the senses, words and mind.

Chapter Sixteen

brahmānanda-prakaraṇam
TOPIC OF THE BRAHMAN-BLISS

Ribhu:
I shall now tell you about the Bliss of Brahman, rare to come by in all three worlds, just by hearing which one can attain eternal Liberation.

2. I am, indeed, the Self that is supreme Bliss, ever Bliss only. I am of the nature of complete Bliss. The world[1] is all Consciousness-Bliss.

[1] *jagat, universe*

3. I am, ever, endless[1] Bliss. This world[2] is Knowledge-Bliss. I am of the nature of Enlightened Bliss. This mind is ever Bliss.

[1] *infinite* [2] *jagat*

4. I am just simple[1] Bliss. I am just Knowledge alone. Try to be of this conviction for the extinction[2] of the phenomenal world.

[1] *kevala, lone* [2] *cessation*

5. I am, indeed, ever the True, the Supreme Light, ever characterized by Existence and such. I am ever the Self, devoid of existence and such, ever the Light, the desirable[1].

[1] *dear, beloved*

6. The self of the illusory phenomenal world does not exist. The illusion of the mind does not exist. The self of what is called illusion does not exist. The mistaken self of the mind does not exist.

7. There are none in this world who are more ignorant, nor are there any who are most ignorant among men. I, indeed, am the Supreme Brahman. I, indeed, am ever myself.

8. Here[1] and hereafter[2] do not exist, indeed. I alone exist. I am Brahman. I am pure. All is Brahman alone.
[1]*This* [2]*another, beyond*

9. All the world[1] is ever unreal. Thought alone is the entire world. Thought alone is said to be the phenomenal world. Thought alone is the cause of the body.
[1]*jagat*

10. Thought alone is the great fault. Thought alone is the little boy; thought alone is this great man. Thought alone is the great unreality.

11. Thought alone is the illusory self. Thought is like the horns of a hare. Thought is ever nonexistent. This is the truth. It is like the son of a barren woman.

12. Thought is the void; there is no doubt of this. Brahman, indeed, is all the world.[1] I, indeed, am sentience.[2] I, indeed, am the attributeless.
[1]*jagat* [2]*caitanyaṁ*

13. The mind, indeed, is worldly existence.[1] The mind, indeed, is the mandala. The mind, indeed, is bondage. The mind, indeed, is sin.[2]
[1]*saṁsāra* [2]*the fall*

14. The mind, indeed, is the great sorrow. The mind, indeed, is the cause of the body. The mind, indeed, is said to be the world of phenomena. The mind, indeed, is the body.

15. The mind, indeed, is the great sattva. The mind, indeed, is the four-faced Lord (Brahma). The mind, indeed, is, verily, Hari directly seen. The mind, indeed, is said to be Siva remembered.

16. The mind, indeed, is said to be magic.[1] The mind is mere sankalpa. The mind only is the great sin. The mind, indeed, is the evil-minded.

[1]*Indra's net*

17. The mind, indeed, is said to be all. The mind, indeed, is the great fear. The mind, indeed, is the Supreme Brahman. The mind, indeed, is all by itself.[1]

[1]*kevalam*

18. The mind, indeed, is of the nature of Consciousness. The mind it is that makes the mind what it is. Consciousness alone is of the nature of the Supreme. Consciousness alone is the supreme abode.

19. At this moment, I alone am the Supreme Brahman. I alone am verily the Supreme Brahman. I alone am the contented Self. I am the embodiment of Bliss.

20. I am the Self with fully matured Knowledge, ever motionless and pure. I, indeed, am the peaceful Self. I am without beginning or end.

21. I am the illumined Self. I am, indeed, Brahman alone. I am everlasting. There is no doubt of this. I am ever Knowledge-loving.

22. I, indeed, am. I, indeed, am the One. I am totally the Immortal. I alone am the self-determined.[1] I alone am the approver.[2]

[1]*self-established*   [2]*the one who assents, shows sympathetic joy*

23. I, indeed, am you yourself. I am the Self of all, devoid of all. I, indeed, am the Supreme Brahman. I am higher than the highest.

24. Ego there is none for me. No sorrow and no faults exist for me. No happiness exists for me. There is no knowledge[1] for me, no thinking[2] for me, no body for me, and no senses for me.
[1]intellect [2]mind

25. Lineage there is none for me. There are no eyes for me, no role[1] for me, nothing of the least or trivial for me. Japa there is none for me. No mantra, no world, no friend exists for me.
[1]adept

26. Relatives there are none for me. No enemies exist for me. No mother and no father exist for me. There is nothing to be experienced for me, no experiencer for me, no activity[1] for me, and no lineage for me.
[1]vṛttiḥ

27. Caste[1] there is none for me. No community,[2] no study of the Vedas are there for me, never for me. Exterior there is none for me. No knowledge[3] is there for me. No place or peer[4] exists for me.
[1]birth [2]color [3]buddhiḥ, intellect [4]age

28. Philosophy[1] there is none for me. No world exists for me. No peace is there for me. No line of descent exists for me. Anger there is none for me; nor is there desire for me. I am only of Brahman alone.
[1]tattvam, truth

29. Being just Brahman alone, I am just myself. There is no attachment or covetousness or stotra (hymn) or scripture[1] for me.
[1]smṛtiḥ

30. Delusion there is none for me. No desire exists for me. No friendship is there for me. There are no qualities for me, no sheaths for me, no childhood for me, no youth for me, and no senility for me.

31. As all are of the nature of Brahman, it is certain that Brahman is one. There is nothing higher than Brahman. There is nothing apart from Brahman.

32. There is nothing as "this" apart from Brahman. Verily, there is nothing as "this" apart from Brahman. There never is anything apart from the Self. I am, indeed, the Self. There is no doubt of this.

33. Apart from the Self, there is no happiness. Apart from the Self, I do not exist, either. I am devoid of grasping or anything to be grasped, devoid of renunciation or anything to be renounced.

34. There is nothing to renounce for me, nor is there anything to acquire. There is no bondage, nor is there anything that can offer liberation. No world exists for me, and there is nothing inferior, nothing superior, and nothing adverse.[1]

[1]detracting, corrupting

35. There is no strength for me. There are no outcastes for me, nor are there castes such as Brahmins. No protection exists for me. There is nothing short[1] for me, nothing weak[2] for me, and no strength for me.

[1]weak, insignificant [2]diminished

36. There is no power for me, no enjoyment for me, no destiny for me, and no separateness for me. Being only Brahman, I am nothing apart from eternality.

37. There is no religion[1] for me and no illusion for me. There is truly no body for me, ever. There is surely no such thing as "I," nor any name such as "Brahman."

[1]doctrine, idea

38. Whatever, whatsoever, phenomenal world there is, whatever, whatsoever, words of the guru there are, I am, indeed. All that is Brahman. All that is considered as Consciousness.

39. Brahman is Consciousness, Consciousness,[1] ever the Reality, ever the Reality.[2] One is oneself Brahman. One is oneself the Supreme.

[1]*cinmayaṁ* [2]*sanmayaṁ*

40. One is oneself Liberation. Oneself is continuity. Oneself, indeed, is empirical knowledge.[1] Oneself, indeed, is atheism.

[1]*vijñānaṁ, awareness*

41. Oneself is ever the essence. One is oneself the Supreme. Oneself is the Self of the Void. Oneself is the mind-captivating.

42. Sitting in Silence, indeed, is the holy ablution. Sitting in Silence, indeed, is the japa. Sitting in Silence, indeed, is the worship. Sitting in Silence, indeed, is the highest.

43. Inquiring constantly[1] with the mind, be of the certitude that I am Brahman. There is no doubt that I am Brahman. Remaining Silent, thus, is the japa.

[1]*always*

44. All is only Brahman; nothing else exists. All is of the nature of the tapas filled with Knowledge. There is nothing, indeed, as oneself. [I am] of the nature of the all-transcendent.

45. I am the true nature that transcends words. Doing japa with words is meaningless. This is the highest explanation of the mind. A difference such as "I and this" does not exist for me.

46. All beings are like corpses. All groups are as corpses. The world is ever unreal. All the universe is unreal.

47. Being a thing apart is unreal. There is no such word as "unreal." Being something is unreal. You, yourself, are ever Brahman alone.

48. The Vedas and the branches of the Vedas are unreal. The conclusions of the scriptures[1] are unreal. This listening is verily unreal. Reflection on that is unreal.

[1] *śāstraniścayaḥ*

49. Profound meditation, too, is unreal. Classification as a particular group is unreal. Classification into different groups is unreal. This declaration is the truth. This is the truth. There is no doubt of this. All is Brahman, ever Brahman, ever Brahman. Brahman is one, the changeless Consciousness.

50. Verily, this universe is born out of the sport of the mind. It manifests itself in fullness by the compassion of the Lord of the universe. Only by following the pure words arising from the crest of the Vedas and acting according to the injunctions of the scriptures does Liberation follow, not otherwise.

Chapter Seventeen

ātma-vaibhava-prakaraṇam
TOPIC OF THE GLORY OF THE SELF

Ribhu:
Hear this, which is exclusive, deep,[1] secret, most marvelous, this which is highly mysterious and ever instantly conferring Liberation.

[1]*kevalamatyantaṁ*

2. Easy is the Knowledge of Brahman. It is easy, auspicious, and the best. It is easy for them who are established[1] in Brahman, and it gives Knowledge of everything.

[1]*abide*

3. It is easy for them who have fulfilled their duties, easy for them abiding in themselves, easy and causeless, and easy for them who are established in Brahman.

4. It is easy for them who are without thought, for them who are themselves That, itself, for them who are without the cycle of recurrent birth.[1] Thought is said to be this world.[1]

[1]*saṁsāra*

5. This world[1] has not been created. This is only Brahman. It is not even the mind. This is, indeed, Brahman. There is nothing to fear. This is Brahman and nothing else.

[1]*saṁsāra*

6. All this that is unreal is, indeed, Brahman. It is Brahman that is to be sought. Brahman is, indeed, [all] these bodies. All this is Brahman alone. There is not a blade of grass [apart].

7. I am Brahman alone. I am not anyone else. This is, verily, Brahman. There is no world.[1] This space[2] is unreal; it is Brahman alone. Action is unreal; it is Brahman alone.

[1]*jagat* [2]*sky*

8. These great personages are, indeed, Brahman. This love is ever Brahman. This limitless universe is, indeed, Brahman. I, indeed, am Brahman. There is nothing to fear.

9. I am, indeed, Brahman and also ever the mind. I, indeed, am Brahman. I am, verily, not this. Whatever is illusory is Brahman, and that is verily myself. This apprehension is verily Brahman, myself.

10. Brahman, indeed, is entirely the settled conclusion. Brahman, indeed, is the seat[1] of the mind. Brahman, indeed, is all the abodes. Brahman, indeed, is the mandala of sages.

[1]*abode*

11. I am, indeed, Brahman. There is nothing else. Worship of the Guru is also Brahman. Brahman, indeed, is nothing else. Brahman, indeed, is all ever.

12. Brahman, indeed, is the triad of guna-s. Brahman, indeed, is of the form of Hari. There is no word other than Brahman. There is not a moment for me apart from Brahman.

13. I am Brahman, indeed. There is no other word. I am Brahman, indeed. There is nothing else heard. I am Brahman, indeed. There is no equal. All is only Brahman, indeed.

14. I am Brahman, indeed. There is no experience for me. I am Brahman, indeed. There is nothing separate from me. I am Brahman; indeed, nothing else is. Only Brahman, indeed, is of the nature of Brahman.

15. Brahman alone ever manifests.[1] Brahman alone is the greatest happiness. Brahman alone is the manifold. I am Brahman alone, the great love.

[1]*shines*

16. Brahman alone is to be worshipped by Brahman. Brahman alone is the Guru of Brahman. Brahman alone is the mother of Brahman. I am, indeed, Brahman, the father and the son.

17. Brahman, indeed, is Brahman and its deity. Brahman, indeed, is Brahman and its origin. Brahman is the Self of the nature of meditation. Brahman, indeed, is the guna of Brahman.

18. The Self, indeed, is the ever-present Self.[1] There is nothing other than the Self. The Self is, verily, ever the Self. The Self, indeed, is the Guru of the Self.

[1]*sarvanityātmā*

19. The Light of the Self has become "I." The Self is ever itself. I am, indeed, Brahman indicated by "That you are." I, myself, indeed, shine as the illuminator.

20. I, myself, am the peacefulness of the individual soul. I, myself, am of the nature of Isvara. I am Brahman, the Supreme Brahman. I alone am, and I am immutable.

21. I, myself, am the destruction and the ultimate conclusion. I, myself, am the Self that illuminates. I, myself, am the Self of the luminous nature. I am, myself, intensely pure.

22. I, myself, am the eternal Self. I am the pure without aversion or desire. I, myself, am the Vedas.[1] I am without a body or such.

[1] *chandaḥ, pleasing*

23. I am the faultless Self. I reach out like space. "This one" and "the other nearer" do not exist. This is without any differences.

24. Brahman alone manifests as thought. Brahman alone is Siva, ever. Brahman alone manifests as intellect, and Brahman alone is Siva, ever.

25. Brahman alone shines as the rabbit on the moon, ever. Brahman alone is the gross. Brahman, indeed, is never anything different. Brahman is its own Guru.

26. I am the Light of the Self. I, as myself, never am. I am, myself, the Supreme Brahman. I am, myself, immutable Consciousness.

27. I am, myself, the self-illumined that shines everywhere by itself. I am, myself, Brahman. I, myself, am the body. I, myself, am the fullness and the highest of men.

28. I am, myself, the Brahman of "That you are." I, myself, shine as the illuminator. I am the peace of the individual soul. I am myself of the nature of Isvara.

29. I am, myself, the Supreme Brahman. I am, myself, the only one and that which is immutable. I am the revealed Ultimate.[1] I am the established Ultimate.[2] I am, myself, the Self that illumines.

[1] *established result* [2] *conclusion*

30. I am the Self of the nature of Light. I, myself, am absolutely immaculate. I, myself, am certainly the eternal Self. I, myself, am the pure, the lovable, and the unlovable.

31. I, myself, am, indeed, rooted in myself. I am, myself, without a body. I am the faultless Self. I am, myself, spread out[1] like space.

[1]*abide*

32. I am undivided and full, filled with the essence of the indivisible. I am, indeed, the indivisible Bliss. I am of the nature that is unlimited (uninterrupted).

33. Being of this certitude, I am the complete Self. I am Brahman and not separately myself. I, indeed, am the eternal Self. I am, indeed, the ancient.

34. I am, indeed, that Brahman. I am Brahman, the Lord of the universe. I am, indeed, Brahman without distortions. I am, indeed, Brahman, the unafflicted.

35. I am, indeed, Brahman, the space of Consciousness. I am, indeed, Brahman, the perpetual. I am, indeed, Brahman, the great Bliss. I am, indeed, Brahman, which is ever of the Self.

36. I am, indeed, Brahman, the limitless[1] Self. I am indeed Brahman, the supreme joy. I am, indeed, Brahman, the totally silent,[2] the completely inactive.

[1]*infinite* [2]*the great silent one*

37. I am Brahman only. All this is illusory. I am, indeed, Brahman. The world is unreal. I am Brahman alone. I am not the body. I am Brahman alone, the great nonduality.

38. Brahman alone manifests as thought. Brahman alone [manifests] as Siva, ever. Brahman alone manifests as Knowledge. Brahman, itself, [manifests] as the result.

39. Brahman, itself, manifests as a form. You are that Brahman. There is no doubt of this. Brahman, itself, manifests as time. Brahman, itself, [manifests] as all.

40. Brahman, itself, manifests as the sentient beings, and Brahman, itself, manifests as the insentient. Brahman is all as Omkara. Brahman, itself, is of the nature of Omkara.

41. Brahman alone is Brahman as sound. There is nothing else different or nondual. It is the truth. It is the truth. Again, it is the truth. There is nothing apart from Brahman.

42. Brahman itself is the Self of all. There is nothing apart from Brahman. All is illusory. The phenomenal world[1] is illusory, as [all are] only appearances like the pot and such ever.

[1]*jagat*

43. I am, indeed, Brahman. There is no doubt of this. Because I am only Consciousness, I ever exist. I am, indeed, Brahman because of my pure nature. I, myself, am great because I am the seer.

44. I am, indeed, the Supreme Brahman. I am higher than the highest. I myself transcend the mind. I am beyond the universe.

45. I am, verily, the eternal Self. I am of the nature of illusion. I am Bliss. I am supportless. I am only Brahman and nothing else.

46. I am nothing else but Brahman. I am nothing else but immutable Consciousness. Outside[1] of the Self, all else is insignificant. I do not exist apart from the Self.

[1]*other than*

47. Apart from the Self, I have no body. I am, indeed, the Self. I have no blemish. My mind is only [concentrated] in the Self. I am, indeed, the Self. It is not different.

48. I am, indeed, the Self. I am the Void. I am, verily, the Self. There is nothing mine, ever. I am, indeed, the Self. There are no qualities for me. I am the Self. There is nothing different anywhere.

49. You are completely nonexistent. All, like these, are totally nonexistent. This is totally nonexistent. Even an atom is non-existent—completely so.

50. I am, indeed, the Self, the Supreme Brahman. The triad of worlds is all illusory. I am, indeed, the Supreme Brahman. I, indeed, am the Supreme Guru.

51. The concept of the individual soul is ever unreal. The concept of the existence of Siva is also likewise. The concept of Vishnu is also misapprehension. All is like the horns of a hare.

52. I, indeed, am the ever full. I, indeed, am interstice-less. Ever satisfied and formless, I am, indeed, Brahman. There is no doubt of this.

53. I am, indeed, the supremely blissful. I, indeed, can cease to exist in a moment. I am you; you are I; you and I do not exist, do not exist, indeed.

54. I am surely beyond the range of words. Words and mind, indeed, do not exist. They are imagined. I am, indeed, Brahman, the Self of all. I am, indeed, Brahman, the spotless.

55. I am Brahman alone, just Consciousness. I am Brahman alone, the everlasting. This never is. I alone am the ever established.

56. This is joy. I am Brahman. This is joy. I am insentient. This doubtlessly is Brahman. This is the truth. This is the truth, again and again.

57. Thus, the glory of the Self has been proclaimed. This teaching is rare to come by in all the worlds. By hearing this once, one becomes Brahman himself.

58. Those who are tired by worldly existence, with their minds set on peace and self-control and who resort to the destroyer of Antaka (death) (Siva), the Lord of the moon who ever shines inside oneself, attain their peace, indeed, by the words of the crest of the Vedas.

Chapter Eighteen

sarva-prapañca-heyatva-prakaraṇa-varṇanam
DESCRIPTION OF THE TOPIC OF ALL PENTADS TO BE DISCARDED

Ribhu:

I shall tell you the great secret, hidden even in the Vedas,[1] by hearing which you, yourself, shall become Brahman, indeed.

[1] *vedānta*

---

2. I am Existence-Consciousness-Bliss alone. All is pervaded by Existence-Consciousness. Seeing that as Brahman itself, you shall become Brahman yourself.

3. I am Brahman. This is Brahman. All the multiplicity is Brahman. There is no doubt of this. Existence is Brahman, ever Brahman. I am Brahman alone.

4. The Guru is Brahman. Guna is Brahman. All is Brahman. I am the higher [Knowledge]. Brahman is infinite. I am Brahman. All is Brahman. I am the lower [knowledge].

5. The Supreme Brahman is to be known through the Vedas. Brahman is to be known specially through Knowledge. The Self is Brahman. I am Brahman. The beginning and the end are Brahman. I am He.

6. Reality is Brahman, ever Brahman. There is nothing else. It is always the Supreme. I am Brahman, but "I" do not exist; there is nothing as egoism.

7. I am Brahman. This does not exist. This Self is ever the greatest. Brahman-Self is to be comprehended through the Vedas.[1] All else is like the horns of a hare.

[1]*vedānta*

___

8. There is no past and no future. Brahman remains constant. I am full of Consciousness. I am only Consciousness. The destruction of the inert body is insignificant.

___

9. The least thought whatever, the least momentary thought whenever—any thought—is something afar. I am of the Self, which is Truth, Knowledge, and Infinity. I am not of the nature of untruth, insentience, and sorrow.

___

10. The Self is real. Indeed, the body is only the infinite Self. There is no doubt of this. Whatever words are heard are unreal. They are nonexistent. I am the Light of the light.[1]

[1]*mahomahaḥ, Great Light (a name of Siva)*

___

11. Enumeration, such as one and so forth, is unreal. Brahman, indeed, is the Reality. I am ever real. All is, indeed, unreal, being ever only but manifestations of[1] the Supreme.

[1]*arisen from*

___

12. Though bereft of all limbs, I am, indeed, supreme because of eternal existence. All that is seen is naught for me. I say so because of being Consciousness alone.

___

13. There is nothing to be acquired for me. I say so because of being Consciousness alone. Nor is there anything to be pointed out as "this." "This" is nowhere, nowhere ever.

___

14. Because of the teaching of the [good] Guru, I am, verily, the attributeless Brahman. Empirical knowledge[1] is Brahman with attributes. I am the embodiment of knowledge.[1]

[1]*vijñānaṁ*

___

15. I am attributeless. I am partless. I am the creator. I am the sustainer. I am the God. I am full of wealth.[1] I am pure. I am devoid of anything.

[1] *the perfectly full substance*

16. I am the essence. I am devoid of the essence. I am the fourth state. I am the feeling of auspiciousness. I am desire. I am actionless. I am the embodiment of perennial purity.

17. I am devoid of codes of conduct and their fruits. I am Brahman alone. All this is the Supreme Brahman. This is the Self. There is no wonder in this.

18. The Self is of the nature of the full and the not-full. It is ever the nature of the Self of all. The Self is the Principle[1] of Supreme Bliss without any limitations[2] at any time.

[1] *Truth* [2] *interruptions*

19. Joined with the bhava of "I," united with the bhava of "I," have the attitude that I am, indeed, the one Self, pure by nature.

20. Look upon the Self of all as peaceful. The "principle of peacefulness" is a blemish of the mind. Renouncing the thought that I am the body, be of the certitude that I am Brahman.

21. I am Brahman, only Brahman, and nothing apart from[1] Brahman. I am not this, I am not this, I am not this—remember this ever.

[1] *other than*

22. I am He-am-I; I am He-am-I; I am Brahman—contemplate thus. Consciousness am I; Consciousness am I; I am Brahman; Consciousness am I; Consciousness am I—declare thus.

23. This is not, this is not. This ever is not; this is not you or me—contemplate thus. All is Brahman. There is no doubt of this. All is known to be nothing.

24. All is a built-up structure of words and meanings. The apprehension of all the worlds does not exist. All the holy waters are, indeed, unreal. All the temples of the gods, too, are unreal.

25. All being only Consciousness, the name "all" never is. Renouncing all forms, be of the certitude that all is Brahman.

26. All is Brahman. That is the Truth. The phenomenal world and prakriti (manifestation), verily, do not exist. Renounce the remembrance of prakriti and resort to the remembrance of Brahman.

27. Then, renouncing even that, be firm in your own nature. Renouncing further this established nature, remain only as the Self.

28. Renouncing the renunciation even, ever leave off[1] the idea of any difference. Surrounding yourself yourself, abide in yourself yourself.

[1]abandon

29. What the finger points out as this, the seen, is a deceased[1] thought. This is only of[2] words and speech.

[1]dead [2]This word is the lamentation by

30. All is supposition. There is no doubt of this. All is unreal. There is no uncertainty of this. All is insignificant. There is no doubt of this. All is delusion. There is no doubt of this.

31. You and I are Brahman. There is no doubt of this. This is only Brahman. There is no uncertainty of this. All is the mind. There is no doubt of this. All is Brahman. There is no uncertainty in this.

32. If illusion manifests itself apart from Brahman, all is illusion from one end to the other. There is neither body nor the five elements nor the mind, which is a mere misconception.

33. Nor is there the existence of the intellect or the senses. Nor is there liberation that is just Brahman. If that exists, there is neither a moment's doubt (fear) nor sankalpa.

34. If the ego exists, know that it is unreal. If conceit exists, it is unreal. There is no remembrance or thought, no doubt, and no decay.

35. The prana ... (missing phrase) if there is a nose, there is a sense of smell. If there is an eye, there is form. If there are ears, there is the bhava of hearing.

36. If there is skin, there is the existence of touch. If there is a tongue, there is the ability to taste. If there is a jiva, there is life. If there are feet, walking is present.

37. If there are hands, there is the existence of action. If there is a creator, creation is possible. If there is a thing to be protected, there is Vishnu the protector. If there is something to be consumed, the consumer, Siva, exists.

38. All is Brahman. There is no doubt of this. All is Brahman alone. If there is a thing to be worshipped, worship also is present. If there is a manifestation, there is the manifester, Siva.

39. All is illusory. There is no doubt of this. All is Consciousness alone. If the cause is real, the effect also will result.[1]

[1]become

40. If all these do not exist,[1] I am, without nonexistence. I am only Brahman, the goal. This only is the endless sorrow. This, indeed, is the changeless, never-ending joy.

[1]If there is "is not,"

142

41. Life,[1] itself, is endless; there is the possibility[1] of endless struggle. All is total impurity. The Supreme, [though], is the completely pure.

[1]*birth*

42. Wrong imagination is endless. I am totally pure. Error is ever endless. Goodness is ever endless.

43. Brightness is ever endless. Impurity is ever endless. I am, also, ever endless. This, also, is ever endless.

44. Brahman is ever endless. The world is ever endless. What has been said so far is no cause for fear. I do not have any differences in the least.

45. There is no reality or unreality. Indeed, "reality" and "unreality" are words. They are nonexistent. They are nonexistent. There is no doubt of this. I am, indeed, Brahman. There is no doubt of this.

46. There is entirely nothing of the nature of cause and effect. There is no doubt about this. Likewise, there is no doer, enjoyer, or activity. There is nothing to be enjoyed; nor is there the satisfaction of enjoyment.

47. All is Brahman. There is no doubt of this. The term "all" is not real. The past, the future, and the present, as well as activity, are ever nonexistent.

48. Neither differences of reality and unreality nor differentiation into the real and the unreal, nor qualities, nor the differentiation of qualities exist. Purity and impurity do not exist, do not exist in the least.

49. There is nothing. There is nothing in the least of which to speak, nothing of talk at all. There is nothing at all of strength or weakness or you or me.

50. Neither is there anything to be grasped; nor is there anyone to grasp. There is never anything to be disregarded. For
the Self, there are neither holy rivers nor any form of ablution,
neither gods nor worship of gods.

51. There never is, never is in the least, any cause for life[1] or
death. There never is, never is, any truth or form of truth in
the least.

[1]*birth*

52. There are no mothers or fathers or bodies in the least.
There is neither the form of the seer nor the form of the seen.
There is nothing in the least here.

53. The effects of delusion[1] or the existence of any delusion[1]
is not here in the least, not in the least. Knowledge or differences of knowledge are not here in the least, not in the least.

[1]*māyā, illusion*

54. I have explained to you the need for rejecting the entire
phenomenal world. Whosoever hears this, even once, attains
the status of the Self.

55. Skanda:

That maya, with the triad of guna-s, becomes dissolved by
the worship of the lotus feet of the parent of the Lord of the
gana-s (Ganesa), with the moon as his crest-jewel, and not
by any other means. The goddess of Knowledge shines like
a streak of lightning in the innermost recesses of the heart of
one whose no small tapas she blesses with a look of utmost
compassion; that one's Liberation is permanent.

Chapter Nineteen

nāma-rūpa-niṣedha-prakaraṇam
TOPIC OF THE NEGATION OF NAME AND FORM

Ribhu:
All is Brahman, I tell you. All this is nonexistent. The phenomenal world is a falsity. I am Brahman. I have no thought.[1] I am Brahman. There is no insentience for me.

[1] *There is no thought for me*

2. I am Brahman. I have no mistake.[1] I am Brahman. I have no results. I am Brahman. There is no word for me. I am Brahman. I have no second.

[1] *fault*

3. I am Brahman. I have no permanency. I am Brahman. I have nowhere to go. I am Brahman. I have no mother. I am Brahman. I have no father.

4. I am Brahman. For me, there is no such thing as "He is this." I am not, indeed, Vaisvanara (Cosmic Self). I am Brahman, the Space of Consciousness. I am Brahman. There is no doubt of this.

5. I am in the interior of all. I am the perfectly full Self, inmost of all, inmost of the mind. I am, indeed, the inmost of the body. I am ever the immovable.

6. One who knows this is liberated. This Knowledge is difficult to obtain. Only one in many hundreds of thousands has this discrimination.

7. By just a look at him, the deceased ancestors are satisfied. The sight of such wise men is punya. It is equal to bathing in all holy waters.

8. A man will become liberated while yet alive only by offering worship to such wise men. By offering food and charity to such wise men, a man will immediately become liberated.

9. I am Brahman. There is no doubt of this. I, myself, am the supreme Guru. I am peaceful. I am pure. I myself am the core of the guna-s.

10. [I] transcend the qualities, transcend humanity, transcend the highest, transcend the mind, transcend the highest of the high, transcend intellect, and transcend the essence.

11. [I] transcend contemplation, transcend the mind, transcend the Vedas, transcend knowledge, transcend the body and such, and transcend wakefulness, dream, and deep sleep.

12. [I] transcend "the supreme, primal, unmanifest state." Such is the conclusion of Knowledge. Whoever, renouncing this and leaving[1] all, like a mute,

[1]abandoning

13. is silently Brahman oneself—the Supreme Brahman, the eternal Brahman—even an atom of the greatness of such a wise one is clearly evident

14. and is incapable of being described by Hari or by Hara or by Brahma or by the gods, even in hundreds of crores of kalpa-s.

15, 16. The wisdom[1] that I am Brahman is rare to come by in all the three worlds. It is rare to have a look at great people[2] of such discrimination and abidance as only

Brahman and converse with them and touch their feet. If one has a bath in the water that has at any time touched their feet, one becomes Brahman oneself.

[1]Knowledge [2]souls

17. All is illusory. There is no doubt of this. All is Brahman alone. This explanation is said to be the summary of all the settled conclusions.

18. The man who reads with devotion this rare exposition attains Brahman. I say that all is Brahman; there is nothing else. The entire world is a falsity.

19. Brahman alone is this world[1]-form. Brahman alone is the supreme abode. I am, indeed, the Supreme Brahman. Even "I," indeed, is to be excluded.

[1]jagad

20. I am just Consciousness,[1] excluding all. I am the [Supreme] Chetana (sentience), excluding all. I am the peaceful Self, excluding all. I am the embodiment of all auspiciousness.

[1]cinmātraṁ

21. I am Brahman, the Supreme Brahman. This is not real for me, not for me. There are no past and future for me and no castes for me. There is no doubt of this.

22. I am, indeed, Brahman. Not even the least thing exists for me. I am Brahman. [I am] the supreme tapas. All this is of the nature of Brahman, of the nature of the afflictionless Brahman.

23. Brahman, itself, manifests as different. Brahman is nothing different. It is the Supreme. The Self, itself, manifests as if dual. The Self is the supreme abode.

24. Brahman is thus devoid of differences. Differentiation is the great fear. I am, indeed, the Self. I am pure. I am,[1] indeed, the triad of worlds.

[1]*The Self alone is*

25. The Self, indeed, is everywhere. Nothing else is so. All is Brahman and none else. I, myself, shine ever. I am, indeed, Brahman. I am the Supreme.

26. I am pure, the Supreme Brahman, and devoid of action and inaction. I am ever of the nature of the pure One, ever only Consciousness alone.

27. Definitely, I am the Supreme Brahman. I am the reality. I am all. I am indestructible. [I am] the Supreme Brahman. I am Siva. I am the summit.

28. I am of an equanimous nature. I am peaceful. I am merged[1] with That, immutable Consciousness. I am certainly ever Brahman and eternal. I am ever with the characteristics of only Consciousness.

[1]*completely devoted to*

29. I am ever of the nature of the undivided One. I am always beyond measure. Ever am I of the nature of the One and the pure. [I am] always only Consciousness alone.

30. I am ever the real measure, ever the Existence, and the illuminator. I am ever of the nature of the settled conclusion. I am always pure[1] and auspicious.

[1]*holy*

31. Whoever has this certitude is the liberated. Whoever is always thus is the superior. One who has this conviction is always the Supreme Brahman, indeed.

32. One who has the certitude that I am Brahman is the wise man[1] who is, himself, Brahman. He alone who has the certitude that he is Brahman[2] is the Purusha in this world.

[1] jñānī   [2] "I am Brahman"

33. That man alone is the wise one.[1] He is liberated while yet alive. He is of the Self. I am, indeed, Brahman, the great Self, of the nature of Existence-Consciousness-Bliss.

[1] jñānī

34. I am not the individual soul. There are no differences for me. I am not thought, nor am I the mind. I am neither flesh nor have I bones, nor am I the body with the ego.

35. Not thought out and not measurable, I am not all. I am transcendent. I am of the nature of All-Knowledge. I am not all, at any time.

36. I am not dead. I have not another life. I am not just Consciousness. I am not. I cannot be spoken of, nor am I liberated. I am not enlightened, ever.

37. I am not a void. I am not an ignoramus. I am not all. I am transcendent. I am ever Brahman alone. I am not the essence, [nor] Sadasiva, [ever].

38. I am not the nose, nor am I the scent. I am not a symbol. There are none dear to me. I am not the individual soul or its essence. I am not Varuna (the deity of water), nor am I the terrestrial globe.

39. I am Brahman. There is no doubt of this. I am without any name or form. I am not the ear, nor am I the sound. I am not any of the directions, nor am I a witness.

40. I am not you, not heaven, and not air; nor am I a witness of these. I am not the organ of excretion or the excretion. I am not death, nor am I a witness.

41. I am not a mystery, nor am I joy. I am not Prajapati (progenitor of the human race) or other gods. All is Brahman. There is no doubt of this. Indeed, all is Brahman alone.

42. I am not the mind, not sankalpa, not the moon; nor am I a witness either. I am not the intellect and not the senses. I am not Brahma, the creator, nor do I have a definite form.

43. I am not the ego. I am not Rudra. Neither am I an experiencer[1] nor a witness. I am not thought, nor am I Vasudeva, the supporter, nor this Isvara.

[1] *a desirous mind*

44. I am not the universe. I am not the waking state. There is nothing of any gross body for me. I am not the apparent jiva, nor am I of the phenomenal world.[1]

[1] *one with worldly life*

45. I am not a God that is the highest truth, nor am I an insentient sheath of matter (lit., of food). I am not a sheath of prana, nor am I one with the sheath of the mind.

46. Nor am I the sheath of intellectual knowledge, nor am I one with the sheath of bliss. I am Brahman alone. There is no doubt of this. I am without any name or form.

47. Having heard all this about the duality of name and form, all this should be forgotten in a second and abandoned like a scrap of wood or rusted iron.

48. All this is ever unreal, always, like the son of a barren woman. This is just like the horn of a hare. It is just like the horn of a man.

49. It is like[1] a flower in the sky. It is just like a mirage, like a city of gandharva-s (celestial beings) in the sky, and just like various kinds of wizardry.

[1] *resembles*

50. What is thought of as the pentad of the forms of gods is completely unreal. Duality is brought into use only at the time of initiating the disciple in instruction. It is not Absolute Truth.

51. When the mother is dead, people should be called in for crying [over the loss] and distributing dravya (goods or money). The pentad of dravya-s (substances: the elements earth, water, fire, air, space) is solely like their cries (unreal).

52. This nonduality has been explained by me to the one in eagerness who forgets all else. Be of the certitude that I am Brahman. Be of the conviction that I am Brahman.

53. Indeed, I am also Bliss. Indeed, I am nothing else. Indeed, I am Consciousness alone. Indeed, I am Brahman. Be of this certitude.

54. I am the spotlessly pure. I am without the characteristics of life.[1] Indeed, I am Brahman, the Self of all, shining as "I."

[1] *jīva*

55. Indeed, I am Consciousness alone. Indeed, I am the attributeless. I am all-pervasive[1] Brahman. I am Consciousness alone and ever peaceful.[2]

[1] *universal* [2] *sadāśivaḥ*

56. I am the Self, which is of the nature of eternal auspiciousness. I am the man who is ever in Liberation. Being of this certitude, ever abide in your Self, by yourself.

57. I am, indeed, Brahman. There is no doubt of this. There is no name or form for me. This explanation, in this form, is rare to come by in all the Vedas. Whoever hears this once himself becomes Brahman.

58. What is intensely and highly dear to the heart of that foe of Manmatha (god of passion)—whom the twice-born realize by the great yaga-s glorified by the words of the Vedas and by the experience of vrata-s (vowed observances), charities, fasts, yama, and other rigorous practices—is the worship of Siva as a linga. By that alone, Isvara quickly gives the gift of the great Knowledge that destroys all delusion.

Chapter Twenty

rahasyopadeśa-prakaraṇam
TOPIC OF THE SECRET INITIATION
(SPIRITUAL INSTRUCTION)

Ribhu:
Nidagha! Listen. I shall tell you what is rare to come by in all the worlds. [All] this is Brahman. The highest[1] is Brahman. Only Existence-Consciousness-Bliss is.

[1]*supreme*

---

2. The variety of persons of the world, the variety of actions and causes, anything apart from Brahman—all are unreal. All is, indeed, Existence-Consciousness-Bliss.

3. I am Brahman, always Brahman. I am, indeed, Brahman. Time is Brahman. A moment is Brahman. I am Brahman. There is no doubt of this.

4. The Veda is Brahman. The highest is Brahman. Truth is Brahman, [as is also] the higher than the highest. Brahma is Brahman. Hari is Brahman. Siva is Brahman, the changeless Consciousness.

5. All the Upanishads are Brahman. Equanimity is Brahman. I am equanimous. The unborn is Brahman. The essence is Brahman. The sky is Brahman. Brahman is higher than the highest.

6. Truti (a fleeting moment) is Brahman. The mind is Brahman. A group of separate, individualized things is Brahman, the ever joyful. [All] this is Brahman. The highest is Brahman. The [highest] Truth is Brahman. Brahman is ever the japa.

7. I am, indeed, Brahman, the [first] letter "a." I am the letter "u." There is no doubt of this. I alone am Brahman, the letter "m" (a, u, m constitute the sacred Aum). I am Brahman and the mantra. I am the supreme father of the human race (Manu).

8. I alone am Brahman, the letter "si." I alone am Brahman, the letter "va." I am ever Brahman, the letter "ya" (si, va, ya with namah is Sivayanamah, the sacred five-letter mantra). I am also the panchaksara (the great five-letter mantra: Namah Sivaya), the Supreme.

9. The exhaled breath, in reality, is Brahman.[1] The inhaled breath is Brahman, always[2] is Brahman. The retained breath is Brahman. I am all. I am Brahman, the substratum everywhere.

[1]Sadbrahman [2]everywhere

10. Brahman alone is. Nothing else is. All is only Existence-Consciousness-Bliss. One who has this certitude is one liberated at once. There is no doubt of this.

11. Some great ignoramuses talk only about duality. They are not fit to be spoken to, not fit to be honored, and not fit to be bowed to.

12. They are fools, bigger fools, to be considered as unworthy of attention, the biggest of fools. Such people are not for me ever. I am Knowledge alone.

13. There is no fear for me as all is only of the nature of Consciousness and of Bliss. Such a thing as "I," indeed, does not ever exist, nor does anything such as the highest exist ever.

14. Even Brahman is also nothing else. All that is is only Existence-Consciousness-Bliss. It transcends time, transcends happiness, and transcends all. It is the Transcendent.

15. It ever transcends the impermanent and the permanent. Brahman, which alone is, is boundless. Brahman alone exists. There is nothing else. Whatever is all is only of the nature of Existence-Consciousness-Bliss.

16. The [conceptual] knowledge that duality is real is only due to the intellect of duality. Forget that. All is only Brahman. Nothing else exists. All is Brahman alone.

17. Transcending the intellect, transcending the mind, transcending the Vedas, the Supreme, and also transcending oneself, transcending all people, transcending individual souls, attributeless,

18. transcending wooden [inaction], transcending art, transcending dance, the highest happiness—perceive all as Brahman alone, and be attuned[1] only to Brahman.

[1]*completely devoted*

19. Attuned[1] always only to Brahman, I am Consciousness alone. There is no doubt of this. I am only the Light and Bliss, only my own blissful Self.

[1]*completely devoted*

20. I am only the Self that is the Bliss of the Void. Remember that I am Consciousness alone. I am just Existence, here, always beyond time and qualities.

21. I am of the nature of eternal Reality, just the Self of pure Bliss. I am devoid of the manifold world. I am just Existence-Consciousness-Bliss.

22. I am just the Bliss of certitude. I am just the Bliss of solitude.[1] I am just the Supreme Bliss. I, indeed, am the perfectly full Bliss.

[1]*kevala*

23. I am settled about[1] the extent of duality. I am the definition of sovereignty. Being of this certitude, be as you please in all the three [states or times].

[1]*I am established over, or I am established regarding*

24. Being the Self, of the nature of firm certitude, filled with the Reality of firm certitude, being the peaceful Self of firm certitude, with a mind of firm certitude,

25. being the perfectly full Self of firm certitude, the pure[1] one of firm certitude, the jivatma of firm certitude, the auspicious one of firm certitude,

[1]*blemishless*

26. the jivatma of firm certitude has all doubts destroyed. Firm certitude here is alone the hallmark of the Knowledge of Brahman.

27. Firm certitude here is alone the hallmark of the Knowledge of the teaching. Firm certitude here is alone the cause of attaining the treasure of Liberation.

28. Ever acting in this manner alone enables the firmness that I am only Brahman. I am only Brahman. There is no doubt of this. I am just Existence-Consciousness-Bliss.

29. I am of the nature of the Bliss of the Self. Be of the conviction that nothing else exists. Then, renouncing even that conviction, be firm as just the One.

30. Then, renouncing even that, ever remain without any attributes. Renouncing even this attributeless-ness, one should transcend all words.

31. Renouncing even the transcendence of words, focus on just being Consciousness. Renouncing even the transcendence of the Self, focus on only Brahman.

32. Renouncing being only Consciousness alone, also, focus on just the all-silence. Renouncing the all-silence also, focus on ineffable quiescence.[1]

[1]*great silence*

33. Renouncing this ineffable quiescence[1] also, take refuge in quiescence of the mind. Renouncing the quiescence of the mind also, take to the quiescence of the jiva.

[1]*great silence*

34. Renouncing the quiescence of the jiva, too, focus on the void of the jiva. Renouncing the abandonment of the void, exist as you are.

35. Renouncing also that existence, which is beyond the range of words and mind, you should not speak of anything afterward or perceive anything afterward.

36. Or else, with total renunciation of everything, focus on "I am Brahman." Always remembering this, always thinking of this, be ever of the conviction of being without any qualities.

37. Ever remain the knower of the Truth, ever the wise,[1] ever the highest, ever blissful, ever transcendent, ever devoid of defects,

[1]*jñānī*

38. ever peaceful, ever satisfied, ever the Light, ever the essence, ever the eternal, ever the pure, ever the wise,[1] ever the dissolved,

[1]*enlightened*

39. ever Brahman, ever joyous, ever blissful, ever supreme, ever oneself, ever the Void, ever the Silent,[1] ever the auspicious (Siva),

[1] *maunī*

40. ever all, ever the friend, ever the ablution, ever the japa, ever forgetful of all, ever renounced in Silence.[1]

[1] *maunaṁ*

41. Renouncing attachment to the body, renounce the very substance of thought. Always be of the conviction that I am the Self, I am myself.

42. Remaining thus, you will become liberated, with no activity or inquiry. What little exists is all Brahman, indeed, Existence-Consciousness-Bliss.

43. I am Brahman. This is Brahman. You are Brahman always. You are [that which is indicated by] Prajnanam Brahman (Knowledge, or Consciousness, is Brahman) alone. You are Brahman. There is no doubt of this.

44. Be of this firm certitude and do good to yourself. Brahman is the jewel of the mind. The Supreme is the jewel of the mind.

45. The doer is the adornment of the mind. I am, indeed, Brahman, being the seer. Brahman is Existence-Consciousness-Bliss, of the nature of Existence-Consciousness-Bliss.

46. All is Existence-Consciousness-Bliss—Existence-Consciousness-Bliss, indeed. The individual soul[1] is Existence-Consciousness-Bliss—of the nature of Existence-Consciousness-Bliss.

[1] *jīvātmā*

47. Nonduality is Existence-Consciousness-Bliss. Sankara is Existence-Consciousness-Bliss. Empirical knowledge[1] is Existence-Consciousness-Bliss. The object of enjoyment is Existence-Consciousness-Bliss.

[1] *vijñānaṁ, awareness*

48. The perfectly full Self is Existence-Consciousness-Bliss. The generative cause is Existence-Consciousness-Bliss. The sportive Self is Existence-Consciousness-Bliss. Existence-Consciousness-Bliss is the treasure.

49. All the limbs are Existence-Consciousness-Bliss. The sandal paste is Existence-Consciousness-Bliss. The settled conclusion is Existence-Consciousness-Bliss. The creator of the Vedas is Existence-Consciousness-Bliss.

50. The meaning of all the scriptures is Existence-Consciousness-Bliss. The text is Existence-Consciousness-Bliss. The homa is Existence-Consciousness-Bliss. The ruler is Existence-Consciousness-Bliss.

51, 52. The perfectly full Self is Existence-Consciousness-Bliss. The one that fulfills is Existence-Consciousness-Bliss. Existence-Consciousness-Bliss alone is reality. What has been said here should never be discussed by the person of discrimination with those whose minds are given to the pleasures of the world. Nothing of this should be read aloud among the ignorant, nor should any of this be given to the totally foolish whom one may meet as a fellow traveler en route.

53, 54. By hearing this just once, one becomes Brahman oneself. If a woman desires to learn this, it should be from the mouth of a brahmin. All being Consciousness, the difference of being a woman also disappears. Even if endowed with a study of the Vedas, if there is absence of real Knowledge, the twice-born (brahmin with sacred thread) is really not twice-born.

159

55. Only the real aspirants after Liberation are truly endowed with the sacred thread of Brahman. This entire secret has been told by Bhagavan Sankara Himself, indeed.

56. To enjoy the fruits of the worship of the feet of the moon-crested Lord Siva, the concentrated Bliss, without any sensory organs, there is no other way such as yoga, or hearing of scriptures, let alone action, but only skillfully instructed, inner experience.

ahaṁ brahma-prakaraṇa-nirūpaṇam
TOPIC OF THE DEFINITION OF I AM BRAHMAN

Ribhu:
Again and again, I say unto you the highest truth: anything apart from the Self is unreal, indeed. There is no word for unreality. Reality being ever existent, there is no word for it.

2. I shall declare the definition[1] of the Self for one eager for Brahma-abhyasa (practice of Brahman). I shall speak of it immediately with an auspicious beginning.

[1] *nirṇayam, complete ascertainment*

3. All is Brahman. I, indeed, am only Consciousness. There is nothing else. I, indeed, am the Supreme Brahman. I am, also,[1] the Consciousness-Self.

[1] *indeed*

4. There is nothing as "I" or "mine." There is nothing as my being a wise man.[1] I am pure. I am of the nature of Brahman. I am Bliss. I am unborn. I am uncreated.

[1] *jñāni*

5. I am a god. I am the divine sun. I am the fourth state. I am the present and the future. I am the creator. I am the complete. I am the innermost of the innermost.

6. I am immortal. I am perpetual. I am the totally supreme. I am of the nature of the high and the low. I am of the nature of the essence of the eternal and the transient.

7. I am devoid of qualities and absence of qualities. I am the essence of the fourth state and the other than the fourth. I am devoid of space[1] and the absence of space.[1] I am of the nature of the essence of knowledge and ignorance.

[1]tranquility

8. I am devoid of time and timelessness. I am devoid of the Self and non-Self. I am devoid of the acquired, the un-acquired, and the like. I am all-void and immutable.

9. I, indeed, am myself.[1] I, indeed, am myself without interstices, and I am also not without interstices. I am permanent. I am without a goal. I am the Self. I am the perfectly full.

[1]"I"

10. I am the one without the term "and others." I am the first of "and others," and I also do not exist. I am devoid of the phrase "and others." I am unconquerable.

11. I am without discontinuity. I am the past; I am the future; I am the present. I am devoid of worldly existence. I am without any definitions or indirect attributes derived therefrom. I am actionless. I am that which moves quickly.

12. I do not have the nature[1] of space and others. I am of the untouched[2] nature of space. I am of the nature of the innermost of the innermost. I do not have anything as the innermost of the innermost.

[1]form [2]imperishable, solid

13. I am of the nature of all settled conclusions. I am devoid of all defects. I am never the liberated. I am never the one in bondage.

14. Doing only thus, ever remember I am, indeed, Brahman. By this much, itself, you will certainly become liberated.

15. I am Consciousness alone. I am all peace—Siva (Sivo'ham). I alone am ever the auspicious. I am of the nature of Truth. I am liberated and am ever beyond the range of words.

16. I am always the complete,[1] devoid of all knowledge and conditionings. I am devoid of other activities of the mind. There is no such thing as my having a mind.

[1]*paripūrṇa*

17. There is nothing in the least that exists. Loving talk is nonexistent, indeed. For me, really, there is no such thing as dear to the Self or the non-Self.

18. This is sorrow; this is happiness; this shines [of itself]. "I," indeed, do not exist. I am of the nature devoid of all. I am the Cetana devoid of all.

19. Indescribable, indescribable, I am, indeed, the essence of the Supreme Brahman. I am Brahman. There is no doubt of this. I am higher than the highest.

20. I am the Self that is Consciousness. I am never the body. I am not the subtle body, either; nor am I the causal body.

21. Leaving "I" aside,[1] I am the highest.[2] I am of the nature of Brahman. I am devoid of, and transcendent of, desire and others. I am beyond differentiations of time.

[1]*having abandoned "I"* [2]*Supreme*

22. It is to be understood that this is, indeed, Brahman. It cannot be perceived, nor is it, indeed, the negation of anything. That I am Brahman should be a state of utter tranquility with all doubts subdued.

23. It is certain there is nothing for me, because of my being thought-less and decay-less.[1] Consciousness am I, Consciousness am I. I am Brahman-Consciousness. Consciousness am I. Ever, I am Consciousness.

[1]*indestructible*

24. Thus, with this conviction, divested of doubt, be at ease. Renouncing all connections,[1] always be at one with the Self.

[1]*sangam*

25. I shall tell you what is meant by sanga: the certitude of I am Brahman; I am the Truth; I am the Supreme Self; indeed, I, myself, am myself by myself.

26. I am not the body, the prana, the pairs of opposites, and not even purity. This, indeed, is satsang. This, itself, is purity.

27. In the company of the great, the great conviction of being Brahman is the highest state. I am rooted in[1] peace. I am Brahman. There is no doubt of this.

[1]*the origin of*

28. I am of the nature that has renounced all. I am without thought and others. This, indeed, is satsang. I shall be this always.

29. I am without all sankalpa-s (determinations, concepts). I am without any[1] modes. I am immortal. I am unborn and eternal. I am beyond the fear of death.

[1]*all*

30. I am the all-auspicious nature, ever of a loving disposition. I am with parts, with blemish, and I am beyond blemish. Ever, I am the companion.

31. I am only boundless Being. I am of the nature of real Knowledge. I am other than sound. I am sound, and I am without any name or form.

32. I am devoid of total identity with anything. I am devoid of beginning, middle, or end. Thus, by such steadfast practice and by personal experience and

33. by the repeated daily[1] conviction of being the Self, be happy. Thus, with the Self attaining such Bliss, there shall be no rebirth.

[1]eternal

34. He shall become instantly liberated. He is established as the nature of Brahman. This universe is of the nature of the Self. I am the great nature of the Self.

35. There is the Self alone. Nothing else has been created. The Self alone is the mind. The Self alone manifests as thought. The Self alone sometimes manifests as memory.

36. The Self it is that manifests as the intellect.[1] The Self, indeed, manifests as anger. Always, the Self, indeed, is sravana. Likewise, the Self, indeed, is manana, also.

[1]modes of mind

37. The Self it is that is ever the introduction.[1] The Self alone is the conclusion. The Self, indeed, is ever the equal of all around. The Self, indeed, is the fruit or apurva (unseen potency).[2]

[1]commencement [2]unprecedented result, unforeseen consequence

38. The Self it is that manifests as the arthavada. It is, indeed, the attainment of the Supreme Self. Brahman appears as desire and fructified karma; the Supreme appears as desire and fructified karma.

39. Brahman appears as the beginning of desire for the Supreme. The power of desire is only Consciousness. The power of desireless-ness is, indeed, the Self. The power of desire for the Supreme is imperishable.[1]

[1]unchangeable

40. The Supreme Self is the sovereign. All things are of the Supreme Self. All association is only the Supreme Self. Fruitfulness[1] is of the Supreme Self.

[1]*purpose, cause*

41. Brahman alone is the supreme connection.[1] Whatever arises out of karma is also the connection with Brahman. Brahman, itself, manifests as arising out of delusion. The pairs of opposites are only Brahman and nothing else.

[1]*saṅgam, contact, agreement*

42. The certitude that all is Brahman immediately confers Liberation, indeed. It is savikalpa samadhi; it is nirvikalpa samadhi.

43. What is connected with sound is only Brahman. What is connected with seeing is only Brahman. Brahman is the original samadhi. Brahman is the middle samadhi.

44. Brahman, indeed, is certainly the Void. Hence, it is said to be impossible to meditate upon it.[1] Being rid of the attachment[2] to the body is said to be the meditation of renunciation.[3]

[1]*non-samadhi* [2]*concept, self-conceit* [3]*that sāmādhi of vairāgya*

45. By this conviction, the peaceful jivanmukta is in samadhi. Intense, overall[1] peacefulness is the samadhi while alive.[2]

[1]*total, entire* [2]*of Liberation in the body*

46. This is told for the benefit of those intent on practice. This is that with which all this is connected. Forgetting, again forgetting, renouncing and again renouncing everything,

47. leave off all activities[1] with the attitude that I am established as the Void. Forgetting, also, that I exist, forget, also, that I am manifest.

[1]*vṛttim*

48. Leaving aside[1] that I am conscious, leave aside[2] also that I am only Existence. Renouncing renunciation itself, renounce having any attitude or conviction.

[1]*abandoning* [2]*abandon*

49. Leaving aside[1] all of the mind, quickly cast off remembrance, too. Even the least remembrance [of ignorance] is the great ocean of samsara here.

[1]*abandoning*

50. Remembrance in the least here becomes the great misery. Thought is the great defect and the bondage to worldly existence. The mind is the cause of hundreds of births.

51. The knot of the heart is the fructified demerits of karma, of sins such as killing of brahmins and others. Likewise, remembrance is here the cause of bondage-and-liberation.

52. This explanation of "I am Brahman" destroys all misery. It effaces all the illusory manifold world [of karma]. It ever confers instant Liberation. Merely hearing this, one becomes Brahman alone oneself.

53. The mind, by devotion, and in a mode of contemplation of the honored feet of the one with the lotus-petal eyes, shall attain freedom from the distress of wandering in endless births. Abandoning all these trivialities by firm determination, one of high discipline and charged with devotion to Siva may attain exalted peace by the love of Siva, the ocean of compassion.

Chapter Twenty-Two

brahmaṇaḥ sarva-rūpatva-nirūpaṇa-prakaraṇam
TOPIC OF THE ASCERTAINMENT OF BRAHMAN BEING ALL FORMS

Ribhu:
I shall tell you about the well-known Self, the illuminator of all the worlds, with all manner of forms, ever settled everywhere, dense and great.

2. I am that Brahman. There is no doubt of this. Being of this conviction, stand firm. I am Consciousness alone; I am Consciousness alone. Whatever is manifold is I myself.

3. I am the end of words. I am God, Consciousness, indeed, beyond the mind. I am, indeed, Consciousness, the Supreme Brahman. Consciousness is the abode of all.

4. This gross body is only Consciousness. The subtle body is only Consciousness, indeed. Consciousness is the instrumental cause, and that am I. The body is, indeed, only Consciousness.

5. The undivided mode, the best, the middling, and the bad [are Consciousness]. I, indeed, am Consciousness devoid of a body. The subtle body is, indeed, Consciousness.

6. Consciousness is the cause, and that am I. I, indeed, am Consciousness alone, without an intellect. I, indeed, am Consciousness without any bhava, Consciousness alone, indeed, without any defects.

7. There is nothing such as "the existence of Brahman." There is no such thing as "Brahman does not exist." There is nothing, indeed, as "is" or "is not." I, indeed, am only Consciousness.

8. All is nonexistent, nonexistent indeed. Being with form is nonexistent, nonexistent, indeed. Whatever is, in the least, is nonexistent. I, indeed, am only Consciousness.

9. Comparison and contrast, as well as the defects of beginning, middle, and end, are all only of the nature of Consciousness. I, indeed, am only Consciousness.

10. All that are separate,[1] real and unreal, and what makes for cause and effect, are nonexistent, nonexistent, indeed. I alone am.

[1] different, another

11. Impurity, purity, nonduality, duality, the one, and the many are all nonexistent, nonexistent, indeed. I alone am.

12. The unreal and the real,[1] what are not pairs of opposites, what are pairs of opposites, what is higher than the highest are all nonexistent, nonexistent, indeed. I alone am.

[1] the untrue and the true

13. The past, the future, and the present, delusion and nondelusion, the equal and the unequal are all nonexistent, nonexistent, indeed. I alone am.

14. A kshana, a lava, a truti are all Brahman. [What is denoted by] the word "you" and by the word "That," likewise, are all nonexistent. All is nonexistent, nonexistent, indeed. I alone am.

15. The word "you" and the word "That" and their merging together[1] are all only I, myself. All are nonexistent, nonexistent, indeed. I alone am.

[1] oneness

16. Bliss, great bliss, all bliss, the true,[1] [and] the great are all nonexistent, nonexistent, indeed. I alone am.

[1]*nijam, innate, constant*

17. I am Brahman, this is Brahman, the sanctified letter "kam" is Brahman. All are nonexistent, nonexistent, indeed. I alone am.

18. Vishnu, indeed, is the Supreme Brahman. Siva and Brahma are only myself.[1] All are nonexistent, nonexistent, indeed. I alone am.

[1]*I*

19. The ear is Brahman, the Supreme Brahman. The sound and auspicious words are Brahman. All is nonexistent, nonexistent, indeed. I alone am.

20. "Touch" is a word for Brahman. So also, is "skin." "Skin" and "Brahman" are interchangeable. All are nonexistent, nonexistent, indeed. I alone am.

21. Let the nature of the Supreme be likewise united with the eyes. All are nonexistent, nonexistent, indeed. I alone am.

22. Brahman alone is all, always only Existence-Consciousness-Bliss. All are nonexistent, nonexistent, indeed. I alone am.

23. I am only Bliss, full of Consciousness. I am this universe, all this, always. All is nonexistent, nonexistent, indeed. I alone am.

24. All that is present in the least is Brahman. I am that Brahman. There is no doubt of this. All is nonexistent, nonexistent, indeed. I alone am.

25. Whatever name is uttered by the mouth,[1] and whatever is thought of by the mind is all nonexistent, nonexistent, indeed. I alone am.

[1]*speech*

---

26. Whatever is imagined as the cause, whatever remains always silent, whatever is experienced by the body, and whatever is contemplated upon by the senses is all nonexistent, nonexistent, indeed. I alone am.

27. Whatever is prescribed in the Vedas as Veda-ordained action, whatever is defined in the Sastra-s as ordained by the Sastra-s, the settled conclusion arrived at by the instructions of the Guru, whatever illuminates the pure and the impure,

28. the concept of desire, the separate comprehension of Brahma and other gods, the apprehension of jivanmukti (Liberation while alive), the understanding of videhamukti (Liberation beyond the body),

29. the sankalpa that there is Brahman, the idea about the enlightened knower of Brahman, the determination[1] as the better, the idea about the best,

[1]*sankalpa*

---

30. the sankalpa that I am Brahman, also the notion that I am Consciousness, the sankalpa about great knowledge, the notion about the great delusion,

31. the determination[1] about the great Void, the notion of great thoughts, the determination[1] about the great world, the conception of the great Truth,

[1]*sankalpa*

---

32. the determination[1] about the great form, the notion of the great form, all sankalpa by thought, and all sankalpa by the mind

[1]*sankalpa*

171

33. are all nonexistent, indeed, nonexistent. All are only Brahman alone. All duality is of the nature[1] of the mind. All sorrow is of the mind. I am only Consciousness. There is no doubt of this. The triad of worlds is entirely only Consciousness.

[1] *a form*

34. What little is spoken, what little is mental japa, what little is mental activity—all is Brahman alone.

35. "All is nonexistent" is the good[1] mantra. Jiva is of the nature of Brahman. "All is Brahman alone"—this mantra, indeed, is the best of the best.

[1] *true*

36. The unuttered mantra is the good[1] mantra. Absence of any mode is the greatest. The determination that all is Brahman—that, itself, is the highest state.

[1] *true*

37. The determination[1] that all is Brahman is the same as singing the name "Mahadeva." The determination[1] that all is Brahman is equal to the great worship of Siva.

[1] *saṅkalpa*

38. The experience that all is Brahman is all-embracing.[1] There is no doubt of this. The determination[2] that Brahman is all is said to be total renunciation.

[1] *the form of all* [2] *saṅkalpa*

39. The determination[1] that Brahman is all destroys existence and nonexistence. The determination[1] that all is Brahman is itself Mahadeva, the great Lord. There is no doubt of this.

[1] *saṅkalpa*

40. The determination[1] that Brahman is all liberates one from the existence of time. The determination[1] that all is Brahman liberates one from existence as a body.

[1] sankalpa

41. The determination[1] that all is Brahman is of the nature of Existence-Consciousness-Bliss. I am all; indeed, [I am] Brahman alone. All is, indeed, only Brahman alone.

[1] sankalpa

42. What little there is as "this" is, undoubtedly, Brahman. Hell and its suffering are misapprehensions. Heaven is said to be a misapprehension.

43. Brahma and Vishnu are misapprehensions; the form of Siva is also a misapprehension. Virat, Svarat, Samrat, the Sutratma are all misapprehensions.

44. The gods and actions pertaining to the gods, the movement of the sun and the moon, the sages, the Manu-s, [and] the siddha-s are all undoubtedly, misapprehensions.

45. All the gods and demons are misapprehensions, their wars and origins, too. The legends of the birth of the incarnations of Vishnu and their dissolution are, likewise, misapprehensions.

46. The creative activities of Brahma and the lore about Rudra are all full of misapprehension. It is by misapprehension that the worlds are considered to be fourteen.

47. The division into castes and orders of life is a misapprehension. There is no doubt of this. The worshipful meditation on Brahma, Vishnu, Isa, Rudra, and others is a misapprehension.

48. So, also, there is only misapprehension of yantra and mantra. There is no doubt of this. Brahman is beyond the range of words. All is just Brahman alone, indeed.

49. All is nonexistent, indeed. All is nonexistent, indeed. I, indeed, am only Consciousness alone. Say so and stand firm. You shall instantly become liberated.

50. Whatever has been told so far is nonexistent. There is no doubt of this. The more quickly this enters into you, the more quickly there is the firm certitude of Brahman.

51. Firm certitude is, here, the foremost cause. It is this certitude now that later becomes[1] natural,[2] indeed.

[1]will become [2]svayam

52. The world, which is afflicted with sorrow, which is considered as a creation separate from the feet of Lord Siva, which is full of mental modes, which is not blissful with the thoughts of the Supreme, and which is subject to the sextet of states, will, [upon one's] abandonment of all modes, dissolve, along with the eyes and minds and words of its beings in the dense, immaculate mass of Mahesvara, like the river merging indivisibly with[1] the ocean.

[1]dissolving indivisibly in the ocean

Chapter Twenty-Three

jñānāmṛta-manomaya-prakaraṇa-varṇanam
DESCRIPTION OF THE TOPIC OF THE NECTAR OF KNOWLEDGE AND ALL BEING FULL OF THE MIND

Ribhu:
I shall now speak about Existence-Consciousness-Supreme Bliss, naturally ever full of happiness. It is itself the essence of the essence of all Vedas and Purana-s.

2. There is no difference, duality, or pairs of opposites. There is nothing different or devoid of differences. [All] this, indeed, is the Supreme Brahman, unaffected[1] [by desire or anger]. It is to be reached by[2] Knowledge.

[1]*not afflicted* [2]*connected to*

3. There is never anything as "I." There is nothing else. There is nothing decayless and no highest of the high. All this, indeed, is the unaffected Supreme Brahman. It is to be reached by Knowledge.

4. There is no exterior, no interior, no "I," no sankalpa, and no form. All this, indeed, is the unaffected[1] Supreme Brahman. It is to be reached by Knowledge.

[1]*unafflicted*

5. There is no existence, no renunciation, no word,[1] no defective meaning of words. All this is, indeed, the unaffected[2] Supreme Brahman. It is to be reached by Knowledge.

[1]*talk* [2]*not afflicted*

6. There are no qualities, no indirect statements, no certitude of the modes of the mind, no japa, no limitation, nothing pervasive, and no unreal results.

7. There is no guru, no disciple, nothing fixed, nothing good or bad,[1] nothing manifold in form, no separate form,[2] no liberation, and no bondage.

[1]*auspicious or inauspicious* [2]*no single form, no other (another) form*

8. There is no meaning of the word "I" or for the word for "that," no senses, no objects, no doubt, nothing trivial, no certainty, no action to be completed,

9. no nature of peace, no nonduality, nothing upward, nothing downward, no characteristic, no part that is sorrow, no happiness, no indecisiveness,

10. no body, no linga, no cause or absence of cause, no sorrow, nothing ultimate,[1] no "I," no secret, no highest state,

[1]*close*

11. no sanchita [karma]; no agami [karma], no truth, no you and I, no ignorance, no empirical knowledge,[1] no dullard, no one who knows,

[1]*vijñāna*

12. no lowly hell, no end, no liberation, no holiness, no desire, no learning,[1] neither you nor I, no philosophy[2] or a god,

[1]*knowledge* [2]*tatvaṁ*

13. no indication of good or bad, no death, no life, no satisfaction, nothing enjoyable, no undivided single essence, no nonduality,

14. no sankalpa, no manifest world, no sovereigns of the wakeful state, nothing whatever of the defect of equality, no misapprehension of what is counted as the fourth,

15. nothing as all, nothing with impurities, nothing desired, no law,[1] no worship, no manifest world, no plurality, no admixture of other talk,

[1]*precept of conduct*

16. nothing such as satsang or absence of satsang, no Brahma, no inquiry, no endeavor,[1] no speaker, no ablution, no holy waters,

[1]*practice*

17. no punya,[1] no sin, nor any activity that is a cause of error, nothing originating from the inner[2] nature or from the external nature or of divine origin,

[1]*merit* [2]*one's own*

18. no birth or death anywhere, no wakeful and dream and deep sleep states, no earth, no nether-world, no victory or defeat,

19. no weakness,[1] no fear, no desire[2] or quick death, nothing unthinkable, no person at fault, no misapprehension of the Vedas and religious lore (nigama and agama),

[1]*hīnaṁ, exclusion, inferiority* [2]*rati, pleasure, sexual enjoyment*

20. no sattvic (peaceful) state, no rajasic (energetic, active) state, no tamasic (dull) state, no such qualities, no Saiva, no Vedanta, no study[1] of these, no thinking of these,

[1]*tasting*

21. no bondage, no liberation, no aphorism of identity (of individual and supreme selves), no female form, no male form, no state of being neither male nor female, no permanent state,

22. no encomium, no criticism, no eulogy,[1] no hymn, no worldliness, no religiosity,[2] no scripture, no commandment,

[1]*stotram* [2]*vaidikam*

23. no drinking, no fasting—none of these—no joy, no exu-
berant merrymaking, no attitudes or absence of attitudes, no
family line, no name, no form,

24. nothing excellent, nothing vile, no blessing or curse,[1] no
purity or elimination of impurity, no individual soul, no control of the mind,

[1]better or worse

25. no such term as invocation of peace, no peace, no control of the mind and restraint of senses, no play, no phases
of existence, no modifications, no defects,

26. nothing in the least, nothing of where I am, nothing of
what is called maya, no results of maya, no dharma and such
in the least, no observance of dharma,

27. no youth, no boyhood, no senility, no death and such,
no relative, no non-relative, no friend, no brother,

28. no all, no nothing, no Brahma[1] or Vishnu[2] or Siva, no
guardians of the eight directions, no [cosmic] experiencer of
the waking state or dreamer,

[1]viriñco [2]keśavaḥ

29. no [cosmic] experiencer of the deep-sleep state, no fourth
state, and no brahmin or kshatriya or highly learned. All this
is, indeed, the Supreme Brahman, the affliction-less nectar
of Knowledge.

30. There is nothing such as the one who appears again or
the one who follows. There is no event that will occur again,
no mark of time, no "I," no cause of a conversation,

31. nothing upward, no inner faculty (mind, intellect, ego,
thought), no talk of only Consciousness, no duality that I am
Brahman, no duality that I am only Consciousness,

32. no sheath of food, no sheath of prana or the mind, no sheath of intellectual knowledge, no separate sheath of bliss,

33. nothing of the nature of knowledge, nothing knowable, no teaching—all of which is a misapprehension—none to be troubled, none to trouble, no illusion, no definition of the triad of knowledge,

34. no perceiver,[1] no perception,[2] no object of perception, and no appearance of results. All this, indeed, is the Supreme Brahman, the affliction-less nectar of Knowledge.

[1]conceiver [2]correct perception

35. There is nothing mysterious,[1] nothing explicit,[2] nothing great, nothing trivial of atomic proportions, no manifest world as at present,[3] no manifest world, ever,

[1]secret [2]evident [3]idea

36. no world[1] of the inner faculties, no mind,[2] no misapprehension of the world,[3] no world[1] of thought,[4] no manifest world[1] of intellect,[5]

[1]saṁsāra [2]mano [3]jagatām [4]cittarūpa [5]buddhi

37. no world[1] of the nature of jiva-s, no remembrance[2] of the nature of vasana-s (past impressions), no world[1] of differentiation by characteristics, no remembrance[2] of the nature of ignorance,

[1]saṁsāra [2]saṁsṛtiḥ, world, course of transmigration

38. no world[1] of the nature of the Vedas, no remembrance[2] of the sastra-s and agama-s, no world to show that there is something apart, no differentiation of something apart,

[1]saṁsāra [2]saṁsṛtiḥ, world, course of transmigration

39. no cognition of difference or nondifference, no imagining of defects or absence of defects, no world[1] of peace or peace-less-ness, no remembrance[2] of qualities and absence of qualities,

[1]saṁsāra [2]saṁsṛtiḥ, world, course of transmigration

40. no feminine gender, no masculine gender, nothing neuter, nothing stationary, nothing mobile, no sorrow or happiness, ever,

41. nothing of the nature of the virtuous or unvirtuous,[1] no certitude of the fit and the unfit, no activity[2] of a dual nature, no characteristic of the witness mode,

[1]learned or uneducated, disciplined or ill-behaved [2]mode

42. [nothing] of the mode of the undivided nature, [nothing] of the joy of the one undivided essence, nothing of the [notion that] I am the body, nothing of the declaration that I am Brahman,

43. no mode of the certitude of the undivided, no one great undivided essence, no coming into being of all modes, no destruction of all modes,

44. no inquiry into all modes, no release from all modes, no culmination of the destruction of all modes, no voiding of all modes,

45. nothing of all the modes in their thousands that are destroyed moment by moment, no witness of all modes, no bhava (feeling) of oneself being Brahman,

46. no universe, no mind, no ultimate,[1] no performance of action, ever, no criticism or praise, no characteristic of the unfettered,

[1]anto, final end

47. no mark of a virtuous person, no marks of a person of good qualities, no signs of absorption in meditation,[1] no piling up of sins,[2]

[1]*samādhi* [2]*no continuing bondage of prārabdha*

48. no thoughts of Brahman or of the Self, the true, no indications of the dream of the Supreme, none deemed as the most desirable, none to be excluded, none the best or excellent, and no meaning of [the words] "that Supreme."

49. Whoever is devoid of the Knowledge of the Self is, indeed, a great sinner. Whoever is thus devoid of Knowledge is a very sick person, indeed.

50. I am Brahman. There is no doubt of this. [I am][1] of the nature of the one undivided essence. [I have] the certitude of personal experience[2] that Brahman alone is all, indeed.

[1]*The Self is* [2]*Self-experience*

51. [Such a man] is instantly liberated. There is no doubt of this. Instantly, he becomes the embodiment of the highest Knowledge.[1] He, indeed, is the wise man[2] in this world. He is, indeed, Paramesvara.

[1]*prajñāna* [2]*jñānavān*

52. [All] this, indeed, is the Supreme Brahman, the nectar of Knowledge, filling the mind. Whoever hears this explanation is Brahman, indeed.

53. Neither the state of being one nor the state of being many, neither an atom nor the immense, neither the cause nor the effect, neither the universe nor the lordship of the universe, ever tasteless, smell-less, formless, neither bound nor liberated—may we become that shining Light, unconnected with birth, senility, or sickness and such, ever in the joy of the highest happiness, that blissful Sadasiva.

Chapter Twenty-Four

ānanda-rūpatva-nirūpaṇa-prakaraṇam
TOPIC OF THE DEFINITION OF THE NATURE OF BLISS

Ribhu:

I shall speak about the true explanation of the mind full of Brahman-Bliss. All this is, indeed, full of eternal Bliss devoid[1] of cause and effect.

[1]*free*

2. I am, indeed, the undecaying Bliss. I am the illuminator of the Bliss of the Self. I am of the nature of the Bliss of Knowledge. I am ever the Bliss at which to aim.

3. I am devoid of the joy of relating to things. I reveal the illusory joy. I am the happy Self that is devoid of activity.[1] I transcend the bliss of being devoid of activity.[1]

[1]*vṛtti, mode*

4. I am the Self that illumines the joy of insentience.[1] I am the essence of the Bliss of the Self. I am devoid of the bliss of the Self. There is no embodiment of the Bliss of Self.

[1]*the inert*

5. I am devoid of the joy of action. I have[1] the portion of bliss that comes from action. I am devoid of the bliss of the guna-s. I am of the nature of the secret joy.[2]

[1]*am* [2]*bliss*

6. I am of the nature of the hidden joy.[1] I am the great one of the Bliss of [all]-doing. I am devoid of the bliss of knowing. I am without any joy[1] to be hidden.

[1] *bliss*

---

7. I am ever of the nature of eternal joy.[1] I am the natural[2] joy[1] of exhilaration. I am the bliss of the world. I am the great Bliss. I am the great One transcending the world.

[1] *bliss* [2] *innate*

---

8. I am the bliss of difference. I am the Bliss of Consciousness. I am the Bliss of happiness. I am nondual. I am the bliss of action. I am decayless Bliss. I am without the bliss of [diverse] modes.

---

9. I am all Bliss. I am undecaying Bliss. I am the Bliss of Consciousness. I am immutable. I am the true Bliss. I am the highest Bliss. I am the Bliss of the present.[1] I am higher than the highest.

[1] *immediate*

---

10. I am the bliss of speech. I am the great Bliss. I am the Bliss of peace.[1] I am nondual. I am the Bliss of peace.[1] I am devoid of the bliss of the future and of the bliss of the beginning.

[1] *śiva, Siva*

---

11. I am the pure Self, the highest[1] Bliss. I am the Bliss of Consciousness. I am nondual. I am the bliss of modes. I am the highest[1] Bliss, transcending knowledge and blemishless.

[1] *supreme*

---

12. I am the Bliss transcending [all] causes, the Bliss of Consciousness. I am nondual. I am all Bliss, the highest Bliss, of the conviction that I am[1] the Bliss of Brahman.

[1] *the Self is*

13. I am the bliss of life and the bliss of dissolution. I am of the nature of the Bliss of Consciousness. I am the Self of the nature of pure Bliss. I am the bliss of the intellect,[1] filling the mind.[2]

[1]buddhi [2]manomayaḥ

14. I am the bliss of sound.[1] I am the great Bliss. I am the Bliss of Consciousness, the nondual. I am the Self of bliss and absence of bliss. I am devoid of the bliss of differences.

[1]śabda

15. I am the Self reveling[1] in the bliss of duality. I am the Bliss of Consciousness and nondual. Be of the conviction that I am, indeed, all such great Bliss,

[1]prabhāva, that is the power

16. that I am, indeed, the Bliss of peace, the illuminator of the Bliss of Consciousness, the one Bliss, the highest Bliss, the one and only immutable Consciousness.

17. I am the one and only great Self, the one which cannot be enumerated. I am the great Bliss of the one Truth, devoid of differences of interpretation.

18. I am devoid of any conquest of bliss. I am without any conquest by bliss. I am rendered absolutely peaceful by bliss-less-ness. I am peaceful for I am peace itself.

19. I am peaceful in the bliss of "my-ness." I am the original illuminator. I am ever at peace with my body. I am devoid of the [position] "I am peaceful."

20. I am Brahman alone, not of this world[1]—thus, also, I am peaceful. I am the innermost of the innermost. Indeed, I am the innermost of the innermost of the innermost.

[1]saṁsārī

21. I am the one and only great Bliss. I am the one and only imperishable[1] One. Brahman is just one syllable[1] [Om]. The decayless[1] is just one syllable[1] [Om].

[1]akṣara

_____

22. There is only one great Self. There is only the One that fascinates[1] the mind. I am the only One without a second. [I am] the only One and none other.

[1]removes

_____

23. [I am] the only One. [I am] not the world and others. [I am] the only One and not the intellects. I am the only One and highly peaceful. [I am] the only One and the blissful[1] Self.

[1]happy

_____

24. [I am] the only One, not one with desire. [I am] the only One, not the angry. [I am] the only One, not one with greed. I am the only One, not one infatuated.[1]

[1]mohakaḥ, deluded

_____

25. I am the only One. I am not deluded. [I am] the only One. There is no other essence for me. [I am] the only One, not the thinking[1] self. [I am] the only One and not another.

[1]citta

_____

26. [I am] the only One, not the substance of goodness.[1] [I am] the only One, not old or immortal. [I am] the only One, the perfectly full Self. I am the only One, the motionless.

[1]sattātmā

_____

27. [I am] the only great Bliss. I am the only One. I have the only One. I am devoid of the concept that I am the body. I am permanently [of the Realization] that I am at peace.

28. I am at peace, for I am Siva. It is natural[1] that I am the Self alone. I am at peace, for I am the Self,[2] ever pure, in the core of my heart.

[1]*kramaḥ, a progression to* [2]*jīva, life*

29. Thus, be of such conviction without a doubt[1] and, immediately, you are liberated in Non-duality. Let one, unwavering, at least daily read such words aloud.

[1]*fear, hesitation*

30. It has been said in the scriptures that the world of beings moves by the flow of time and by prescribed rules. This is a mistaken notion, because of the insentience of the world. All this is, on the other hand, by the will of Isvara.

Chapter Twenty-Five

ātma-vailakṣaṇya-prakaraṇam
TOPIC OF THE SELF BEING WITHOUT CHARACTERISTICS

Ribhu:
I am, indeed, Brahman. I am, indeed, Consciousness. I am blemishless. I am one without interstices. I am, indeed, of a pure nature. I am of the eternal nature. I am the highest.[1]

[1]*supreme*

2. I am of the eternally pure[1] nature. I am the embodiment of eternal Consciousness. I am of the nature without beginning or end. I am without the duality of beginning and end.

[1]*blemishless*

3. I am of the perpetually happy nature. I am one with the nature of perpetual Bliss. I, indeed, am the primordially liberated. I am causeless.

4. I, indeed, am the Supreme Brahman. I, indeed, am myself,[1] indeed. Being of this perpetual bhava and happy in your own pure Self,

[1]*aham, I*

5. be established in happiness; be established in happiness; be in a state of happiness for a long, long time. You are not different from all that is to be known. There never is anything of thought.[1]

[1]*imagination*

6. There never is anything called mind. There never is any remembrance.[1] There never is, there never is, there never is the world,[2] indeed.

[1]*saṁsṛtiḥ, world, course of transmigration* [2]*jagat*

7. There never can be any talk about[1] the world. How, then, can there be any word[2] about the body? Brahman alone is all—only Consciousness. I, indeed, am the only One.[3]

[1]*dispute about, attachment to* [2]*talk* [3]*kevalam*

8. There is no such thing as thought either. The thought that there is thought is itself nonexistent. The bhava of there being anything is nonexistent. The talk about the existence of the world is false.

9. One who says that things exist, the talk that things exist, the attitude that the world is, that there is a protector of the world other than one's own Self, the certitude that I am the body,

10. the notion that this man is indeed a great candala (polluted person), the certitude that this person is a great brahmin—is all nonexistent. Of the world or the mind or the intellect,

11. be of[1] the immediate, pure conviction that nothing exists, nothing exists. Be of the conviction that there is nothing to be seen, nothing [to be seen], nothing, nothing, indeed.

[1]*lit., do, make*

12. I, indeed, am the Supreme Brahman. I, indeed, am the partless. I only am. There is no doubt of this. I, indeed, am the happiest of the happy.

13. I, indeed, am the divine Self. I, indeed, am Kevala (the only One). I am immeasurable[1] by words. I am, indeed, and not another.

[1]*inaccessible*

14. I, indeed, am the Self of all. I am ever loving.[1] I am the Self of faith.[2] I am without any modes.

[1]dear [2]bhāvātmā, the Self of existence, the Self of a state

15. I, indeed, am without limitations.[1] I, indeed, am without any discontinuity. I, indeed, am unaffected by thought.[2] I, indeed, am the good[3] Guru.

[1]uninterrupted [2]unconcerned [3]true

16. I, indeed, am ever the Witness. I am, indeed, myself[1] only. I am not hidden; nor am I unhidden, nor am I the always shining one.

[1]I

17. I am not insentient nor am I only Consciousness. Wherever, in whatever measure, That, indeed, is. I am not the prana-s, nor am I insentience, for such are always a total misapprehension.

18. I am intense[1] Bliss. I am completely spotless. I am the Self that completely knows [all]. I am the harbinger of complete auspiciousness.[2]

[1]complete [2]completely śāṅkaraḥ

19. I have no recollection that I am anything in the least. I am, indeed, bereft of anything before me. I am bereft of happiness and good.

20. Brahman, which is higher than the highest, the man[1] that is higher than the highest—that I am, the higher than the highest, the higher than the highest of all.

[1]spirit

21. I am devoid of all bodies. I am devoid of all action. I am the peaceful Self of all mantras. I transcend all antahkarana.

22. I am devoid of all praise.[1] I reveal[2] all the deities.[3] I am[4] devoid of all holy ablutions. [I am] one. [I am] the foremost.[5] [I am] non-dual.

[1]stotra [2]illuminator of, revealer of [3]deva [4]The Self is [5]summit

23. In the holy center[1] of the Self, in the sacred water of the Self, in the enjoyment[2] of the Bliss of the Self, I repose[3] in myself, in the Knowledge that I am the Self alone.

[1]tīrtham [2]fascination [3]shine and rejoice

24. There is only the Self. The Self, indeed, is the enjoyment. The Self, indeed, is the satisfaction. Happiness is of the Self. The Self, indeed, is the Self of the Self, the Self alone. I, indeed, am the Supreme.

25. I am the Self. I am the Self. I am, I am, indeed, the Self, not of this world. I am the Self of all. I am ever the Self. I am the eternal Self, beyond the guna-s.

26. Being always of this conviction, ever have such conviction for final fulfillment. Only Consciousness stands as the fulfillment. That, indeed, is only by certitude. Even this certitude reaches dissolution. Be happy by yourself alone.

27. The endless scriptures, by their various chapters, describe only you, Bhagavan, the only One, as Vishnu, Indra, Brahma Sun, Fire, Wind, the Lord of beings and the gana-s (retinues), O Sambhu, the eminent!

Chapter Twenty-Six

tanmaya-bhāvopadeśa-prakaraṇam
TOPIC OF THE INSTRUCTION OF ABIDING
AS THAT ITSELF

Ribhu:
I shall tell you now about being wholly That itself. This is
rare to come by, even for yogis. This is the secret of[1] [all] the
Vedas, of[1] [all] the scriptures. This is very rare to come by,
[indeed].

[1]*in*

---

2. That which is the Supreme Brahman, the Self of all, of the
nature of Existence-Consciousness-Bliss, the Self of all, the
Supreme Self—ever abide as That itself.

3. All this is of the nature of the Self, which is without beginning or end and which is insuperable. This is neither action
nor inaction. Ever abide as That itself.

4. That in which there is no fear of duality, in which nonduality awakens, in which peacefulness and non-peaceful-
ness both do not exist—ever be That itself.

5. That in which there is nothing of sankalpa, in which misapprehension does not exist, in which, likewise, there is no
thinking—ever abide as That itself.

6. That in which there is nothing, indeed, in Brahman, in which having any bhava[1] is a delusion,[2] in which the entire world[3] does not exist—ever abide as That itself.

[1]or, bhāvi, becoming, future [2]vikalpanam [3]jagat, universe

7. That in which existence or nonexistence and delusions[1] due to misapprehensions of the mind, and even the word "misapprehension," do not exist—ever abide as That itself.

[1]vikalpanam

8. That in which there is no pleasure,[1] in which there is no imagination[2] that I am the body, and in which all sankalpa has been relinquished—ever abide as That itself.

[1]sukhaṁ [2]rūpakam

9. That in which a bhava [inclusive] of Brahman does not exist, in which defects are not present, and in which there is no fear of the pairs of opposites—ever abide as That itself.

10. That in which the actions of speech and body and the eon itself have ended in dissolution, and in which the manifest universe is yet unborn—ever abide as That itself.

11. That in which there is no manifestation of delusion,[1] in which there is not the least activity of illusion,[1] in which there is nothing seen or unseen—ever abide as That itself.

[1]māyā

12. That in which there is no wise man or vidya (wisdom), in which there are no such things as one's own side and an opposing side, and in which there are no defects or non-defects—ever abide as That itself.

13. That in which there is no differentiation, [such] as being Vishnu, in which Brahma does not exist, and in which there is no differentiation as Sankara—ever abide as That itself.

14. That in which there is no differentiation as truth[1] and non-truth, in which there is no such state as understanding,[2] and in which there is no such idea[2] as "jiva"—ever abide as That itself.

[1]sat [2]kalanā, the state of being with, having, impelling

15. That in which there is no meditation on Sankara, in which there is no supreme abode,[1] and in which there is no state[2] of comprehension[3]—ever abide as That itself.

[1]state [2]form [3]kalanā

16. That in which there is no microcosm or macrocosm, in which there is no imagining of happiness,[1] and in which the manifest world is a fallacy—ever abide as That itself.

[1]being pleased

17. That in which there is no conception[1] of a body, in which there is no jubilance, and in which there is no awareness of thought[1]—ever abide as That itself.

[1]kalanaṁ

18. That in which there is no intellect or empirical knowledge,[1] in which there is no Self in the sheath of mind, and in which there is no conception[2] of desire—ever abide as That itself.

[1]vijñānaṁ, awareness [2]kalanaṁ

19. That in which there is no liberation or repose, in which there is no bondage or separation, and in which there is no permanent knowledge—ever abide as That itself.

20. That in which there is no conception[1] of time, in which there is no bhava of sorrow, and in which there is no conception[1] of the body—ever abide as That itself.

[1]kalanaṁ

21. That in which there is no dispassion of the jiva, in which there is no misunderstanding[1] of the scriptures, and in which I, being the Self, am myself[2]—ever abide as That itself.

[1]vikalpanam [2]I

22. That in which there is no jivanmukti, in which there is no liberation from the body, and in which there is no activity by sankalpa—ever abide as That itself.

23. That in which there is no conception[1] of beings, in which there is no existence of anything separate,[2] and in which there is no differentiation as the jiva either—ever abide as That itself.

[1]kalanaṁ [2]other

24. That in which Brahman is a state of Bliss, in which joy is a state of Bliss, and in which the quality of Bliss is eternal—ever abide as That itself.

25. That in which there is no manifestation of things, in which there is no victory or defeat, and in which there is no utterance of statements—ever abide as That itself.

26. That in which there is no branch of inquiry into the Self, in which there is no urge for sravana, and in which there is no great bliss—ever abide as That itself.

27. That in which there is no classification such as the same group or different groups, and in which no internal difference arises—ever abide as That itself.

28. That in which there is neither the terror of hell nor the treasures[1] of heaven and in which there is no world of Brahma—ever abide as That itself.

[1]enjoyment

29. That in which there is no union with Vishnu, in which there is no Kailasa mountain, in which there is no sphere of the egg of the cosmos[1]—ever abide as That itself.

[1]*brahmāṇḍamaṇḍalam*

30. That in which there is no praise, in which censure exists not, and in which there is not the mistake of regarding them as on a par either—ever abide as That itself.

31. That in which there is no bhava of the mind, in which there is no misapprehension,[1] and in which there is no experience or suffering—ever abide as That itself.

[1]*savikalpanam*

32. That in which there is no fear of sin, nothing of the five great sins, and in which there is no defect of attachment—ever abide as That itself.

33. That in which the triad of afflictions does not exist, in which there are never the three states of the jiva, and in which the universe is known to be a delusion[1]—ever abide as That itself.

[1]*vikalpa*

34. That in which knowledge has not arisen, in which there is no error of conceiving of the world, and in which there is no manifestation of activity—ever abide as That itself.

35. That in which there is no domain of the mind, in which, indeed, there is the greatest happiness, and in which exists the permanent[1] abode—ever abide as That itself.

[1]*everlasting*

36. That in which the cause of all is peace, in which all is happiness, and having reached, wherefrom none reverts—ever abide as That itself.

37. By knowing which all is renounced,[1] by knowing which nothing else remains,[2] and by knowing which there is nothing else to be known[3]—ever abide as That itself.

[1]*released, relinquished* [2]*exists* [3]*no other knowledge*

38. That in which no defect has arisen, that which is the place that is changeless,[1] and in which, indeed, the jiva is destroyed—ever abide as That itself.

[1]*unmoving*

39. That in which, indeed, the Self is ever satisfied, in which, indeed, there is changeless bliss, and in which, indeed, there is changeless peace—ever abide as That itself.

40. That in which, indeed, there is all happiness, in which, indeed, there is the definition of the real, and in which, indeed, there is certainty [of Existence]—ever abide as That itself.

41. That in which I am not, and in which you are not, in which you, yourself, are not, indeed, yourself, and in which, indeed, there is certain peace—ever abide as That itself.

42. That in which, indeed, you are eternally joyful, in which, indeed, happiness is attained,[1] and in which there is no fear of sorrow[2]—ever abide as That itself.

[1]*becomes extensive and intense* [2]*suffering*

43. That in which there is the fullness of Consciousness, in which there is, indeed, an ocean of Bliss, and in which, indeed, there is the direct presence of the Supreme—ever abide as That itself.

44. That, indeed, in which one, himself, is, indeed, That itself and in which there is no difference between oneself and one's Self—ever abide as That itself.

45. That in which, indeed, there is supreme Bliss, in which oneself is the supreme happiness, and in which, indeed, there is the understanding of differenceless-ness—ever abide as That itself.

46. That in which there is not even an atom, in which there is no blemish of the mind, in which there is nothing like "I do" (lit. "I give")— ever abide as That itself.

47. That in which thought is dead, in which one's body and mind are dead, and wherein memory finally dissolves—ever abide as That itself.

48. That in which, indeed, "I" is surely dead, in which desire meets[1] its dissolution, and in which, indeed, Supreme Bliss is—ever abide as That itself.

[1]*comes to*

49. That in which the trinity of gods has its dissolution, in which the bodies and such perish, and in which there are no interactions[1]—ever abide as That itself.

[1]*worldly, everyday interactions*

50. Immersed wherein there is no fatigue,[1] immersed wherein one does not see, and immersed wherein there is no life[2] and such things—ever abide as That itself.

[1]*trouble* [2]*birth*

51. Immersed wherein nothing shines, wherein wakefulness does not exist, and wherein, indeed, delusion meets its death—ever abide as That itself.

52. That in which, indeed, time finds its death, in which yoga finds[1] its dissolution, and in which satsang ceases to be—ever abide as That itself.

[1]*comes to*

53. That in which, indeed, the Brahman-nature exists, wherein, indeed, there is only Bliss, and wherein, indeed, there is the supreme Bliss—ever abide as That itself.

54. That in which the universe never exists, in which the [manifest] world does not exist, and in which there are no inner faculties—ever abide as That itself.

55. That in which, indeed, there is only joy, in which it, itself, is entirely only bliss, and in which, indeed, it itself is supreme Bliss—ever abide as That itself.

56. That in which there is only the Consciousness of Existence, in which Consciousness alone is all there is, and in which shines the fullness of Bliss—ever abide as That itself.

57. That in which there is the direct presence[1] of the Supreme Brahman, in which one evidently[1] is oneself the Supreme, and in which serenity is the supreme goal—ever abide as That itself.

[1] sākṣāt

58. That in which lies the direct meaning of the undivided, in which exists the very goal, and in which destruction and such exist not—ever abide as That itself.

59. That in which, evidently, there is only oneself, in which only oneself, evidently, prevails, and in which exists, evidently, the great Self—ever abide as That itself.

60. Wherein the Supreme Truth evidently is, wherein evidently oneself is the great, and wherein Knowledge evidently exists—ever abide as That itself.

61. Wherein the transcendence of qualities evidently is, wherein blemishless-ness evidently is, and wherein eternal purity evidently is—ever abide as That itself.

62. Wherein the great Self itself is present, wherein the joy of joys is present, and wherein, indeed, jnana (wisdom) and vijnana (knowledge) are present—ever abide as That itself.

63. That in which, indeed, oneself is the Light, in which oneself, indeed, is the non-dual, and in which, indeed, there is supreme Bliss—ever abide as That itself.

64. Thus the bhava of becoming That itself has been proclaimed. Be thus always—ever, ever. I am Brahman, Existence-Consciousness-Bliss. I am undivided and ever joyful.

65. I am Brahman alone, which is Knowledge. I am the supreme Peace. I am Consciousness. I am devoid of thought.[1] I am not "I." I abide as He Himself.

[1] the mind

66. I am That. I am Consciousness. I am He. I am spotless. I am the highest. I am the highest. I am the Supreme. Thus, casting aside[1] everything, be happy.

[1] abandoning

67. All this is the remnant of thoughts, the muddying of purity. Thus, renouncing all and forgetting everything, like mere dead wood,

68. leaving aside the body like a corpse, being ever like a piece of wood or iron, and renouncing even remembrance, firmly abide only in Brahman as the goal.

69. Whoever hears this explanation even once, even though he may be connected with great sins, shall, casting off all, reach the Supreme.

70. Though, in parts, they deal with upasana (meditation) on You, do not the Vedas proclaim You as the unattached, as especially connected to the vessel of the heart of all, existing as the Self, and of the nature of the undivided?

Chapter Twenty-Seven

brahmaika-rūpatva-nirūpaṇa-prakaraṇam
TOPIC OF THE DEFINITION OF BRAHMAN BEING THE ONLY ONE

Ribhu:
I shall tell you about the Supreme Brahman being the only reality and about the incomparable renunciation[1] of the world, by hearing which just once, Supreme Brahman-hood[2] can be attained.

[1]*abandonment* [2]*Brahman-Existence*

2. Beyond Brahman is only Brahman, attributeless, eternal and pure,[1] permanent, equanimous, and complete. Nothing exists apart from[2] Brahman.

[1]*blemishless* [2]*other than*

3. I am Reality, the supreme joy,[1] the pure, the eternal, the taintless. All is Brahman. There is no doubt of this. I am that Brahman. There is no doubt of this.

[1]*bliss*

4. I am, indeed, the undivided Essence. I am always complete and perfectly full. Brahman is all. Nothing else exists. All is Brahman. There is no doubt of this.

5. I am always the Self alone. All is all of the time Brahman. I am of the nature of Bliss alone. I am nothing else. Nothing in the least is permanent.

6. I am of the nature of pure Bliss. I am the pure Knowledge of the Self. I am of the nature of the One-nature. I am devoid of the nature of multiple existences.

7. I am pure Knowledge inside.[1] I, indeed, am the goal sought. All is Brahman. There is no doubt of this. That Brahman am I. There is no doubt of this.

[1]*pure, interior Knowledge*

8. I am devoid of varying[1] interpretations. The [sense of] one-ness also does not exist. All is Brahman. There is no doubt of this. That Brahman am I. There is no doubt of this.

[1]*multiple*

9. I am of all manner of forms. I am also devoid of being all. All is Brahman. There is no doubt of this. That Brahman am I. There is no doubt of this.

10. I am of the nature of blemishless Knowledge. "I," indeed, does not exist. I am of the nature of pure Brahman. I am beyond[1] the term "pure."

[1]*exclude, devoid of*

11. I am of the nature of eternal Bliss. I am ever the Bliss of Knowledge. I am subtler than the subtlest. I am devoid of subtlety and other such [qualities].

12. I am only undivided Bliss. I am of the nature[1] of undivided Bliss. I am ever of this immortal nature. I am ever the embodiment[1] of the One.[2]

[1]*vigrahaḥ* [2]*kaivalya*

13. This is all the Bliss of Brahman. All never exists, never exists. I am devoid of jiva-hood.[1] I am devoid of Isvara-hood.[2]

[1]*jīvatvadharma* [2]*īśvaratva*

201

14. I am of the true nature of the Vedas and scriptures. [I am] the cause of the remembrance of the scriptures. [I am] the cause and effect of the world, and [I am the triad of] Brahma, Vishnu, and Mahesvara.

15. I am the distinction between the direct word and the derived meaning, the gross and the subtle bodies, the states of wakefulness, dream, and deep sleep, and the [cosmic] experiencer of the waking state, the [cosmic] dreamer, and the [cosmic] sleeper.[1]
_____
[1]*prājña-taijasa-viśva*

16. I am the embodiment[1] of all scriptures. I am all Bliss, always. I transcend the meaning of name and form. I transcend all imagination,
_____
[1]*true nature*

17. [concepts of] duality and nonduality, joy and sorrow, gain and loss, success and failure. All is Brahman. There is no doubt of this. I am that Brahman. There is no doubt of this.

18. The difference between the serene[1] and the energetic,[2] the doubts and desires[3] of the heart, the seer and the seen and the all-seer, [the effect of] the elements, living beings and gods—
_____
[1]*sātvikaṁ* [2]*rājasaṁ* [3]*consequences, effects, results*

19. all are Brahman. There is no doubt of this. I am that Brahman. There is no doubt of this. I am, verily, of the nature of the Fourth State, indeed. I am ever of the nature of Knowledge.

20. Ignorance, indeed, does not exist. Where is its activity? All is Brahman. There is no doubt of this. I am that Brahman. There is no doubt of this.

21. The display of the activities of the mind or of the intellect does not exist, indeed. I am without the concept of a body or an imaginary concept of the intellect.

22. All is Brahman. There is no doubt of this. I am that Brahman. There is no doubt of this. I am of the nature of the certainty of the intellect. Oh! Even this certainty passes away.

23. Egoism of many forms and the attitude that "I am the body"—all are Brahman. There is no doubt of this. I am that Brahman. There is no doubt of this.

24. I am Brahman, moreover, one-eyed and deaf. I am the highest. All is Brahman. There is no doubt of this. I am that Brahman. There is no doubt of this.

25. The equations of "I am the body" and that of the body to the Supreme Self—all is Brahman. There is no doubt of this. I am that Brahman. There is no doubt of this.

26. The equation that I am all and the equation of all to the Supreme Self—endeavoring to be of this conviction and being established as "I am Brahman"

27. is, indeed, the firm bhava (conviction). Truly, truly, I am the Supreme. It is, indeed, this firm conviction that gives certitude to the words of the Sadguru (true Guru).

28. Stand, stand firm always, in the universal sovereignty of the firm conviction of being the Supreme. I am, indeed, the Supreme Brahman, illuminating the Bliss of the Self.

29. The worship of Siva, the [notion that] I am Siva, Vishnu and the worship of Vishnu, whatever little conveys any knowledge, whatever little gives any conviction,

30. "you are, indeed, That" and "I am, indeed, you"—no such thing exists. This is the focus.[1] This is the thing to be seen: No such thing exists at all.

[1] *the thought, the mind*

31. Even if concepts of reality and unreality remain, no difference exists between one and the other. All this is of the nature of joy, and all this is also not of the nature of joy.

32. Millions of differences, an occasional difference—all differences—do not exist. Brahman is Bliss. There is no doubt of this. I am that Brahman. There is no doubt of this.

33. The difference as Brahman, the difference as the fourth state, the difference as jiva—all are difference-less. This has, indeed, not arisen. Nothing at all ever is.

34. The indication "He is a god" exists not at all, not at all, ever. Only if it exists, is it to be described in speech. If it exists not, how can it be described in speech?

35. There is never any such thing in me as supreme or distinguished. The mind and fickleness[1] do not exist, do not exist at all. There is no doubt of this.

[1] *unsteadiness*

36. Thus, indeed, ever perfectly full, be established in desire-less-ness[1] and be of a serene mind. "I am all, Brahman, perfectly full"—thus, also, there is never any such thing.

[1] *motionless-ness*

37. Nor, indeed, is there any such thing as "I am bliss," "I am the best," "I am the Brahman-Bliss," "I am the great Bliss," or "I am the Bliss of the indivisible Self."

38. This Great Destroyer does not ever exist in the least. There is no understanding such as, "This is all," or any misapprehension as, "There is nothing as bliss."

39. All is Brahman. There is no doubt of this. I am that Brahman. There is no doubt of this. The concept of definitions and the thing defined, the seer, the seen, and the seeing,

40. total absence,[1] and all manner of experiences ever—all are Brahman. There is no doubt of this. I am that Brahman. There is no doubt of this.

[1] *nonexistence*

41. The secret, the mantra, the attribute, the scripture, the truth, the proficiency in the Vedas, the body, death, birth, cause, effect, the sanctified, the auspicious,

42. desire, anger, covetousness, infatuation, pride, jealousy, the defect of duality, fear, sadness—all, indeed, never exist.

43. This never is, never is, never. All is Bliss. The reflection of "This is Brahman," the thinking that "I am Brahman,"

44. the reflection that "I am Brahman," the effacement of your being Brahman, and the "reality and unreality"[1] do not affect[2] the Brahman-Knowledge.

[1] *true and untrue* [2] *trouble*

45. The Supreme Self is one, indeed, devoid of any weariness of being one. All is Brahman, ever Brahman. That Brahman is myself.[1] There is no doubt of this.

[1] *I*

46. The form of the jiva, the concept of jiva, the word "jiva"— all these[1] do not exist. The form of Isvara,[2] the concept of Isvara,[2] and the word "Isvara"[2] are all imagined.

[1] *triad of words* [2] *īśa*

47. There are no alphabets, nor the entirety, no word with direct meaning and derived explanation, and nothing in the least of the heart, mantra, tantra, thought, or intellect.

48. There is none such as the ignoramus, the wise man, the discriminating, the pure, the certitude, pranava (Om), the exalted, "this," "the Self," the guru and the disciple,

49. stillness, tranquility, the great quiescent stillness, silence, bhava of silence, the light and the illuminating, the inquiry into the Self and the non-Self,

50. the yoga of meditation, the raja yoga, and experience of the eight limbs of yoga. All is Brahman. There is no doubt of this. That Brahman am I. There is no doubt of this.

51. The talk of existence and the talk of nonexistence, too, the statement "I am of the nature of the fifty letters of the alphabet" or "of the sixty four arts"—

52. all is Brahman. There is no doubt of this. I am that Brahman. There is no doubt of this. I am, indeed, Brahman, the Self immediately present. I am, indeed, Brahman, the immutable Consciousness.

53. Remote am I from the knowledge of the scriptures, remote from the knowledge of the Vedas. All that has been said is the Supreme Brahman. There is not a shred of doubt of this.

54. All is Brahman. There is no doubt of this. I am that Brahman. There is no doubt of this. I am, indeed, Brahman, the Self immediately present, the immutable Consciousness.

55. Thus has the nature of Brahman been lovingly taught to you. Whoever is aware always that "All is Brahman; there is no doubt about this," whoever hears daily about this, is blemish-free and Consciousness alone.

56. Those who do not sully their hearts by their doubts and doubt-engendering actions, which are affected by the multitude of mutations of the world, attain videhamukti by the Grace of Lord Siva.

Chapter Twenty-Eight

mahāvākyārtha-nirūpaṇa-prakaraṇam
TOPIC OF THE DEFINITION OF THE MEANING OF
THE GREAT SAYINGS

Ribhu:
I shall now tell you the highly[1] secret, which reveals the very Brahman, itself, the meaning of all the Upanishads, rare to come by in all the worlds.

[1]*complete*

2. Prajnanam Brahman (Absolute Knowledge is Brahman) is a certitude consisting of two words. There are four sentences that are great aphorisms, occurring in the *Rig, Yajur,* and *Sama* (Vedas).

3. I am Absolute Knowledge. I am Brahman.[1] This world[2] is mere[3] Knowledge. The entire world[2] is, indeed, only Knowledge. Nothing exists besides Knowledge.

[1]*My supreme Knowledge, indeed, is I am Brahman.* [2]*jagat*
[3]*only*

4. All that is seen is of the nature of Knowledge and, indeed, Knowledge without any interspace. What is of Knowledge and of Brahman are mine, indeed, and not separate.

5. The jiva is associated[1] with Absolute Knowledge, and Isvara is associated[1] with Brahman. The undivided meaning of this is their identity. It is pervaded by the undivided Essence.

[1]*śabdasya, of the word*

6. Being in the undivided mode while [apparently] in a form is called jivanmukti. The Reality that is the one undivided Essence is called videhamukti.

7. I am Brahman. I am not of this cycle of birth and death.[1] I am Existence-Consciousness-Bliss. I am attributeless. I am partless. I am one of Supreme Bliss.

[1] *saṁsārī*

8. I am eternal. I am delusionless.[1] I am Consciousness. I am ever Consciousness. The mind, which is in what is called the undivided state,[2] exists as the Brahman-Self,

[1] *undifferentiated* [2] *vṛtti*

9. just as salt becomes one and undivided with water itself, one undivided essence. I shall tell you about the characteristics of Liberation out of the body.

10. Leaving aside[1] the words "Absolute Knowledge" and, indeed, the word "Brahman," leaving aside[1] "I am," "I am great," "I am determined,"[2]

[1] *abandoning* [2] *established, accomplished one*

11. leaving aside[1] all remembrance and bhavas created by thought, leaving aside[1] everything internal, and being in a state of complete voidness,

[1] *abandoning*

12. leaving aside[1] even the state of silence, then the vikalpa about silence, and the world, which is imagined by the mind and is a reflection of that thought,

[1] *abandoning*

13. leaving aside[1] the egoism that I am the body, which is called the state of duality, and abiding in the firm conviction[2] that I am Brahman, the witness of all,

[1] *abandoning* [2] *certainty*

14. and being ever doubtless about Brahman, is called the witness-state.[1] The state[1] of duality, the witness-state,[1] and the nature of the undivided state,[1] which is

[1]vṛtti

15. the one undivided Essence—there are, thus, three such states in the world. The first is a belief in duality. The second is the doubt of being the witness.

16. In the third state alone, firm certainty is said to exist. Having inquired into and tested the meaning of all three and setting them aside,[1] attain certitude.

[1]abandoning

17. Reaching the nature of the one undivided Essence, ever move about, being only That itself. This sentence[1] is for practice always and is the basis[2] of practice.

[1]statement [2]cause

18. This one, which is the supreme sentence[1] for reflection, is like the sandalwood tree (which is subjected to test before acceptance). The state exemplified by the three words [aham brahma asmi (I am Brahman)] should be reasoned out.

[1]statement

19. The meaning of the word "aham (I)" is the jiva. Isvara[1] is the meaning for the word "Brahman." As for the word "asmi (am)," it is the state of being of the undivided nature.

[1]īśa

20. Casting aside[1] the three words and inquiring with the mind and attaining the one undivided Essence is the characteristic of Liberation out of the body.

[1]abandoning

21. I am Brahman, Consciousness alone, of the nature of Existence-Consciousness-Bliss. The sentence,[1] "I am Brahman," should always be heard continuously.

[1]*statement*

22. "I am Brahman; I am eternal; I am peace; I am the Supreme; I am attributeless; I am desireless; and I am without parts" should ever be remembered.

23. "I am the Self, indeed. There is no doubt of this. I am the one undivided Essence." Thus, with this Knowledge, one should uninterruptedly consider oneself as the Supreme Self.

24. As this is a statement to be experienced, one should always experience it. The first as well as the second aphorisms should be remembered as statements to be experienced.[1]

[1]*practiced*

25. The third sentence reads on the face of it[1]—tat tvam asi (You are That). It consists of three words: tat (That) tvam (you) asi (are).

[1]*The third statement is the universal conclusion*

26. The meaning of the word "That" is Isvara. For the word "you," the meaning is jiva. The meaning of the word for identity ("are") is the one undivided Essence.

27. Of the dual mode, the witness mode, and the mode of undivided Existence, the undivided one is Existence-Consciousness-Bliss, and it is certain: That you are.

28. You are Brahman. There is no doubt of this. You, indeed, are changeless Consciousness. You, indeed, are Existence-Consciousness-Bliss. You, indeed, are the undivided certainty.

29. If this is so said by the Guru, he, indeed, is the great[1] Guru. By being convinced[2] that I am Brahman, the good[3] disciple becomes the Supreme Self.

[1]*supreme* [2]*certain* [3]*true*

30. None else is a Guru, nor any other a disciple. You yourself are Brahman, the Supreme Guru. He who ordains[1] all the Gurus is the Supreme Guru.

[1]*initiates and instructs*

31. Be convinced[1] that whoever tells you that you are Brahman is, indeed, the Guru. Likewise, you are that Brahman. Indeed, you are the Sadguru, too.

[1]*certain*

32. Whoever gets conviction in the words of the Sadguru, attaining the certitude of Truth, always makes for Liberation. There is no need to debate on this.

33. The mahavakya-s, the statements of the Guru, the statements such as "That you are"—whoever hears these and thinks of these is practicing listening. There is nothing else said to be listening.

34. [For] all the statements of Vedanta, the substratum[1] is the nondual Brahman. Hearing so from the mouth of the Guru is hearing this from Brahman.

[1]*stand, abode*

35. There is no one else who is a speaker of mantra except the Guru. There is only one Sadguru. By whomsoever it is said, "You are Brahman," he, indeed, is the Sadguru.

36. This is sravana to Vedanta. Nothing else is called sravana. Thinking on this by reasoning is called manana.

37. Thus are tested the sandalwood tree and what is heard. Even while[1] saying that you are Brahman, a doubt is felt.[2]

[1]*though* [2]*seen*

38. Only after testing is there conviction (about the sandal-wood tree). Thus, the Self also is tested. By way of reasoning, I say this here: I am not the body because of its being subject to destruction.

39. The gross body and the subtle body are due to the gross, the subtle, and the causal. As all three are not in the fourth state, all is only Consciousness, indeed.

40. All these are nonexistent like the pot, because of insentience and of being the seen. I am, here, only Consciousness, and, being of the nature of the seer, not connected therewith.

41. Existence-Knowledge-Infinity are the natural[1] qualities of the Self, and, ultimately, insentience,[2] sorrow[3] and such are the manifested qualities of the world.
[1]*sahajā* [2]*jaḍa* [3]*suffering*

42. "Hence, I am, indeed, Brahman and all this is false[1]"—thus reflects daily[2] he who knows Brahman best.
[1]*asatya* [2]*nityaṁ, always*

43. I shall now speak about constant meditation[1] and the characteristics of double renunciation. The listening to "You are Brahman," and the reflection that "I, indeed, am,"
[1]*nididhyāsanaṁ*

44. the renunciation of the concept of different items belonging to the same category, belonging to different categories, or the internal differences of a single category,

45. renouncing all renunciations and being devoid of even the fourth state, and being of the essence of Brahman-Consciousness alone is declared to be sakshatkara (direct perception).

46. It is declared that "That you are" is the great aphorism of upadesa (instruction). Likewise, "I am Brahman" has been defined as an aphorism of experience.

47. What arises from the statement "Absolute Knowledge is Brahman" is said to be for spiritual exercise, for practice. What arises from the statement "This Self is Brahman" is said to be a statement of perception.[1]

[1] darśanaṁ, revelation

48. Ayam (This) is one word and with Atma and Brahma (Self is Brahman) makes three words. The meaning of the word "this" is the jiva and that of Atma (Self) is the supreme Isvara.

49. Likewise, the meaning of Brahman is being in the undivided state. The merging together of all three words is the one undivided Essence.

50. The Self is, itself, the one undivided Essence, eternal, pure, and liberated. That, itself, becomes all. There is no doubt of this.

51. God is the undivided Essence. The words are: one is "this," one is "Self," one is "Brahman."

52. The meaning of "this" is the individual self; "the Self" denotes Isvara. The meaning of "I am" is the undivided meaning, the undivided Essence.

53. [First] the dual mode, [then] the witness mode, [then] the undivided mode, then the undivided Essence—then be of the conviction "He is I."

54. Thus, the implied meanings of the four statements have been explained. The statements are [loaded] with conditionings. The denoted meaning is the simple, unconditioned[1] state.

[1] kevalaṁ

213

55. The individual self is conditioned by littleness of knowledge and such [characteristics]. Isvara is conditioned by omniscience and such. The individual self, being the lower, Isvara with sentience, and I being the witness,[1]

[1]*parokṣakaḥ, imperceptible*

56. all should be renounced as void with the certitude that I am Brahman. I am Brahman. There is no doubt of this. I am of the nature of Existence-Consciousness-Bliss.

57. Having reached the state of "I am one with the Supreme," be in your highest, natural state. All this is a great illusion, nonexistent, nonexistent. There is no doubt of this.

58. All is nonexistent. There is no confusion in this. All is Brahman. There is no doubt of this. The undivided meaning is Oneness. That itself I am. There is no doubt of this. This all-pervasiveness[1] is Brahman. That Brahman I am. There is no doubt of this.

[1]*expansiveness*

Suta:
59. Become the enlightened one, with realized Wisdom, with a happy heart and the miseries of worldly existence removed by the conviction of being the exalted essence in this world that has arisen from the face of the one (Brahma) who has come out of the Supreme. Those with their bodies besmeared with ashes, filled agreeably with the love of intense joy, worship the serpent-bedecked Siva, who gives pleasure to and protects beings in the entire universe.

Chapter Twenty-Nine

sarva-mithyātva-nirūpaṇa-prakaraṇam
TOPIC OF THE DEFINITION OF THE ILLUSORINESS OF ALL

Ribhu:
I shall tell you again about the rejection[1] of the unreal and the certitude of Brahman, by just hearing which a man shall immediately become liberated.

[1] *abandonment*

2. The existence of thought, the existence of the mind, and the state of Brahman being anything different are all illusory. There is no doubt of this. I am Brahman. There is no uncertainty in this.

3. The existence of the body, the existence of characteristics, the existence of attitudes, and remaining as the decay-less are all illusory. There is no doubt of this. I am Brahman. There is no uncertainty in this.

4. The seen, the seeing, the seer, and the doer, the doing, and the deed are all illusory. There is no doubt of this. I am Brahman. There is no uncertainty in this.

5. Being one, being two, being separate, and determinations such as "is" and "is not" are all illusory. There is no doubt of this. I am Brahman. There is no uncertainty in this.

6. The differences of scriptures, the differences of Vedas, and the concept of differences in liberations are all illusory. There is no doubt of this. I am Brahman. There is no uncertainty in this.

7. The differences of groups, the differences of castes, and determinations such as purity and impurity are all illusory. There is no doubt of this. I am Brahman. There is no uncertainty in this.

8. The undivided mode and the one supreme, undivided essence are all illusory. There is no doubt of this. I am Brahman. There is no uncertainty in this.

9. Misconceptions such as the high and the low, and misconceptions such as punya and papa[1] are all illusory. There is no doubt of this. I am Brahman. There is no uncertainty in this.

[1] *merit and sin*

10. The duality of imaginary thought and absence of imaginary thought and the concept that it is the mind that thinks are all illusory. There is no doubt of this. I am Brahman. There is no uncertainty in this.

11. The achieved, the achievable, the means of achievement, the precepts,[1] and the attitude of Being[2] are all illusory. There is no doubt of this. I am Brahman. There is no uncertainty in this.

[1] *śāsanaṁ, corrections. Printed Sanskrit text says nāśanaṁ, destruction* [2] *concept of Brahman*

12. Knowledge of the Self, the nature of the mind—wherefrom can all these arise[1] in the absence of the mind? All are illusory. There is no doubt of this. I am Brahman. There is no uncertainty in this.

[1] *be*

13. Ignorance is a state of mind. Wherefrom can this arise in its absence? All are illusory. There is no doubt of this. I am Brahman. There is no uncertainty in this.

14. Serenity and control of the senses are states of the mind. Wherefrom can they arise in its absence? All are illusory. There is no doubt of this. I am Brahman. There is no uncertainty in this.

15. Bondage and liberation are states of the mind. Wherefrom can they arise in its absence? All are illusory. There is no doubt of this. I am Brahman. There is no uncertainty in this.

16. All are illusory, the world[1] is illusory, and the body is illusory because of their insentience.[2] All are illusory. There is no doubt of this. I am Brahman. There is no uncertainty in this.

[1]jagat [2]inertness

17. The world of Brahma (the Creator) is ever illusory. The nature[1] of the intellect is likewise. All are illusory. There is no doubt of this. I am Brahman. There is no uncertainty in this.

[1]form

18. The world of Vishnu is ever illusory; even so that of Siva always. All are illusory. There is no doubt of this. I am Brahman. There is no uncertainty in this.

19. The world of Rudra is ever illusory, because it is of the nature of the ego. All are illusory. There is no doubt of this. I am Brahman. There is no uncertainty in this.

20. The world of the Moon is ever illusory, being a delusion of the nature[1] of the mind. All are illusory. There is no doubt of this. I am Brahman. There is no uncertainty in this.

[1]form

21. Associated with the ear and sound, the world of Akasa (space)[1] is ever illusory. All are illusory. There is no doubt of this. I am Brahman. There is no uncertainty in this.

[1]diśo

217

22. Associated with eyes and form, the world of Surya (the Sun) is ever illusory. All are illusory. There is no doubt of this. I am Brahman. There is no uncertainty in this.

23. The world of Varuna (water) is ever associated with the tongue and taste. All are illusory. There is no doubt of this. I am Brahman. There is no uncertainty in this.

24. Associated with skin and touch, the world of Vayu (wind) is ever illusory. All are illusory. There is no doubt of this. I am Brahman. There is no uncertainty in this.

25. The world of smell of the asvin-s (divine doctors), associated with the duality of smell, also, is entirely illusory. There is no doubt of this. I am Brahman. There is no uncertainty in this.

26. Being of speech with words, the world of Agni (fire) is ever illusory. All are illusory. There is no doubt of this. I am Brahman. There is no uncertainty in this.

27. Associated with hands and feet, the world of Indra is ever illusory. All are illusory. There is no doubt of this. I am Brahman. There is no uncertainty in this.

28. The great world of Upendra (Vishnu in dwarf incarnation), associated with feet and movement, is entirely illusory. There is no doubt of this. I am Brahman. There is no uncertainty in this.

29. There never is any Mrityu (god of death) associated with the organ of excretion, which is only an outlet. All are illusory. There is no doubt of this. I am Brahman. There is no uncertainty in this.

30. The maharloka, the great world of Prajapati, the secret bliss, and that which is associated with secrets and enjoyment are all illusory. There is no doubt of this. I am Brahman. There is no uncertainty in this.

31. All are illusory. There is no doubt of this. It is certain that all is the Self. Fortitude, tranquility, clear understanding of the scriptures,[1] and the word of the preceptor,

[1]*faith*

32. the urge for liberation, liberation itself, living in order to attain liberation, the determination that he who is endowed with the four means is the truly qualified person,

33. the worthy conviction of the identity of the individual soul[1] and Brahman, the certitude that space is Brahman, the teaching of the "Brahmana-s" (chapters of the Vedas relating to action) and of Vedanta, and the teacher thereof, are all called bondage.

[1]*jīva*

34. If the removal of all [conceptual] knowledge occurs, the result is the attainment of joy.[1] Thus, it has been said by all the ancient Vedas that all is ever unreal.

[1]*bliss*

35. The nature of the meaning of all the Vedas and their definite conviction is so: Brahman alone is the Supreme Reality. All else is ever unreal.

36. Listening to endless[1] words and the inquiry into endless[1] meanings are entirely illusory. There is no doubt of this. I am Brahman. There is no uncertainty in this.

[1]*many*

37. The words regarding Brahman should not be thought of lightly. This is something great. At the time of Brahmopadesa (ordination into Brahmin-hood), no doubt, all has been said:

38. "I am, indeed, Brahman," and "all this is duality," the concept[1] of the mind-stuff, "I am mere Consciousness," and "all this is duality," the concept[1] of "the individual self is Brahman,"

[1]*attitude*

219

39. the mantra of "I am Consciousness alone," thinking about cause and effect, "decay-less joy and knowledge," "the undivided essence without a second,"

40. "the highest is Brahman," "this is Brahman," "peace is Brahman," "oneself is the world," the knowledge of the inner senses, the control of the external senses,

41. all the prescribed periods of ordination,[1] equality, distinction, the great creation, earth, water, fire, wind, space, mind and intellect,
[1]*initiation, spiritual instruction*

42., 43. the difference between cause and action, the imagining of the one way of the sastra-s, doubt and contrast, sankalpa, cause, and misapprehension—none of these is of the nature of Reality. There is never anything called "reality,"[1] because of the asseveration that I am Brahman, this is Brahman, all is Brahman.
[1]*named "truth"*

44. There is nothing apart from the Self. All is illusory. There is no doubt of this. Whatever great mantras exist, erudition, purity, auspiciousness, inauspiciousness,

45. differences of regions,[1] differences of things, and differences of awareness do not exist. Individuality apart from the Self, definitions other than the Self,
[1]*places*

46. names and forms apart from the Self, good and evil[1] apart from the Self, the existence of things apart from the Self, the three worlds apart from the Self,
[1]*bad, inauspicious*

47. joy and sorrow apart from the Self, thinking apart from the Self, the manifest world apart from the Self, success and failure apart from the Self,

48. the worship of deities apart from the Self, the worship of Siva apart from the Self, great contemplation[1] apart from the Self, and the distribution into parts apart from the Self

[1]*meditation*

49. are entirely illusory. There is no doubt of this. Brahman is all. There is no uncertainty in this. All this is said by the Lord. Ever contemplate[1] on this single-mindedly.

[1]*meditate*

50. Hearing well this once is the end of the knot of the heart, the destruction of the accumulated karma of the ignorant, and the Liberation of the great.

51. The karma of millions of births will be burnt to ashes. This is the truth. This is the truth. Again, this is the truth: that all these perish. Liberation ensues instantly. There is no doubt about this. There is nothing auspicious or inauspicious.

52. Where is the visualization of differences? Look at the remarkable conviction of identity in the crest of the Vedas, which removes sorrow and delusion. Like the thread of the web of the spider, the world has its dissolution in the great Lord from whom it came into existence and by whom it was sustained.

Chapter Thirty

saccidānanda rūpatā-prakaraṇam
TOPIC OF THE NATURE OF EXISTENCE-CONSCIOUSNESS-BLISS

Ribhu:
I say unto you, there is only the Supreme Brahman. This world is not born. I am just the state of Existence, only Bliss. This world[1] is not created.

[1]*jagat*

2. I am only the Self, the Supreme Brahman. All that is seen in this world[1] is nothing else. I am just the state of Existence, only Bliss. This world is not created.

[1]*saṁsāra*

3. I am the state of Existence, only Bliss. I am of the nature of the state of Consciousness, only Bliss. I am myself,[1] the only One. I am higher than the highest.

[1]*"I" alone*

4. I am only the one Existence-Consciousness-Bliss. I am Brahman alone. I exist and ever shine. This form is unreal, wherever it may be.

5. What is you is also the Supreme Brahman, of the nature of Consciousness-Bliss. The nature of Consciousness, the infinite[1] Consciousness, Consciousness alone, is the greatest joy.

[1]*space of*

6. I am only the Self. I am not unreal. I am Kutastha (the unchangeable Absolute), the supreme Guru. Time does not exist. The world[1] is nonexistent. It is a false conception.

[1]*jagat*

7. I myself am the Supreme Brahman. I am the ever peaceful.[1] I am just pure Consciousness. I am the experience of pure Existence.

[1]*śiva, Siva*

8. I am only nondual Bliss. I am immutable. I am great. All is ever Brahman alone. All is spotless[1] Brahman alone.

[1]*the blemishless*

9. All is Brahman alone and nothing else. All sentience[1] is Brahman alone. I am of the all-illuminating nature. I am, indeed, the mind dear to all.

[1]*awareness*

10. I am the one who shines alone. I am devoid of the settled and the unsettled.[1] I am of the nature of the inner pervader of all and of the characteristic of the witness of all.

[1]*siddhāsiddha*

11. It is certain that I am of the nature of tranquility, inquiry, and joy. I am the Supreme Self. I am the Supreme Light. I am the Supreme, devoid of anything else.

12. I am of the wholly full nature. I am the Supreme Self, the untouched. I am of the nature of all the Vedas. I am the conclusion of all the scriptures.

13. I am of the nature of the joy of the world. I am the definition of the best joy. All is Brahman alone. There is no world. Brahman alone is the cause of all.

14. All is Brahman alone. There is nothing created. All is Brahman alone. I am the superior. I am the ever decay-less,[1] the eternal, the harbinger[2] of all good.

[1]*imperishable* [2]*cause*

15. I am the light of Truth and Knowledge. I am the embodiment of the paramount Knowledge. I am the illuminator of the fourth state, and [I am] other than the fourth state. I am devoid of the settled and the unsettled and such.[1]

[1]*siddhāsiddhādi*

16. All is ever Brahman alone. All is Brahman without any interspace. All is Brahman, the infinite[1] Consciousness. The eternal Brahman is taintless.

[1]*space of*

17. All is Brahman, transcending qualities. All is only Brahman alone. All is Brahman alone. Have this certitude, always.

18. Being of this definite conviction that all is Brahman, be happy in the certitude that all is Brahman.

19. All is ever Brahman. Existence and nonexistence are only Consciousness. This disputation about duality and nonduality is unreal, unreal. There is no doubt of this.

20. I am only all-Knowledge. It is certain that all is Brahman. I am He who is the most mysterious of the mysterious. I transcend all qualities. [I am] nondual.

21. Inquire into all comparisons and contrasts, actions and inaction. I am of the nature of Existence-Consciousness-Bliss. This world[1] is not born.

[1]*jagat*

22. All this is Brahman alone. This world[1] is infinite[2] Consciousness. Brahman alone is the great[3] Bliss, all-pervading like space.

[1]*jagat* [2]*the space of* [3]*supreme*

23. Brahman alone is Existence-Consciousness-Bliss, ever immeasurable by words. Brahman alone is all this. "It exists" and "It exists not" say some.

24. It is a concept of "bliss" for some. "It is real, and it is unreal," say a few. Brahman alone is all this and is ever alone real.

25. Brahman alone is all this. Brahman is a mass of Consciousness, of the nature of Bliss. Brahman is the Reality and the Truth. I am the great and the immemorial.

26. Brahman alone is Existence-Consciousness-Bliss. It exists like the warp and woof. Brahman alone is Existence-Consciousness-Bliss. Brahman is of the nature of all and is immemorial.

27. Brahman alone is Existence-Consciousness-Bliss, the supreme Bliss, the immutable. Brahman alone is Existence-Consciousness-Bliss, transcending maya (illusion), taintless.

28. Brahman alone is Existence-Consciousness-Bliss, Existence alone, the Bliss of bliss. Brahman alone is Existence-Consciousness-Bliss, of the one single nature of Consciousness alone.

29. Brahman alone is Existence-Consciousness-Bliss, devoid of all differences. Brahman alone is Existence-Consciousness-Bliss, existing as the manifold.

30. Brahman alone is Existence-Consciousness-Bliss. It is the doer. It is time.[1] Brahman alone is Existence-Consciousness-Bliss, of the nature of the supreme Light.

[1]*favorable opportunity*

31. Brahman alone is Existence-Consciousness-Bliss, eternal, motionless, and immutable. Brahman alone is Existence-Consciousness-Bliss. It is the limit of words.

32. Brahman alone is Existence-Consciousness-Bliss, ever the natural Self. Brahman alone is Existence-Consciousness-Bliss and does not act and does not stand still.

33. Brahman alone is Existence-Consciousness-Bliss, neither moving nor standing still. Brahman alone is Existence-Consciousness-Bliss. There is nothing apart from Brahman.

34. Brahman alone is Existence-Consciousness-Bliss, neither white nor black. Brahman alone is Existence-Consciousness-Bliss, the substratum of all, the immutable.

35. Brahman alone is Existence-Consciousness-Bliss, neither silent nor speaking. Brahman alone is Existence-Consciousness-Bliss, neither he nor you nor I—nothing in the least.

36. Brahman alone is Existence-Consciousness-Bliss, greater than the greatest, devoid of any sacrificial fire. Brahman alone is Existence-Consciousness-Bliss, the great celebration, transcending all tattva-s.

37. Brahman alone is Existence-Consciousness-Bliss, pervading the great space. Brahman alone is Existence-Consciousness-Bliss, always of the nature of the Guru.

38. Brahman alone is Existence-Consciousness-Bliss, always of the nature of purity. Brahman alone is Existence-Consciousness-Bliss, pervaded by pure Consciousness.

39. Brahman alone is Existence-Consciousness-Bliss, of the nature of the self-illumined. Brahman alone is Existence-Consciousness-Bliss and is, also, certainly, the cause itself.

40. Brahman alone is Existence-Consciousness-Bliss, shining by itself. Brahman alone is Existence-Consciousness-Bliss, existing as the manifold.

41. Brahman is of the nature of Existence-Consciousness, of the nature of the substratum of a chimera. Brahman alone is Existence-Consciousness-Bliss. All is nonexistent. I do not exist.

42. Brahman, beyond the measure of words, is of the nature of Existence-Consciousness-Bliss. I am of the nature of Existence-Consciousness-Bliss. This world has not come into being.

43. Brahman alone is ever the reality, ever free, and ever untainted. Brahman alone is Existence-Consciousness-Bliss, the only one that is ever blissful.

44. Brahman alone is Existence-Consciousness-Bliss, fuller than the fullest, and the great. Brahman alone is Existence-Consciousness-Bliss, the Isvara that pervades all.

45. Brahman alone is Existence-Consciousness-Bliss, manifest with name and form. Brahman alone is Existence-Consciousness-Bliss, the endless,[1] the blissful, and the pure.

[1]*infinite*

46. Brahman alone is Existence-Consciousness-Bliss, bestowing great[1] Bliss. Brahman alone is Existence-Consciousness-Bliss—the only Truth, transcending "reality" and "unreality."

[1]*supreme*

47. Brahman alone is Existence-Consciousness-Bliss, greater than all and immutable. Brahman alone is Existence-Consciousness-Bliss, of the nature of Liberation, the auspicious and the inauspicious.

48. Brahman alone is Existence-Consciousness-Bliss, without any limitations at any time. Brahman, indeed, is all this, the pure, the enlightened, and the stainless.

49. I am of the nature of Existence-Consciousness-Bliss. This world has not come into being. This explanation is the Truth, granting instant Liberation,

50. effacing all sorrow, conferring all Knowledge, making for constant Bliss, truly bestowing peace and self-control.

51. One whose heart is constantly in contact with the lotus feet of Mahesvara, the destroyer of Antaka (death), and has his mind full of the divine feet before which large multitudes bow shall come within the fold of the grace emanating from Lord Siva.

Chapter Thirty-One

dṛṣṭāntair-brahma-sādhana-prakaraṇam
TOPIC OF THE ATTAINING OF BRAHMAN, WITH EXAMPLES

Ribhu:
Hear about the Knowledge of Brahman, which is wonderful and is difficult to obtain and which, by hearing once, Supreme Liberation is attained.

2. It is the truth, it is the truth that the world exists not; nor do sankalpa, understanding, and such exist. The Knowledge of Brahman is ever enveloped in[1] Bliss itself.

[1] *of the nature of*

3. It is blissful, changeless, peaceful, of one nature, and affliction-less. The phenomenal world of the mind exists not. Truly, there is nothing of action that can be reality.

4. The concept of the world is unreal. There is nothing of form to be seen. Sankalpa is of the nature of unreality. The world is not [the result] of its activity.

5. All is thus unreal. Time, Isvara, the creator, and the world are concepts like the fear of the son of a barren woman.

6. The world appears in front of me like the top of a peak in the illusory city of Gandharva-s in the sky (castles in the air). The world would exist if one could get satisfaction from drinking of the waters of a mirage.

7. Let this be like a man being killed by the peak of a mountain and not by an arrow. If the city of the Gandharva-s would be real, let the world exist always.

8. Truly the world becomes real if the sky is an ocean of blue. The world would exist if the silver in the oyster shell could become a real ornament,

9. if a man could enter into the transmigratory cycle by being killed by the snake that is an illusory superimposition on a rope, if burning flames of fire could be quenched by an arrow of flowers,

10. or if cooking could be done by a log that is the stem of a green plantain tree. Brahman, the eternally blissful, is ever alone by itself.

11. The world would be real if instant satisfaction could be had from a bevy of virgins. Brahman, the eternally blissful, is ever alone by itself.

12. The creation of the world would be present if there were a crow-swan in an illusory forest. The world would be, if the basic mantra (which is usually solemn in nature and has involved pronunciation) for establishing a powerful force could constitute a pleasing conversation.

13. The world would be if a man who died a month ago were to return. Any bit of the world could exist if buttermilk could attain the nature of milk.

14. The world would be if the milk coming out of the udder of a cow were to flow back into the teats. Let the world ever be if . . . (missing phrase)

15. The world would be if an elephant gone mad could be tied by the hairs of a tortoise. The world would be if the Meru mountain were to be dragged by lotus tendrils.

16. The world would be if an ocean river were to be dammed by a garland of waves. The world would be if a lotus were to grow in a flaming conflagration.

17. All this would be if Indra's mansion were to materialize on a huge mountain. Brahman is ever blissful and is ever alone by itself.

18. This world would be if a fish were to come and stay on a lotus seed. This would be if the sun were splintered and swallowed up. This would be if the mountain Meru had a tail.

19. It is as if it were imagined that a lion is killed and consumed by a mosquito. The world would be if all the three worlds were contained inside the hollow of an atom.

20. The world would be if a dream object were to continue in the waking state. Let this world ever be if the flowing river stands still.

21. The world would be if one confirmed blind becomes an expert in the scrutiny of gems. The world would be if Rahu, "the shadow planet," were to be seen without the sun and the moon.

22. The world would be if there is growth from a decayed seed or if anything born of the mind were to grow. The world would be were the indigent to experience the pleasures of the affluent.

23. The world would be if the milk that has been milked out were to flow back again (into the teats) or if there is only a mirror and no reflection.

24. The world would be if the sky were to disappear and only its reflection remain. There is no elephant in the womb of a gnat; likewise, there is no world inside us.[1]

[1] the Self

25. Just as the scriptures are revelations,[1] the world is all Brahman. Just as cotton consumed by fire ceases to exist and leaves no residue,[2] so is the world nonexistent.

[1]happened as related in the tantras [2]ash

26. Brahman is supreme. Brahman is the supreme Light, the highest of the high, and beyond all. The concepts of difference, duality, or nonduality never exist.

27. The misery of the world is the [many] modes of the mind. Destruction of it arises only if it exists. Bondage is born of sankalpa. If it exists, be of the conviction of being Brahman.

28. There is the attitude of duality if there is nescience, action, body, and such. The mind is the mighty disease. If you are afflicted by it, Brahman is the physician therefor.

29. If "I" becomes the enemy, be of the conviction "I am Brahman." If there be the misery of "I am the body," be of the certitude that I am Brahman.

30. If there be the goblin of uncertainty, destroy it by Brahman alone. When possessed by the ghost of duality, have recourse to the sacred ashes of Nonduality.

31. If there be the ghost of non-Self, bind it by the spell[1] of the Self. Brahman is ever blissful and ever alone by itself.

[1]mantra

32. Thus, Brahman, itself, has been established by sixty-four examples. Whichever man hears this daily is liberated. There is no doubt about this.

33. He has accomplished his objective. There is no need for further inquiry about this.

34. Your lotus feet, Mahesvara! without form, without scent, ever in the recesses of the heart, always a source of joy to the knowledgeable, glowing with effulgence and blooming with luster, and shedding brightness around, transcend mind and speech.

Chapter Thirty-Two

brahmabhāvanopadeśa-prakaraṇam
TOPIC OF THE INSTRUCTION IN BRAHMAN-CONVICTION

Ribhu:

Nidagha! Listen to what I [have to say]. This is highly secret, conferring instant Liberation on men. All is the Self. All this is nothing else. I am the undivided Supreme Self.

2. I, indeed, am the Supreme Brahman, of the nature of Existence-Consciousness-Bliss. I am. I am great. I am peaceful.[1] I am the highest.[2]

[1]*śiva, Siva* [2]*supreme*

3. The Supreme Brahman cannot be seen. There is nothing else that exists in its own nature. All is nonexistent, indeed, nonexistent, indeed. I am Brahman alone.

4. I am the peaceful and the Supreme Brahman, ever eternally pure. All is nonexistent, indeed, nonexistent, indeed. I am Brahman alone.

5. I am free from all sankalpa. I am devoid of all happiness.[1] I am the substance[2] of time, action, the world, duality, the seer, and the seen.

[1]*being pleased* [2]*form*

6. I am bliss, ever happy, the lone, the beloved of the world, of equanimous nature, eternal, the past and the future, the unborn, and the victorious.

7. I am just Consciousness. Ever liberated [am I], there does not exist anything as the jiva or bondage. Listening and the shad-lingas (sextet of characteristics) do not exist, nor does a world such as this.

8. I am devoid of the mind and the world.[1] The world[2] is always just Consciousness. The mind, indeed, is prone to the body [concept]. Non-inquiry is the great foe.[3]

[1]saṁsāra [2]jagat [3]deceiver

9. Non-inquiry is the misery of the world. Non-inquiry is the [cause of] great fear. Immediately, I am satisfied in all ways. I am the supreme, the great, complete, and perfectly full.

10. I am ever pure, ever knowledgeable, and an expanse of Consciousness and chetana (sentience). This is all the Self, indeed, and nothing else. I am the undivided Supreme Self.

11. I am devoid of all defects. I am spread out everywhere. I am of the nature that transcends words. I am the unbroken Self.

12. I transcend this picture of a world. I transcend the pairs of opposites. I am happy, equanimous, the interior and the exterior, without beginning or end, and not definable by any difference.

13. Ego, strength, all desire and anger, acquisitiveness, Brahma, Indra, Vishnu, Varuna, without certainty[1] of existence or nonexistence,

[1]the uncertainty

14. the reality of jiva, the reality of the world, the reality of delusion[1]—none of these exist; nor does the difference between the guru and the disciple and such exist, nor the decision for action and inaction.

[1]māyā

15. One who says "You are Brahman" or "I am Brahman, all-pervading existence," all Vedanta and superior knowledge,[1] the inquiry into all traditions,

[1]*vijñānaṁ*

16. the reality of the meaning of the word "this," existing with the form of "I," the settled conclusion of the Vedas and Vedanta, the differences of the world—these do not exist.

17. All is Brahman. There is no doubt of this. Indeed, there is no such thing as all. There is only Brahman, the peaceful Self. I, indeed, am perpetual.

18. There are no divisions of the auspicious and the inauspicious, defect and non-defect, for me. The mind-stuff and the world-stuff are the chimera of the unfolding of thought.[1]

[1]*modes of the intellect*

19. Brahman alone ever is, not another. This is the truth, this is the truth, the true word. This duality is the form of the Self, only the Self, and nothing else.[1]

[1]*This is a form of the Self. Duality is false indeed. There is not another soul (spirit)*

20. I am just Existence-Consciousness-Bliss. All is changelessness alone. So, too, is it with Brahma, Vishnu, Rudra, Isvara, Sadasiva,

21. differences such as the mind, the world, and I, the activity of the mind, the fear of the world, all joys, immeasurable[1] joy, and the endless joy of the Self.

[1]*great*

22. Nothing of the world of phenomena exists, even in the smallest or the most insignificant part. There is no existence of the word "world" or even its recollection.

23. Nowhere is there a phenomenal world; it is neither inside nor outside; nor is there anything silent. There is nothing at all as "whatever little" or "at all times."

24. There is nothing at all as "he, by whom," "whenever," "by whatever little," or "he, whose," or pure or impure nature. There is no word about Brahman that is difficult to understand.

25. Nothing can be described as "this" or "that." Brahman alone is all, all of the time. Brahman alone is the entire mind.

26. Bliss, great[1] Bliss, eternal Bliss, is ever nondual. Consciousness alone ever exists. Never, never, is it that I am [someone] different.

[1]*supreme*

27. The phenomenal world never exists. The phenomenal world is only a picture. The mind alone is the world of birth and death.[1] Nothing else is, indeed, birth and death.[1]

[1]*saṁsāraṁ*

28. The mind, indeed, is birth and death[1] and the imagining[2] that I am the body. Sankalpa is the world of birth and death.[1] When it is destroyed, this is also destroyed.

[1]*saṁsāro* [2]*of the form*

29. Sankalpa itself is birth. When it is destroyed, this is destroyed. Sankalpa itself is decay.[1] When it is destroyed, this is destroyed.

[1]*splitting, tearing, poverty*

30. Sankalpa itself is reflection. When it is destroyed, this is destroyed. This is only the Self and nothing else. I am the undivided Supreme Self.

31. Knowledge is ever pervaded by the Self. I am, indeed, ever the great. This is all only the Self and nothing else. I am the undivided Supreme Self.

32. If you thus have this conviction always, you will quickly become liberated. You, indeed, are of the nature of Brahman. You, indeed, are the embodiment of Brahman.

33. Thus, meditating and meditating on the supremely blissful, be happy. The entire world[1] is only happiness. The phenomenal world is only love.

[1]*universe*

34. This world is just insentience.[1] This is ever just Brahman. This is Brahman alone and nothing else. I am the changeless Supreme Self.

[1]*inert*

35. This is only One, ever. This alone is the One without interstices. The Supreme Brahman is only One. Changeless Consciousness is only One.

36. That which transcends attributes is only One. That which causes joy is only One. The great Self is only One. There is only One without interstices.

37. There is only the one nature of Consciousness. There is only one definition of the Self. This is, indeed, Brahman and nothing else. I am the undivided Supreme Self.

38. I am the Supreme Self and nothing else. I am the abode[1] of Supreme Bliss. Being of such conviction, always be ever pervaded by[2] Consciousness.

[1]*mandiram* [2]*of the nature of*

39. Suta:
Worship the destroyer of Manmatha[1] (god of love) and of the world created by Brahma, the bearer of the beautiful golden mountain, the chief of the huntsmen. Even if a little water is sprinkled on the top of the linga, instantaneously, one is totally released from misdeeds. Nothing remains behind.

[1]*pañcabāṇa, having five arrows*

Chapter Thirty-Three

brahmabhāvanopadeśa-prakaraṇam
TOPIC OF THE INSTRUCTION IN BRAHMAN-CONVICTION

Ribhu:

Hear, best among brahmins! The definition of "All-is-Brahman," by hearing which you shall forthwith[1] attain Liberation.

[1]*instantly*

2. All this, indeed, never is. I alone am. The Self, indeed, ever is.[1] The Self, indeed, is of the nature of happiness.

[1]*nāsti, is not, in Sanskrit text corrected to asti, is; or to hyasti, indeed is*

3. The Self, indeed, is the greatest Truth. The Self is the multitude of the world. The Self is the expanse of space. Also, the Self is without interspace.[1]

[1]*interruption*

4. The Self truly is Brahman alone. The Self is of the nature of the Guru. The Self, indeed, is an expanse[1] of Consciousness and is eternal. The Self alone is decay-less[2] and changeless.

[1]*of the nature* [2]*imperishable*

5. The Self alone is the firmly established nature. The Self is the Self alone. There is no doubt of this. The Self is the nature[1] of this world.[2] The Self is itself the Self itself.

[1]*form* [2]*jagat*

6. The Self alone is the harbinger of happiness.[1] The Self alone is the mind and space. The Self, indeed, is any little thing that is. The Self alone is the highest state.

[1]*peace*

7. The Self, indeed, is the form of this universe. The Self, indeed, is the changeless love. The Self, indeed, is nowhere anything else. Anything else, indeed, is the Self, which fills the mind.

8. The Self, indeed, is all knowledge. The Self, indeed, is the greatest treasure. The Self is the nature of beings. The Self is the great cycle[1] [of birth and death].

[1]*wandering, erring*

9. The Self alone is the eternally pure. The Self is the Guru of itself. The Self is the disciple of itself. The Self dissolves in itself.

10. The Self alone is the object of meditation upon itself. The Self alone is the goal of the Self. The Self alone is the sacrifice[1] to itself. The Self alone is the japa of itself.

[1]*homa*

11. The Self, itself, is alone the satisfaction of the Self. There is nothing apart from[1] the Self. The Self alone is the root of the Self. The Self alone is the object of devotion[2] to the Self.

[1]*other than* [2]*spiritual vow, practice of*

12. The Knowledge of the Self is the daily[1] vowed religious observance. The Knowledge of the Self is the highest[2] happiness. The Knowledge of the Self is the great[2] Bliss. The Knowledge of the Self is the great goal.

[1]*eternal* [2]*supreme*

13. The Knowledge of the Self is the Supreme Brahman. The Knowledge of the Self is the greatest vow. The Knowledge of the Self is to be realized by oneself. The Knowledge of the Self is the great treasure.

14. The Knowledge of the Self is the Supreme Brahman. The Knowledge of the Self is the great happiness. The Knowledge of the Self is the great Self. The Knowledge of the Self is the abode of all people.

15. The Knowledge of the Self is the great sacred waters. The Knowledge of the Self confers success. The Knowledge of the Self is the Supreme Brahman. The Knowledge of the Self is the moving and the unmoving.

16. The Knowledge of the Self is the highest science.[1] The Knowledge of the Self is unequalled. The Knowledge of the Self is the highest yoga. The Knowledge of the Self is the supreme path.

[1] *śāstram, scripture*

17. The Knowledge of the Self is the unwavering certitude that the highest is Brahman. The Knowledge of the Self is the destruction of the mind. The Knowledge of the Self is the supreme Guru.

18. The Knowledge of the Self is the destruction of thought. The Knowledge of the Self confers release.[1] The Knowledge of the Self is the destruction of fear. The Knowledge of the Self is conducive to happiness.

[1] *liberation*

19. The Knowledge of the Self is the great light. The Knowledge of the Self is the great auspiciousness. The Knowledge of the Self is the nature of the Truth. The Knowledge of the Self is the beloved of the good.

20. The Knowledge of the Self is the Liberation of the good. The Knowledge of the Self generates discrimination. The Knowledge of the Self is the great dharma. The Knowledge of the Self is ever the japa.

21. The equal of the Knowledge of the Self is only the Knowledge of the Self. Anything equal to the Knowledge of the Self never was and never will be.

22. The Knowledge of the Self is the highest mantra. The Knowledge of the Self is the highest tapas. The Knowledge of the Self is verily Hari. The clearly evident, immediate Knowledge of the Self is the Supreme Siva.

23. The Knowledge of the Self is the great[1] creator, Brahma. The Knowledge of the Self is acceptable to all. The Knowledge of the Self is itself punya. The Knowledge of the Self is the great purification.

[1]highest

24. The Knowledge of the Self is the great holy waters. The Knowledge of the Self is tranquility and other such [merits]. The Knowledge of the Self is the mantra that is dear. The Knowledge of the Self purifies[1] oneself.

[1]sanctifies

25. What, indeed, is the Knowledge of the Self? The "I am Brahman" certitude; "I am Brahman" is the great upsurge of the trusted Knowledge of the Self.

26. It is the clear perception "I am Brahman, I am eternal, I am firmly abiding, I am Bliss, the Supreme Bliss, and I am pure and ever changeless."

27. [It is the clear perception that] I am of the nature of the expanse[1] of Consciousness, permanent[2] Existence-Consciousness-Bliss. I am without modifications. I am peaceful. I am everywhere. I am without interstices.

[1]space [2]everlasting

28. I am always of the nature of happiness. I am devoid of all defects. I am free from all sankalpa, and I am always myself.

29. Read silently to yourself about the experience that all is Brahman. In a moment, all the punya which would result from a million asvamedha (horse sacrifices) can be obtained.

30. Being of the certitude that I am Brahman, the fruit of giving the Meru mountain in charity will result. Even the offering of all the land is trivial compared to being firm that[1] I am Brahman alone.

[1] abidance as
_____

31. Being firm that[1] I am Brahman alone, even millions of gifts are trivial. Being firm that[1] I am Brahman alone, all joy is inconsequential.

[1] abidance as
_____

32. The fruit of the conviction that all is Brahman is [Brahman] itself. The equal of being firm that I am Brahman is only Brahman.

33. Therefore, even while in dream and at all times, sacrificing all by positive effort,[1] I am Brahman. There is no doubt of this. I am my own goal.

[1] abandoning all by striving
_____

34. I, indeed, am never anything else. I, indeed, am ever the Guru. I alone am the Supreme Self. My Self is never another.

35. I, myself, am the Guru; I, myself, am the disciple. Be of this certitude. This which is pointed out, the world,[1] which is limited, never is.

[1] jagat
_____

36. There is no earth, no water, no fire, no air, and no space. All being Consciousness alone, nothing else exists.

37. Being full of this conviction, be happy, released from the body. I am the Self. This is nonexistent, as all is only Consciousness.

38. I, indeed, am the complete[1] Self, the ocean of Bliss, and affliction-less. This never is; being insentient,[2] it is unreal, indeed. This is Brahman, ever Brahman. Be happy that this does not exist.

[1]*pūrṇa* [2]*inert*

39. The liberated are those who, without being overcome by trivial enjoyments, which are as illusory as the horns of a horse, and without wasting their time in fruitless action, study the purport of the Vedas, and, by means of listening and such, realize the nature of the undivided Siva.

Chapter Thirty-Four

sarva-siddhānta-prakaraṇam
TOPIC OF ALL OF THE SETTLED CONCLUSIONS

Ribhu:

Nidagha! Listen. I shall tell you about the secret and the most wondrous. By hearing just one verse thereof, you shall attain instant Liberation.

2. This Supreme Brahman that is seen shines as if seen because of Consciousness. All is because[1] of Consciousness. Nothing else exists.[2]

[1]*the nature* [2]*All being Consciousness alone, nothing else exists.*

3. This, indeed, exists not. This nearer one also exists not. Even an atom—even one—exists not, exists not. There is no doubt of this.

4. Nowhere is there any of this empirical world,[1] not even as a word anywhere, nor is there any built-up[2] form or built-up[2] word or built-up[2] action, nor is there anything separate.

[1]*worldly activity* [2]*fetter of*

5. Action is Existence alone. The certitude that I am Brahman is Existence alone. Sorrow, happiness, knowledge, distinction as what is to be accomplished, and what accomplishes[1] it,

[1]*the means to*

6. the Self, the Supreme Self, and the individual self—there is nothing separate as [all] these. I am the body. I am the form. I am the knowledge and knower.

7. I am the nature of cause and effect and the actions of the inner faculties. Any of these—even one of these—exists not, exists not. Be of this conviction.

8. All is mere sankalpa. The world[1] is entirely Brahman. The Knowledge of Truth is the Supreme Brahman. The meaning of Omkara is the japa that gives happiness.

[1]*jagat*

9. [Concepts of] duality, nonduality, constant duality,[1] and, likewise, honor and dishonor are all due to[2] Consciousness alone. Nothing else exists.

[1]*sadādvaitaṁ* [2]*the nature of*

10. I, the Bliss of the Self, am Brahman. Prajnanam (Absolute Knowledge), indeed, is Brahman. The nature of this, the nature of "I," the inquiry into the likeable[1] and the unlikeable,[2]

[1]*dear* [2]*not dear*

11. whatever takes place in the world, whatever can be imagined as achievable, whatever is intrinsically good, and whatever is composed of Consciousness—you should have the conviction that such are Brahman.

12. I, indeed, am, here, the gross body. I am also the subtle body. Besides, the differences of intellect, the differences of mind, the ego, and also what is insentient,[1]

[1]*inert*

13. all being only Consciousness, there is nothing else. Nothing else exists. Indeed, there is nothing of listening, reflection, and also no inquiry into direct perception.[1]

[1]*sākṣātkāra*

14. I am, indeed, the Self, which is the Supreme. I, myself, am not filled with delusion. Brahman alone is all this. Brahman alone is the supreme abode.

15. Brahman, indeed, is the cause and effect. Brahman alone is the overcoming of the world. Brahman alone is all Consciousness. Brahman constitutes the mind, indeed.

16. Brahman alone manifests as the jiva. Brahman alone manifests as Hari. Brahman alone manifests as Siva. Brahman alone is dear to the Self.

17. Brahman alone manifests as tranquility. There is nothing apart from Brahman. I exist not. This exists not. Nothing else exists. Nothing has been created, not even the highest of the high.

18. This exists not, nor does the meaning of the scriptures exist, nor the mimamsa (interpretation of the Vedic rituals and the settlement of dubious points in Vedic texts), nor creation, nor definitions, nor the Vedas and other scriptures, nor thought, nor my mind.

19. There is nothing mine, nothing such as this, nothing at hand, nothing such as this and that, and no intellect. This is ever certain: nothing ever exists. This is the Truth. The Truth is. There is nothing ever.

20. Even only one does not exist, nor this either. There is nothing inside, nothing outside; there is nothing at all. Not even in the least is there any duality. There is no creation. There is nothing to be seen,

21. no contemplation, no remembrance, no forgetfulness— not even an atom of these. There is no understanding of time or space, no sankalpa, no perception,[1]

_____

[1] knowledge

22. no knowledge,[1] no separate body, nothing as my being knowledgeable, and no transmigration. There is no sorrow for me, no liberation for me, and there is no place, good or evil,[2] for me to go.

[1]awareness [2]causing distress

23. I am not [a concept of] "the Self." I am not the jiva (individual self); nor am I the Kutastha (changeless Absolute). I am motionless. I am not the body. I am not the ears, the skin, or the deities of the senses.

24. All being Consciousness alone, all is ever nonexistent. Being of the nature of the undivided, all is ever nonexistent.

25. The need for humkara (a menacing sound), or the creation of such a menacing sound exists not, exists not, exists not, exists not, ever exists not.

26. Even the least meaning of the word "apart," or anything apart, or the talk of something apart, or anything being real or unreal apart from the Self is all a chimera.

27. "It exists not"—exists not, exists not, indeed. Even the words "exists not" exist not. All being Consciousness alone, all, indeed, is ever nonexistent.

28. All is Brahman. There is no doubt of this. I am Brahman alone. There is no doubt of this. The direct meaning of individual words, the expressed meaning of a collection of words, the speaker, the pair of triads,

29. the differences of knower, knowledge, and the knowable, the measure and the measurable, other such things that are dear, whatever is determined by the scriptures, whatever has been decided by the Vedas,

30. the high and the low, the transcendent, the knowledge that I am the transcendent, the Guru, the instruction by the Guru, the precepts of the Guru—there is none such as the Guru—

31. the nature[1] of the Guru, the sincerity of[2] the Guru, and the Guru himself ever exist not. The Self alone is the Guru of the Self, nothing else being existent. There is no doubt of this.

[1]*form* [2]*faith in*

32. The well-being of the Self is the Self, itself, nothing else being existent. There is no doubt of this. The delusion of the Self is the Self, itself. The Self is nothing else.

33. The happiness of the Self is the Self, itself. Nothing else exists. There is no doubt of this. The power of the Self is in the Self, itself. The fondness[1] of the Self is for[2] the Self, itself.

[1]*love, dearness* [2]*in*

34. The holy ablution of the Self is in the Self, itself. The love of the Self is in the Self, itself. The Knowledge of the Self is the greatest reward.[1] The knowledge of the Self is hard to obtain.

[1]*excellence, fortune*

35. The Knowledge of the Self is the Supreme Brahman. The Knowledge of the Self is the happiest of happiness. There is nothing higher than the Knowledge of the Self. There is no scripture[1] other than the Knowledge of the Self.

[1]*smṛtiḥ*

36. Brahman, itself, is the Self. There is no doubt of this. The Self is, indeed, Brahman, itself. It is itself everywhere. It is itself filled with Consciousness.

37. It is itself the expanse[1] of Consciousness. It is itself without interstices. It is itself not non-Self. It is itself not the lower.[2]

[1]*space* [2]*another*

38. It, itself, transcends qualities. It is itself great happiness. It is itself the Self of peace. It is itself partless.

39. It is itself the Bliss of Consciousness. It is itself the great Lord. It is itself ever the witness. It is itself Sadasiva.

40. It is itself, verily, Hari. It is itself Prajapati. It is itself the Supreme Brahman. It is itself ever Brahman.

41. All is Brahman. Oneself is Brahman. Oneself is Brahman. There is no doubt of this. Have this strong certitude yourself, by all means, always.

42. Inquiring into Brahman, you will yourself become only Brahman. The certitude that I am Brahman is, indeed, the Supreme Brahman.

43. This, indeed, is the great Liberation: the certitude I am Brahman. This, indeed, is fulfillment. This, indeed, is happiness always.

44. This, indeed, is always the Knowledge—oneself being Brahman, oneself being that which is great. I am Brahman—this, indeed, is always the Knowledge, and, by itself, is the great.

45. I am Brahman—this, indeed, is the natural state of Being. I am the everlasting. I am Brahman—this is always the permanent,[1] ever [standing] by itself.

[1]*eternal*

46. I am Brahman—this, itself, is the destruction of bondage. There is no doubt of this. This is the certitude of all the settled conclusions: I am Brahman.

47. This is the settled conclusion of the Upanishads[1]—the certitude I am Brahman. This is the purport of all the Upanishads.[1] The world[2] is entirely just Bliss.

[1]*vedānta* [2]*jagat*

48. The settled conclusion of any great aphorism is the certitude I am Brahman. The settled conclusion of, verily, Siva, himself, is the certitude I am Brahman.

49. The settled conclusion of Narayana is the certitude I am Brahman. The settled conclusion of the four-faced [Brahma] is the certitude I am Brahman.

50. This, indeed, is in the heart of the sages. This, indeed, is the exhortation[1] of the gods. This, indeed, is the settled conclusion of all masters[2]—the certitude I am Brahman.

[1]*spiritual teaching* [2]*deśika, guide*

51. This is, indeed, the great teaching for all beings for all times. "I am Brahman" is the great Liberation. The highest, indeed, is this: I am myself.

52. "I" and this experience, too, are to be kept highly secret. I am Brahman. This, indeed, is ever the knowledge, which is, by itself, the greatest.

53. This, indeed, is the great Light—the certitude I am Brahman. This, indeed, is the great mantra, this, indeed, the great japa.

54. This, indeed, is the great purificatory ablution—the certitude I am Brahman. This, indeed, is the great holy water—the certitude I am Brahman.

55. This, indeed, is the great Ganga—the certitude I am Brahman. This is the supreme dharma—the certitude I am Brahman.

56. This, indeed, is the great infinity[1]—the certitude I am Brahman. This, indeed, is the exalted Knowledge—the certitude I am Brahman, Kaivalya.[2] This, indeed, is the settled conclusion of all—the certitude I am Brahman.

[1]*space* [2]*kevalam*

57. Waving their hands and, with hearts free of concern, carrying water pots, cowherdesses see the golden lotus of Sambhu in the mandala of the sun. Hara, with hands reaching out in all directions, nourishes the world with the mass of herbs enriched by the wealth amassed from the collection of waters arising everywhere.

Chapter Thirty-Five

prapañca-śūnyatva-prakaraṇam
TOPIC OF THE VOIDNESS OF THE PHENOMENAL WORLD

Ribhu:

I shall now speak of there being only Existence-Conscious-ness-Bliss, an explanation that is most wondrous, pure, and explicit, and of the emptiness[1] of the entire empirical universe. It is definite that the Self is all.

[1]*voidness*

---

2. The phenomenal universe is of the nature of the Self, or the manifoldness is of the nature of the Self. All that is manifold is nonexistent, indeed. It is definite that Brahman is all.

3. The eternal experience of bliss, the concept that Brahman is eternal, the empirical universe of the nature of thought, the world of birth-and-death[1] of the nature of thought,

[1]*saṁsāra*

---

4. the existence as "this is," "I am," or "the world is," the faulty notions about one's own inner faculties, the actions of one's inner faculties,

5. any kind of misconception such as one's own life, one's own death, one's own birth, "there is an Isvara," "I am the jiva," or "the world is,"

6. the substance of delusion,[1] the substance of greatness, the substance of thought, full of the world, whatever is shown by the scriptures, whatever is expressed in the Vedas,

[1]*illusion*

7. the exhortation "It is One," talk of duality, any misapprehension that I am Siva, the misapprehension that I am Brahma,

8. the misapprehension that I am Vishnu, the misunderstanding that the world exists, the misunderstanding that some little[1] difference exists, the misunderstanding that some little[1] duality exists,

[1]*slight*

9. the certitude that all is, the certitude that [all] is not, the certitude that all is Brahman, the universe of one's own contemplation,[1] the manifest universe of one's own recollection,

[1]*dhyāna*

10. the phenomenal universe of the nature of sorrow and the manifold universe of the nature of joy, the phenomenal universe of "duality and nonduality," and the manifold universe of "reality and unreality,"

11. the phenomenal world of wakefulness, and, likewise, the manifold world of dreams, the phenomenon of the knowledge of the deep sleep state, or the phenomenon of the knowledge of the fourth state,

12. the phenomenal world of Vedic knowledge, the manifold world of scriptural knowledge, the phenomenal world of sinful thoughts[1] or the manifold world of differing merits,[2]

[1]*buddhi* [2]*puṇya*

13. the phenomenal world of the nature of knowledge, the manifold world of the knowledge of the attributeless, the phenomenal world of qualities or absence thereof, the determination of defects and non-defects,

14. the investigation into reality and unreality, the investigation into the mobile and the immobile, the true conviction that the Self is one, the concept that the Self is important,

15. the certitude that the phenomenal world is nonexistent and that all is Brahman, statements that the "differences arising out of duality and nonduality exist not, exist not,"

16. the certitude that the world[1] is, indeed, unreal and all is Brahman, the ideas of cause and effect, and the unsettling due to[2] multiple differences—

[1]jagat [2]extending

17. renouncing and throwing away thus and all that give various mantras, be steadfastly established in yourself forever.

18. The bhava of silence, action in silence, the yoga of silence, what is dear to the mind, the teacher of the panchakshara mantra (Namah Sivaya), likewise, the giver of the ashtakshara mantra (the eight-letter mantra),

19. and whatever there is of the Vedas and scriptures, whatever differences there are of the teachers,[1] and always—in all the world—the imagining of all ideas,

[1]gurus

20. the manifest world of all speech, the phenomenal universe of all thoughts, the wrong understanding of all forms, the imagining of all reasons,[1]

[1]causes

21. the world of all defects, the world of joy and sorrow, what is to be grasped and what is to be given up, the talk of what is to be grasped, and what renounced,[1]

[1]abandoned

22. the investigation into birth and death, the nature of anamnesis[1] and intellect, desire and anger, covetousness and infatuation, all hauteur and arrogance,

[1]*vāsanā*
_____

23. the duality that occurs in all three worlds, Brahma, Indra, Varuna and others, the organs of perception, sound and others, the directions, the wind, the sun and the gods,

24. the good attitude toward the organs of action, matters of the multitudes of deities, the activities of the inner faculties, the impact of the supernatural,[1]

[1]*matters that pertain to the gods*
_____

25. the differentiations of the mental modes, and the determination of the modes of the intellect, this duality which is mere delusion,[1] the determination of reality and unreality,

[1]*illusion*
_____

26. a little duality, enormous duality, the duality of souls[1]— all is ever unreal. The delusion about the origin of the world, the definition of the guru and the disciple,

[1]*jīva*
_____

27. the secrecy of the meaning of the word "That" and the revelation of the meaning of the word "you," likewise, the concept of the sense of identity of the meaning of the word "are,"

28. the difference and nondifference among differences— none of these or anything else exists. This universe, indeed, exists not. It is definite that all is Brahman.

29. All being Consciousness, He (It), Brahman, alone is, indeed. All this is of the nature of the Self. There is nothing apart from the Self.

30. There exists no reality or unreality apart from Brahman, which transcends the fourth state. Renouncing[1] all, ever be firmly established in your own Self alone.

[1]*abandoning*

31. Thought, time, differences among objects, sankalpa, bhava (attitudes), and yourself—renouncing[1] all, always look upon all as, indeed, Brahman.

[1]*abandoning*

32. Wherever the scriptures are given to differences, wherever the mind is given to differences, renounce all of that always, and be firmly established in yourself.

33. Imaginings due to mental projections, misapprehension due to one's own imagination, limitations due to the ego, the attitude that the body is myself—

34. renouncing all of that, always be firmly established in yourself. The [positive] existence of the universe, the origin of a separate universe,

35. thinking of the [positive] existence of bondage, thinking of the [positive] existence of liberation, the [positive] existence or nonexistence of deities, the delineation of the worship of deities,

36. the deity of the panchakshara, the deity of the ashtak-shara, the existence of the five prana-s, the subsidiary pentad of prana-s,

37. the differentiation as earth and the other elements, enumeration of qualities such as dullness, foolishness and others, the ultimate conclusions of the Vedanta scriptures, the Saiva Agama-s,

38. worldly transactions, empirical reality, defects, developments and dissolutions—renouncing all, always be firmly established in yourself.

39. The joy of the Knowledge of the Self, Brahman, the defect of the lack of Knowledge of the Self, the incoming breath, the outgoing breath, the retained breath, the investigation into shadadhara (the sextet of supports),

40. the dualistic mode that I am the body, the witness attitude of Consciousness, the mode of the undivided nature, the acceptance of[1] the undivided nature,

[1]*agreement with*

41. [all] endless experience included, the certitude "I am Brahman," the best, the mediocre, likewise, the worse than the worst,

42. abuse, praise, all eulogy and condemnation, the philosophy[1] of "I am Brahman," "This is Brahman," "All is Brahman, indeed,"

[1]*truths*

43. I am Brahman, I am young, I am old, I am beyond reality and unreality, the Cosmic Being,[1] the macrocosm, the attitude that the universe is gross,

[1]*universally worshiped*

44. my being a vibration of Bliss, my being devoid of the high and the low, my being the ever blissful Brahman, the embodiment of Existence-Consciousness-Bliss,

45. the nature of the seer, the nature of the seen, the nature of the great Existence, aloneness, total destruction, entering into all beings,

46. the past, the present, the future, and all present activity are ever nonexistent. The concept of time, the concept of the body, the definition of reality and unreality,

47. my being, indeed, a mass of supreme Knowledge, the peaceful and the peace-less, the taintless, recollections about the universe, the investigation into[1] duality and nonduality,

[1]*ascertainment of*

48. the practice in regards to the Saiva Agama-s, the expression "study of the Vedas,"[1] "I am Brahman," "I am pure," "I am Consciousness alone," "I am ever peaceful[2]"—

[1]*listening to Vedanta* [2]*Siva*

49. renounce all these and, as Brahman, indeed, be firmly established in yourself. I am Brahman. There is no doubt of this. [All] this is Brahman. There is no uncertainty in this.

50. Know every moment that the gross body, the subtle body, the causal body, and all this are ever Brahman alone.

51, 52. Know that Siva is certainly the Self. Siva is the jiva. Siva is Brahman. There is no doubt of this. Whoever reads or hears this explanation, either once or always, is, indeed, liberated. There is no doubt of this. Hearing this even for a minute or half minute, he will become merged[1] with Brahman.

[1]*connected, blessed*

53. The name and form of Sankara remove for all time the fear relating to the variety of worlds made up of creation, sustenance, and dissolution. That person who investigates by means of the waves of the words of the Vedas, untrammeled by prior ideas of truth and untruth, and ascertains that this is the Reality, is Siva.

259

Chapter Thirty-Six

sarva-laya-prakaraṇam
TOPIC OF THE DISSOLUTION OF ALL

Ribhu:
I shall tell you about the Supreme Brahman, the misconception-less,[1] the affliction-less. I am, indeed, That alone. There is no doubt of this. All is Brahman alone,

[1]*undifferentiated*

2. Consciousness alone, blemishless, peaceful, of the nature of Existence-Consciousness-Bliss, Bliss, supreme Bliss, without misapprehension,[1] without taint,

[1]*undifferentiated*

3. transcending qualities, transcending people, transcending different states, and immutable. Look upon it thus: I am Consciousness. I am Brahman. I am He.

4. I am of the nature transcending all, devoid of all words and meanings. I am the Truth. I am the destroyer of all. I am pure. I am the Supreme.

5. I am unborn. I am peaceful.[1] I am incorporeal. I am the one inside. I am, indeed, devoid of everything. I am my natural Self only. I am myself That which is great.

[1]*the nature of peace*

260

6. I am, indeed, the Self alone. I am the supreme Self. I am Brahman, indeed. I am the peaceful.[1] I am of the nature devoid of thought. I am devoid of intellect. I am [so].

[1]*Siva*

7. I am the pervasive, the witness, and it is certain that I am Brahman. The elephant rider is without a world, the horseman is without a world,

8. the great emperor is without a world, the weapon-bearing warrior is without a world, the great Lord is without a world, one with the contemplation of the Self is without a world,

9. the great sleeper is without a world, one in his natural state is without a world, the jivatman is without a world, the body is without a world.

10. A god is without the retinue of the world and without the pleasure of the world. One who is prosperous is without a world. The mirror is without a world,

11. the charioteer is without a world, inquiry is without a world, the dweller in the recesses of the cave is without a world, the glowing lamp is without a world,

12. the complete, perfectly full Self is without a world, and the slayer of foes is without a world. Thought is the world; thought is all the three worlds.

13. Thought is the great delusion. Thought is the cycle of creation.[1] Thought is the great sin. Thought is the merit.

[1]*transmigration*

14. Thought, indeed, is the great bondage. Thought, indeed, is the liberator. By conviction in Brahman, thought is destroyed. There is no doubt of this.

15. By conviction in Brahman, sorrow comes to an end. There is no doubt of this. By conviction in Brahman, duality is destroyed. There is no doubt of this.

16. By conviction in Brahman, desire is destroyed. There is no doubt of this. By conviction in Brahman, anger is destroyed. There is no doubt of this.

17. By conviction in Brahman, covetousness is destroyed. There is no doubt of this. By conviction in Brahman, the knot is destroyed. There is no doubt of this.

18. By conviction in Brahman, all is destroyed. There is no doubt of this. By conviction in Brahman, arrogance is destroyed. There is no doubt of this. By conviction in Brahman, worship comes to an end. There is no doubt of this.

19. By conviction in Brahman, contemplation[1] comes to an end. There is no doubt of this. By conviction in Brahman, holy ablutions come to an end. There is no doubt of this.

[1] *dhyānaṁ, meditation*

20. By conviction in Brahman, mantra comes to an end. There is no doubt of this. By conviction in Brahman, sin comes to an end. There is no doubt of this.

21. By conviction in Brahman, merit comes to an end. There is no doubt of this. By conviction in Brahman, defects come to an end. There is no doubt of this.

22. By conviction in Brahman, misapprehension comes to an end. There is no doubt of this. By conviction in Brahman, appearances[1] come to an end. There is no doubt of this.

[1] *the seen*

23. By conviction in Brahman, attachment comes to an end. There is no doubt of this. By conviction in Brahman, light comes to an end. There is no doubt of this.

24. By conviction in Brahman, knowledge[1] comes to an end. There is no doubt of this. By conviction in Brahman, existence comes to an end. There is no doubt of this.

[1]*prajñā*

25. By conviction in Brahman, fear comes to an end. There is no doubt of this. By conviction in Brahman, the Vedas come to an end. There is no doubt of this.

26. By conviction in Brahman, scriptures come to an end. There is no doubt of this. By conviction in Brahman, sleep comes to an end. There is no doubt of this.

27. By conviction in Brahman, action[1] comes to an end. There is no doubt of this. By conviction in Brahman, the fourth state comes to an end. There is no doubt of this.

[1]*karma*

28. By conviction in Brahman, the pairs of opposites come to an end. There is no doubt of this. If you inquire with conviction in Brahman, "I am Brahman" is certain.

29. Renouncing[1] even this certitude, be established in the core of your own nature—I am Brahman, the Supreme Brahman, Consciousness-Brahman, Brahman alone.

[1]*abandoning*

30. Knowledge, indeed, is the Supreme Brahman. Knowledge, indeed, is the Supreme Abode. Space is Brahman. The directions are Brahman. The mind is Brahman. I am myself.

31. The trivial is Brahman. Brahman is the Truth. You are that Brahman, indeed. Brahman is unborn. The auspicious is Brahman. The origin is Brahman. I shall tell it.

32. I am Brahman. The oblation is Brahman. Action is Brahman. I ever am. Sound is Brahman. The river is Brahman. Truth is ever Brahman.

33. This is Brahman. The crest is Brahman. That is Brahman. The imperishable[1] is Brahman. Oneself is Brahman. One naturally is Brahman. Indeed, you are ever[2] Brahman.

[1]everlasting [2]the eternal

34. Happiness is Brahman. Love is Brahman. Friendship is Brahman. The ever immortal [is Brahman]. The secret is Brahman. The Guru is Brahman. The luminous, divine law is Brahman.

35. Truth is Brahman. Equality is Brahman. The essence is Brahman. The taintless and the One are Brahman. Hari is Brahman. Siva is Brahman. There is no doubt of this.

36. This is Brahman. My self is Brahman. The world is Brahman. Ever the highest, the Self is Brahman. The Supreme is Brahman. The Self is Brahman without interstices.

37. The unique[1] is Brahman. The long-lasting is Brahman. The entire world[2] is of Brahman. Brahman, indeed, is Brahman. The reality is Brahman. Beyond that is Brahman only.

[1]one [2]jagat, universe

38. Consciousness is Brahman. What is permanent is Brahman. What is to be known is Brahman and nothing else. I, indeed, am Brahman. (Being) the Reality, I, indeed, am without qualities.

39. I, myself, am the eternal Self. Be of this conviction. With a strong vow, be always of the certitude that I am, indeed, the meaning of all scriptures.

40. There is only the Self. There are no other differences.[1] All is illusion. Be of this certitude. The Self, indeed, is myself.[2] I am the Self. There is never, never any non-Self.

[1]There is no difference of another [2]I

41. The world, in truth, shines in the Heart. Even though they be instructed, ignorance does not turn back from the ignorant ones, even by the exposition of the words of the crest of the Vedas. It is by the worship of the Lord of the Universe, by worship of the great linga, by the smearing of sacred ashes, by wearing of garlands of rudraksha (sacred berries), and by meditation on God that one shines as the Self.

Chapter Thirty-Seven

citta-vṛtti-nirodha-prakaraṇam
TOPIC OF THE NEGATION OF MENTAL MODES

Ribhu:
 Listen with joy to this explanation of mine, the quintessence of all essences, the core of the quintessence.

2. Brahman, indeed, is all this. There is nothing apart from Brahman. Being firmly of this certitude, be happy at all times.

3. Brahman, indeed, is all the world. Relinquish the word "world" and, being of the certitude "I am Brahman," renounce the attitude of "I."

4. All reach their end[1] on their own, like a flying bird. They come to an end on their own, like the lotus held in a benumbed hand.

[1]*layam*

5. There is neither you nor me nor this universe. All is Brahman alone. Indeed, there are no beings and no action. All are Brahman alone.

6. Indeed, there are no deity, no activities, no body, no organs,[1] no wakefulness, no dream, no deep sleep, and no fourth state.

[1]*senses*

7. This universe, indeed, exists not. Be of the certitude that all is Brahman. All is illusion, always illusion. Be of the certitude that all is Brahman.

8. The constant inquiry into Brahman is all Brahman, too. Be of this certitude. Likewise, the conviction regarding duality is entirely Brahman. Be of this certitude.

9. The nature of the attitude of always being "I"—all is Brahman. Be of this certitude. [Likewise,] the discrimination between the eternal and the ephemeral—all is Brahman. Be of this certitude.

10. The conviction about existence and nonexistence, also—all is Brahman. Be of this certitude. The division into qualities and defects, also—all is Brahman. Be of this certitude.

11. The division into time and timelessness, also—all is Brahman. Be of this certitude. The experience that I am the jivatma,[1] also—all is Brahman. Be of this certitude.

[1] *jīva*

12. The experience that I am liberated, also—all is Brahman. Be of this certitude. [Likewise,] the understanding that all is Brahman is, also, Brahman. Be of this certitude.

13. The talk that all is nonexistent, also—all is Brahman. Be of this certitude. The inner substance of the deities, [also]—all is Brahman. Be of this certitude.

14. The inner worship of the deities, also—all is Brahman. Be of this certitude. The sankalpa that I am the body—all is Brahman. Be of this certitude.

15. The idea[1] that I am Brahman—all is Brahman. Be of this certitude. The concept[1] of guru and sishya and such—all is Brahman. Be of this certitude.

[1] *saṅkalpaṁ*

16. The idea of equality and inequality and such—all is Brahman. Be of this certitude. The ideas regarding the Vedas and scriptures and such—all is Brahman. Be of this certitude.

17. The idea regarding thought and existence and such—all is Brahman. Be of this certitude. The concept regarding the certainty of the intellect—all is Brahman. Be of this certitude.

18. The ideas[1] regarding mind and misunderstanding[2]—all is Brahman. Be of this certitude. The idea of ego and others—all is Brahman. Be of this certitude.

[1]saṅkalpaṁ [2]vikalpaṁ

19. The idea of the five elements and such—all is Brahman. Be of this certitude. The idea of the reality of the Vedas[1] and such—all is Brahman. Be of this certitude.

[1]śabda, sound, correct expression, verbal authority

20. The concept of seeing and talking—all is Brahman. Be of this certitude. The concept of the organs of action—all is Brahman. Be of this certitude.

21. The concept of the gift of words—all is Brahman. Be of this certitude. The sankalpa about the best of sages and Upendra (the Vamana avatar of Vishnu)—all is Brahman. Be of this certitude.

22. The idea of the mind and intellect and such—all is Brahman. Be of this certitude. Sankalpa and wrong supposition and such—all is Brahman. Be of this certitude.

23. The concept of the shrines of Siva[1]—all is Brahman. Be of this certitude. The idea of the decad of the prana-s and such—all is Brahman. Be of this certitude.

[1]rudra, Rudra

24. Delusion,[1] knowledge, body, and souls[2]—all is Brahman. Be of this certitude. The gross and the aggregate of the gross—all is Brahman. Be of this certitude.

[1]māyā [2]jīvāḥ

25. The idea of subtle, the individual,[1] and the whole[2] and such are entirely Brahman. Be of this certitude. The concept of cosmic ignorance—all is Brahman. Be of this certitude.

[1]discrete [2]aggregate

26. The cosmos and the cosmic experiencer of the waking state—all is Brahman. Be of this certitude. The division into the [cosmic] dreamer and the [cosmic] deep sleeper—all is Brahman. Be of this certitude.

27. The direct meaning as also the indicated meaning— all is Brahman. Be of this certitude. Non-identity of jahallakshana, certainty of identities due to ajahallakshana,

28. total identity due to bhagatyaga [lakshana], all conditionings of Brahman, the indicated meaning, and identity without conditioning—all are Brahman. Be of this certitude.

29. Thus proclaimed all the great ones: All are Brahman alone. Renouncing all, ultimately, be of the conviction I am Brahman.

30. If one sprinkles water on the feet of the Lord with the crest of the moon, lustrous like a lotus on which swarm a scattering of tawny-colored bees, he will attain the great Bliss of Liberation, which is obtained by worshipping Sambhu, anointing Him with a foaming mixture of the best of sugarcane, ghee, curd, best of milk, and such other things.

Chapter Thirty-Eight

grantha-praśasti-nirūpaṇam
DEFINITION OF THE EULOGY OF THE TREATISE

Ribhu:
I am Brahman. There is no doubt of this. I am Brahman. There is no uncertainty in this. I am Brahman, indeed, the eternal Self. I, myself, am higher than the highest.

2. I am Consciousness alone. There is no doubt of this. Having this certitude, renounce even that. True it is. True it is. Again, it is the truth: There is nothing apart from the Self.

3. Catching hold of[1] the two feet of Siva, I say this: There is nothing else. Catching hold of[1] the two feet of the Guru, I say this: There is nothing else.

[1]*touching*

4. Holding a heated axe on my tongue, (a phrase signifying complete truthfulness), I say this. There is no doubt of this. Touching the Vedas and scriptures, I say this. There is no doubt of this.

5. You are definitely the Self, you definitely are. Be happy in[1] this certitude. You are Consciousness. Being Consciousness is the Bliss of Consciousness, indeed.

[1]*by*

6. Brahman, indeed—the Self, which is Brahman—Brahman you are. There is no doubt of this. All this has been said by the Lord. Rare it is even for the yogis to come by this.

7. Exceedingly rare is it always, even for the gods and rishi-s, to come by this. The Knowledge of the Supreme Isvara has been expounded by Siva himself.

8. This Knowledge has been brought from the presence of Sankara in Kailasa. Dakshinamurti taught this to the gods for ten thousand years.

9. Vighneswara (Lord over impediments, Ganesa) taught this for several thousand years. Evidently[1] Siva, himself, also taught this to Parvati for a year.

[1]*The real*

10. In the ocean of milk, Mahavishnu taught this to Brahma. Once upon a time in Brahmaloka, I taught this to my father. (Ribhu is said to be a son born of the mind of Brahma.)

11. Narada and other sages were also extensively taught this. Obtaining it comprehensively, within a short time, I have come here.

12. Millons of sacred streams will not confer what a single quatrain of this can. The fruit of even a gift of land cannot confer anything equal to what this treatise can.

13. The entirety of all charities cannot equal just a single experience of this. There is nothing to equal even listening to half a stanza.

14. If one cannot listen to the meaning of this, he becomes liberated even by silently reading this. Renouncing all, ever, this text should be practiced.

15. Renouncing all mantras, also, this text should be practiced. Renouncing all deities, this text should be practiced.

16. Renouncing all holy baths, also, this text should be practiced. Renouncing all bhava-s, also, this text should be practiced.

17. Renouncing all homa-s (sacrifices in fire), also, this text should be practiced. Renouncing all charity,[1] also, this text should be practiced.

[1] *gifts*

18. Renouncing all worship, also, this text should be practiced. Renouncing all secrecy, also, this text should be practiced.

19. Renouncing all service, also, this text should be practiced. Renouncing all postures,[1] also, this text should be practiced.

[1] *all is-ness, "all is real"-ness*

20. Renouncing all lessons,[1] also, this text should be practiced. Renouncing all practice, also, this text should be practiced.

[1] *reading*

21. Renouncing the guide, also, this text should be practiced. Renouncing the guru, also, this text should be practiced.

22. Renouncing the entire world, also, this text should be practiced. Renouncing all wealth, also, this text should be practiced.

23. Renouncing all resolutions,[1] also, this text should be practiced. Renouncing all merit, also, this text should be practiced.

[1] *saṅkalpakaṁ*

24. This text is the Supreme Brahman. This text should be practiced. Here, indeed, is all the great[1] Knowledge. This, here, is the great[2] abode.

[1] *all* [2] *supreme*

25. Here, indeed, is the highest[1] Liberation. Here, indeed, is the supreme happiness. Here is the repose of thought. Here is the rending asunder of the knot.

[1] *supreme*

26. Here, indeed, is jivanmukti. Here, indeed, is all the japa. Silently reading this text, you shall instantly attain Liberation.

27. Renouncing all sastra-s (scriptures), only this should be practiced always. If read once daily, one will be liberated, indeed.

28. If one hears this even once in the midst of life, he, too, is liberated. The settled conclusion of all scriptures, the epitome of all the Vedas,

29. the quintessence of all essences, the great essence of all essences, there is nothing to equal this text in all the three worlds.

30. It is rare to come by, not being renowned in the world or in the heavens. It is rare to come by in Brahmaloka or in all the scriptures.

31. Brahma[1] once secreted this text and cast it away in the ocean of milk, thinking that none would be liberated by this.

[1] *pitāmahaḥ*

32. Knowing this, and reaching the shores of the ocean of milk, I took hold of this, and seeing what I had caught hold of, he (Brahma) swore at me.

33. Then, I left that world and came here. This Knowledge is extraordinarily wondrous, and this text is, also, extraordinarily wondrous.

34. There are none who know or expound this. Hearers of this text are also rare. This can be attained only by abidance in the Self. There is no competent Guru[1] for finding this,

[1] *sadguru*

35. nor are there any who possess the text. Hence, this has not attained prominence. To you alone has this been revealed. I shall now return to the place from which I came.

36. As soon as this was said, the best among sages, Nidagha, in a flood of tears of joy, fell at the feet of Ribhu, and prostrating full length before him, in bliss, spoke these words.

Nidagha:

37. O Brahman! Having achieved what I sought, I am satisfied.[1] [Indeed, I am.] There is no doubt of this. By the darshan (sight) of your great Self, my life has become fruitful.

[1] *I am one who achieved the goal; I am one who achieved the goal*

38. By reflection on just one sentence, I have become liberated. There is no doubt of this. I bow to your feet, with courtesy,[1] not in Reality.

[1] *as an act of reverence*

39. There is no occasion for this. I, indeed, am not real. You, indeed, are not; nor is there anything of mine. There is not even the word "Brahman."

40. The word "Brahman" exists not, and there is not even the slightest Brahman-bhava (conviction about Brahman). This text does not exist for me. All exists as Brahman.

41. The sentence "All is Brahman" exists not; nor He[1] (Brahman) in "All is Brahman." Enough of the dualistic differentiation as "That" and also the dualistic differentiation as "you"!

[1] *It*

42. Thus, there is nothing in the least, at anytime, anywhere. All is affliction-less Peace. There is only the One and no second. Indeed, there is not even the oneness.

43. [The world] composed of parts and with pairs of opposites, the defect of the world, samsara, the mode of duality, the witness mode, the phenomenal world, the undivided mode, and

44. the undivided essence, do not exist. Nor does the guru or sishya exist. All this is [realized] merely by having darshan of you. There is no doubt of this.

45. Oh, I am the Light of lights, having attained the Brahman-Light. Obeisance to you, good Guru, Brahman! Obeisance to you, dear Guru! Thus prostrating, he stood silent, in complete[1] joy.

[1]*his own*

46. Just as dewdrops on tree leaves vanish when warmed in the hot rays of the sun, so all the accumulation of sins is destroyed on contact with the linga of Sankara and disappears instantaneously. O Conqueror of death, make us happy. The ruler of all the three worlds, O Lord, please protect us!

Chapter Thirty-Nine

nidāghānubhava-varṇana-prakaraṇam
TOPIC OF THE DESCRIPTION OF NIDAGHA'S EXPERIENCE

Ribhu:
Did you listen to my explanation of the Knowledge of Brahman, which is so rare to come by? Did your mind absorb[1] [the Knowledge of] Brahman? What were your thoughts?[2] Tell me.

[1]hold [2]Of what kind is your mind's abidance?

Nidagha:
2. Hear, O worthy Guru! By your grace, I shall speak about Brahman. My ignorance, the great defect, the great block against[1] Knowledge,

[1]obstruction to

3. constant belief in action, the concept of the phenomenal universe being real, and the great fear are all lost instantaneously by your grace.

4. All during this time until now, I had been overpowered by the enemy—ignorance. I have lost the great fear, and my involvement in the philosophy[1] of action is destroyed.

[1]tattvaṁ, principle, doctrine

5. The earlier ignorance in my mind has now changed into Brahman-hood. Earlier, I was as a being of thought. Now, I am filled with Reality.

276

6. The earlier attitude of ignorance has now reached the conviction of Reality. I was remaining like ignorance personified. Now, I am Brahman. I have reached the Supreme.

7. Earlier, I had the misapprehension that I was the mind. Now, I am Brahman. I have reached the Supreme. All defects have fled away. All differences have met their dissolution.

8. All the universe has fallen off. Thought has entirely gone away. All inner faculties have subsided by the real conviction in Brahman.

9. I am, indeed, the expanse[1] of Consciousness. I, indeed, am filled with Consciousness. I, indeed, am the perfectly full Self. I, indeed, am the immaculate.

[1]*space*

10. Even the conviction that I am myself has disappeared. I am the expanse[1] of Consciousness. There is nothing of brahmin-hood.

[1]*space*

11. "I am a sudra by caste;" "I am an outcast;" "I am of high caste;" "I am a householder;" "I am retired into the forests;" "I am one who has renounced the world;" all such ideas are entirely the chimera of thought.

12. The activities prescribed for each order of life are imagined by thought. I am the Self, which should be that at which one aims. I am, indeed, the perfect fullness.

13. I am, indeed, the inner Self. I am the goal. I am, indeed, the substratum of all. I am, indeed, the happy Self.

14. By your grace, I am Brahma (the creator). By your grace, [I am] Janardhana.[1] By your grace, [I am] the expanse[2] of Consciousness. I am all Peace.[3] There is no doubt of this.

[1]*Vishnu, "the one who excites people"* [2]*space* [3]*śiva, Siva*

15. By your grace, I am Consciousness alone. By your grace, there is no world[1] for me. By your grace, I am liberated. By your grace, I have reached the Supreme [State].

[1]*jagat*

---

16. By your grace, I am all pervasive. By your grace, I am unfettered. By your grace, I have crossed over. By your grace, there is great joy.

17. By your grace, I am Brahman. By your grace, you, yourself, are not. By your grace, all this is not. By your grace, there is nothing at all.

18. By your grace, there is nothing in the least that is mine. By your grace, there is no distress for me. By your grace, there are no differences for me. By your grace, there is no fear for me. By your grace, there is no illness for me. By your grace, there is no decay for me.

19. Good souls always praise, again and again, with fervor in their mind, the lotus feet, radiant like the red lotus, of the Consort of Uma, the destroyer of time, the conqueror of Antaka (Lord of death), by worshipping whose feet Hari became worthy of worship, by worship of whose feet Lakshmi became worthy of worship, and by whose command Brahma and others became worthy of worship.

20. What is the use of heaven, with its own frontiers, wherein is collected together all the great enjoyment earned by hundreds of virtuous acts, the source of joy to the gods, since the fall therefrom is full of great, intense sorrow? Therefore, the real joyous festivity, the one mass of immense Bliss, is in the worship of the linga of Sankara, dear to the Consort of Uma, conferring Liberation.

21. Those devotees of Sambhu with love toward Siva who know in their hearts only the imperishable sound of the name of Siva, and who wear the triple stripes of ashes, reach the goal of the lotus feet of Isvara by their hearts' attraction toward meditation and not by yoga and samkhya philosophies.

Chapter Forty

nidāghānubhava-varṇana-prakaraṇam
TOPIC OF THE DESCRIPTION OF NIDAGHA'S EXPERIENCE

Nidagha:
The gross body I see not, nor the subtle, nor the causal. Nor do I see the mind, nor all this filled with insentience.[1]

[1]*Nor do I see the mind, nor do I see all this that is inert.*

2. The expanse[1] of Consciousness I see not. Nor do I see the world anywhere. Hari, I see not, nor do I see Siva.

[1]*space*

3. Remaining in the inner Bliss, not even aroused by "being only That," I do not perceive any difference at any time. Nor do I perceive insentience, nor the world[1] anywhere,

[1]*jagat, universe*

4. nor duality, nor joy, nor sorrow, nor the guru, nor the high or the low, nor qualities, nor the fourth state, nor the intellect, nor doubt,

5. nor time, nor fear, nor sadness, nor the auspicious or inauspicious. None of these do I see. I do not perceive weakness,[1] bondage, or any occurrence.

[1]*affliction*

6. Nor do I perceive any reality of the existence of the body and the organs,[1] nor any reality of things, nor any reality of the mind. Never do I see the stout, the emaciated, or the deformed.

[1] *senses*

7. Neither do I perceive earth, water, or fire. I perceive nothing of passion,[1] of mantra, of guru, of teaching, of steadfastness, or of all.

[1] *delusion*

8. Nor do I perceive the world, listening, nor one-pointed concentration,[1] nor anything else. Submerged in the sea of bliss and not even spurred by the conviction of being just full of That,

[1] *nididhyāsanaṁ*

9. I am blissful. I am endless. I am unborn. I am immortal. Being of the certitude that I am eternal, I am ever perfectly full and possessed of eternal Knowledge.

10. I am complete. I am the fullness of thought.[1] I am sanctified.[2] I am knowledgeable. I am pure. I am completely liberated. I am of all natures. I am immutable.

[1] *the mind* [2] *holy*

11. I am Consciousness alone. I, myself, am He. I am of the nature of Truth, Isvara. I am the high and the low. I am the Fourth State. I am the present.[1] I am the essence.

[1] *gracious, presence, clear*

12. I am Brahman. I am the goal of all. I am always the perfectly full, the imperishable. True Guru! I have told you all about the nature of my experience.

13. I do not prostrate to you. All is the offering to the Guru. My body, offered at your feet, is instantaneously razed to ashes by you.

14. My Self is given by myself, abiding fulfilled in itself. You are I, and I am you. I, indeed, am you yourself.

15. I am submerged in the ocean of identity. You are, indeed, the Knowledge of that identity. I am only the One Consciousness. No movement is possible for you.

16. There is, indeed, no place to go. There is nothing else except this identity. There is no place for you or me to go.

17. There is only one cause. There is only One and no second. There is nothing for you to say, and there is nothing more for me to hear.

18. You, indeed, are not the revered Guru.[1] I am not the disciple. All this is only just Brahman. I am to be measured by this (Brahman-ness), being full[2] of That.

[1]*sadguru* [2]*the nature*

19. I see no difference or nondifference and nothing in the least of action or inaction. If I make obeisance to myself, it is fruitless, indeed.

20. If there is obeisance to you, no fruit will ensue because of differentiation. If there is a difference between you and me, it is certain that no fruit will result.

21. If I make obeisance to you, you will say that I am an ignoramus. If I do it to myself, I become confined.

22. If the prostration is to myself, it is fruitless, being self-centered. There is no prostration to anybody, at any time.

23. Because of always being Consciousness alone, there are never two as you and me, no bondage, none higher, none different, no "I," no this, nothing at all,

24. no second, no oneness, no nonduality, no certitude, no mind, nothing of That, no origin, no happiness, [no] sorrow, no destruction, no firm abidance, and no existence, ever.

25. There is none at all, none at all. There is no doubt of this. Because of the Supreme Self being Kevala (alone by itself), there is no jiva, no Isvara, no sun, no moon, no characteristics of fire,

26. no speech, no organs,[1] no "I," no greatness, no inner qualities, no time, no world, nothing else, nor any non-dual cause.

[1]senses

27. I am not elated[1] or extremely depressed,[2] nor liberated, by your grace. All is nonexistent, nonexistent. All is Brahman alone.

[1]elevated, high [2]exceedingly low, completely forsaken

28. I am Brahman. This is Brahman. I, indeed, am the Brahman-Self. All is Brahman. There is no doubt of this, by your grace, great Lord!

29. You, indeed, are Brahman, the true Guru. Indeed, there is no other true Guru. The Self is the true Guru, Brahman. The disciple, too, is the Self, indeed, the true Guru.

30. The disciple comes into being because of a guru. One without a guru is not a disciple. If there is a disciple, a guru is postulated. In the absence of the disciple, there is no guru.

31. The Self, devoid of guru or disciple, is only itself at all times. I am to be considered to be in the Self, which is Consciousness alone. The Self is only Consciousness and nothing else.

32. I am the Self, Consciousness alone. I am, indeed, One. Nothing else, nothing else, exists. I am ever present everywhere. I do not see anything else of the revered Guru.[1]

[1]sadguroḥ

33. I do not perceive anything else in[1] my mind. I do not perceive anything else at all. Because of the nonexistence of all, I do not perceive [anything]. If all exists, let it come to view separately.

[1]*with*

34. Thus, I perceive Brahman and that there is nothing else, ever. Oh! Difference is to be frowned upon! Oh! Maya does not exist!

35. Oh! The greatness of the true Guru! Oh! The immense joy of Brahman! Oh! The greatness of Knowledge! Oh! The glory of good company!

36. Oh, the effacement of infatuation![1] Oh! I see true joy! Oh! I do not perceive thought! Oh! All is nothing at all!

[1]*delusion*

37. Indeed, I am nowhere else. Indeed, I am Bliss. Whatever certitude exists in my inner faculties has sprung from you.

38. All is Brahman. The Supreme is Brahman. There is no other deity. Thus do I perceive all the time. I perceive nothing else, true Guru!

39. Being of this certitude, I remain in my own nature, in my own Self.

40, 41, 42, 43.
No greater cure will arise through the depths of the Vedic words. The remembrance of the lotus feet of the Consort of Uma confers Awakening—Liberation. When the darkness of the heart, which is due to past impressions[1] of the arising of differences, is destroyed, worship the great effulgent healer, Isvara, in the lotus of the Heart.

[1]*vāsanā*

I adore the indivisible One, Sankara, who burnt the body of Kama in a flash, who is milk-like in appearance, wearing the moon, praised by the poetry of Vedic encomiums.

An excellent heron and a crow being present, both kinds (classes, species) are definite. With [freedom from] great fear and afflictions of the mind (apprehension), by the peace of being endowed with the precepts in the mind, if one has unconstrained meditation upon the feet of the husband (lord) of the daughter of the chief mountain (Himalayas), he, indeed, becomes the foremost in sage-kind (among the sages); it is definite.

Whoever, forsaking the worship of the feet of the Destroyer of the demon of time, resorts to other traditions, with distorted dharma, shall, by giving up the love for the worship of Sambhu, only reap remorse, like the fool who reaps only much grief by a hundred futile attempts to change a she-ass into a mare.

Chapter Forty-One

nidāghānubhava-varṇana
DESCRIPTION OF NIDAGHA'S EXPERIENCE

Nidagha:
Hear, true Guru! There is certitude of Brahman by your grace. Indeed, I am that Brahman. I, indeed, alone am.

2. I, indeed, am the eternal Self. I, indeed, am ever the undecaying. I, indeed, am the peaceful Self. I, indeed, am the partless.

3. I, indeed, am free from thought. I, indeed, am the happy Self. I, indeed, am the Guru yourself. I alone, indeed, am the disciple.

4. I, indeed, am the Self, which is Bliss. I, indeed, am the taintless. I, indeed, am the Self, transcending the fourth state. I, indeed, am bereft of qualities.

5. I, indeed, am the Self without the body. I, indeed, am Sankara. I truly am the complete Self. I, indeed, am Isvara, the Supreme.

6. I, indeed, am the Self, which should be the aim. I, indeed, fill up the mind. I, indeed, am the Self of all. I, indeed, am Sadasiva.

7. I am Vishnu. I am Brahma. I am Indra. I am the gods. I, truly, am the yaksha-s (a category of demigods) and rakshasa-s (demons), pisacha-s (goblins) and the guhyaka-s (class of demigods like yakshas).

8. I am the seas and the rivers. I myself am the mountains. I am the forests and the world.[1] I am all this, indeed.
[1] the Earth

9. I am the ever contented. I am the one with true[1] Knowledge, transcending prakriti. I am, indeed, everywhere. I am, indeed, the all-pervasive.
[1] pure

10. I, indeed, am the great Self. I am of the nature of all that is auspicious. I, indeed, am the liberated, the pure, the Supreme Siva.

11. I am earth. I am wind. I am light. I am space. I am water, the sun, and the moon. I am the stars.

12. I am the worlds and the world-less. I am the one at which to look. I ever am. I am the Self to be seen from the farther shore. I am of the nature of Knowledge.

13. I am the void and the non-void. I am entirely full of all Bliss. I transcend the fruits of the good and the bad. I alone am.

14. I am the divine law. I am the Truth, the Self, of the nature of Existence-Consciousness-Joy. I, indeed, am the Self of Bliss, established as the One, as also the manifold.

15. I am the past and the future, and I am the present always. I am One, and I am [divided into] two. I, indeed, am [divided into] the many. I, indeed, am.

16. I, indeed, am the Supreme Brahman. I, indeed, am Prajapati (the prime progenitor), the Svarat, the Samrat. I, indeed, am thus,[1] ever.

[1]*the womb of the universe*

17. I am Viswan (the cosmic experiencer of the waking state), Taijasa (the cosmic dreamer), Prajna (the cosmic deep sleeper), and also Turya (the cosmic being in the fourth state). I am prana (life). I am also the mind. I am of the category of the sense organs.

18. I am the universe and the worlds. I am, indeed, the Self of space. Whatever is conditioned and whatever is unconditioned—all that, indeed, I am.

19. I am the one free from conditioning, also. I, indeed, am the eternal Bliss. One who has this certitude within ever relishes happiness. Whoever hears this daily is released from all sins.

20. I am eternal. I am without misapprehensions.[1] In the world, the forest of people, I am the sacred and the wise. I am the universe. I transcend the universe. Rid of prakriti, abiding as the One, devoid of the life subject to various kinds of destruction propelled by actions and by one's own knowledge, I am the great mass of Bliss, the Supreme Siva. I am of the nature of Truth.

[1]*differentiation*

nidāgha-kṛta-guru-stuti-varṇanam
DESCRIPTION OF THE PRAISE OF THE GURU
BY NIDAGHA

Nidagha:
In this holy Sivarahasya, which has emanated from Siva, which has been narrated to the Devi by Siva, and by Devi joyously to Skanda—

2. in the sixth part of this, a lotus lit up by six faces, the Knowledge of the Supreme Isvara, the destroyer of the greatest of sins, is heard.

3. This is the sun that dispels the stygian darkness of the great maya. By narrating only one chapter hereof, supreme Knowledge is tasted.

4. Even by listening to the verses, one becomes liberated while alive. There is no doubt of this. The narrator of this treatise is Shanmukha, indeed, Siva himself.

5. Jaigishavya is a great yogi. He also deserves to be heard. Wearing the ashes and holy rudraksha-s at all times, he is always a sage transcending all orders of life.

6. There is no doubt that whoever expounds this treatise is, indeed, the Guru. The expounder of this treatise is, indeed, the Supreme Brahman. There is no doubt of this.

7. The expounder of this treatise is Siva himself and none else. The expounder of this treatise is verily Devi herself. There is no doubt of this.

8. The expounder of this treatise is Ganesha, indeed. There is no doubt of this. The expounder of this treatise is Skanda, indeed, who fought with the demon Taraka.

9. The expounder of this treatise is Nandikesvara. There is no doubt of this. The expounder of this treatise is sage Dattatreya himself.

10. The narrator of this treatise is Dakshinamurti himself, indeed. As for narrating the meaning of this treatise, the rishis and the gods

11. are not capable, O lion among sages! I say this in the name of Siva. The narrator of this treatise should be worshipped by all means as the Guru.

12. The narrator of this treatise is Siva, Vighnesvara himself. The father gives birth; the Guru destroys birth.

13. Practicing in particular that which is contained in this treatise according to the words of the Guru, the disciple should do no disservice to the Guru either by mind or by body.

14. The Guru is, indeed, Siva in person. The Guru is himself Siva. If Siva is angered, the Guru will protect you. If the Guru is angered, no one else can protect you.

15. In the practice of what is contained in this treatise, sincerity,[1] indeed, is the highest motivation. The insincere man does not deserve even an iota of this.

[1] *faith*

16. Sincerity[1] is the greatest harbinger of good, the cause of the identity of the individual self and Brahman, the cause of listening to the teaching that Brahman exists, and the cause of resorting to meditation in such a bhava.

[1]faith

17. Whoever is without the grace of Siva will never know the meaning of this text. The Self is to be grasped by the proper attitude and faith. The Supreme is the One, Siva. This is certain.

18. Renouncing all else, one should resort to meditation on Isvara, the immutable. This Knowledge of Siva is pure and destructive of the pairs of opposites.

19. Such Knowledge of Siva, the ocean of the essence of the Vedas, is not to be found in any other Puranas (legendary lore) or Itihasas (epics).

20. This has been told by Siva himself, without Samkhya and Yoga (systems of Hindu philosophy). Easy to acquire by bhava alone,[1] to be reached by devotion, affliction-less,

[1]bhāvanāmātra

21. conferring great Bliss, it is to be obtained only by direct grace. The meaning of the text, expounded by the great souls, is illuminative.

22. If, after hearing this treatise from the Guru, proper worship is not performed, one would be born as a dog a hundred times and as an outcaste ten million times.

23. If Isvara is not worshipped in the heart after hearing the greatness of this treatise, one is, indeed, born as a boar for millions of years.

24. Whichever brahmin is envious of the narrator of this treatise, he shall remain for eons of time as worms in feces.

25. The knower of this treatise is Brahman. He becomes Brahman himself. What is the need of incessant repetition? This Knowledge confers Liberation.

26. Whoever listens to this, the merit that has arisen out of the waves of the great ocean of Vedanta, emanating from Siva, does not look forward to anything, ever, not even in eons. That Siva is, indeed, the essence of all the Vedas. Even if there be a mountain of chaff all around, will it produce a single grain of rice? It would be a mirage like the magic hallucination of samsara.

27. In this way, avoiding all that is born of duality as non-scriptural and a web of words, always assess, in peace and in an attitude of harmonious comprehension, the assemblage of all these words and thus abide in peace.

28. Considering this world as devoid of reality, and applying yourself accordingly, truly understand the world,[1] always.

[1] *this universe*

Chapter Forty-Three

jñānopāya-bhūta śiva-vrata-nirūpaṇam

DEFINITION OF THE SIVA-VOWS, WHICH ARE THE MEANS TO ENLIGHTENMENT

Nidagha:
Always listening to this treatise and undoing fallacious thoughts, one should, as long as one is in the body, serve the Guru with wealth and worship him.

2. Worshipping him, indeed, always, be of the certitude "I am Brahman;" I am ever complete, eternal, and always of the nature of peace.

3. This, indeed, is the Knowledge of the Self—the determination that I am Brahman. I am of the unfettered nature. Become one who, transcending all caste and [binding] orders of life,

4. wears ashes always, with the uttering of the mantra beginning with "Agni" and other such mantras, and the three stripes with the utterance of the mantra beginning with "Triyayusha" (the triple life or longevity) and "Tryambaka" (triple-eyed).

5. Constant besmearing with ashes is only for those who wear the triple stripes of ashes. The wealth of the grace of Siva accrues [by this]. There is no doubt of this.

6. It is by the grace of Siva that this Knowledge is gained for certain. This sirovrata (chief observance) is now told to you: the simple wearing of ashes.

7. By simply wearing the ashes, this Knowledge is attained. Wearing the ashes a year long,

8. I have reached your lotus feet and have attained my[1] emancipation by you. I am of the nature of the substratum of all, Existence-Consciousness-Bliss alone.

[1]*the Self*

9. I am the Brahman-Self, the good at which to aim, full of the excellence of Brahman. I have attained the experience of Bliss. I am of the nature of Existence-Consciousness-Bliss.

10. I am released from attributes[1] and form and such. I am one liberated while alive. There is no doubt of this. Endowed with the qualities of friendliness and such, I am, indeed, Brahman, the great, the Supreme.

[1]*guṇa*

11. I am ever in samadhi, the best[1] among those liberated while alive. I am Brahman, I am eternal, is said to be the samadhi [state].

[1]*excellence*

12. Among those liberated while yet in the body,[1] the shackles of prarabdha (acquired merits and demerits that have already begun to fructify) persists. Experiencing whatever is received through prarabdha, remain happy.

[1]*while alive*

13. Acclaim and censure will arise everywhere at all times. By the certitude of each one's own mind, it should be deemed "I am liberated."

14. I am, indeed, the Supreme Brahman; I am, indeed, the ultimate goal. One who is of this certitude always is said to be liberated while alive (jivanmukti).

15. Renouncing even this difference, the Master abides in his own nature. I am devoid of the need of sense organs.[1] I am rid of the need of sense organs.[2]

[1]*devoid of the object of sense* [2]*rid of the object of sense*

16. Transcending all the qualities of organs[1] and rid of all the sense organs, I, indeed, am the Master of all, and all abide in me alone.

[1]*sense*

17. I am only Consciousness alone, of the nature of Existence-Consciousness-Bliss. Eschewing all differences always, the difference such as "Brahman" also should be renounced.

18. Being incessantly and always of such conviction, one is, indeed, liberated out of the body (videhamukti). I am Brahman, the Supreme Brahman. I am Brahman, the Lord of the world.[1]

[1]*universe*

19. I am, indeed, the one transcending [all] qualities. I, indeed, am fully pervading the mind. I am in myself, pervading the mind, pervading the prana, full of eternity, full of vision, full of Brahman, full of immortality, immortal Existence, indeed.

20. I am always a mass of Bliss. I am immutable always. I am Isvara, who is the Pranava, and I pervade the Vedas.

21. Bereft of hands and feet, swift and seized, unseeing, I see all as myself. I am all that has gone and all that is to come. I am the Self. Transcending all, I am the present, too.

Chapter Forty-Four

ṛbhu-kṛta-saṁgrahopadeśa-varṇanam
DESCRIPTION OF THE EPITOMIZED INSTRUCTION
BY RIBHU

Ribhu:
Nidagha! Listen. I say this unto you. May you be strengthened by this. Always have this conviction until the grace of Siva is yours.[1]

[1]*extends in all directions*

2. I, indeed, am the Supreme Brahman. I, indeed, am Sadasiva. I, indeed, am Consciousness alone. I, indeed, am the attributeless.

3. I, indeed, am Consciousness. I, indeed, am the partless. I, indeed, am the Void-Self. I, indeed, am the permanent.

4. I, indeed, am the Self of all. I, indeed, am full of Consciousness. I, indeed, am the Supreme Brahman. I, indeed, am the great Isvara (Mahesvara).

5. I, indeed, am the witness of the world.[1] I, indeed, am the true Guru. I, indeed, am the liberated Self. I, indeed, am the blemishless.

[1]*jagat, universe*

6. I, indeed, am the one saying "I, indeed, am." I, indeed, am Sankara. I, indeed, am Mahavishnu. I, indeed, am the four-faced [Brahma].

7. I, indeed, am the pure Self. I, indeed, am ever "I." I, indeed, am the eternal Self. I, indeed, have myself as the goal.

8. I, indeed, am of the nature of the mind. I, indeed, am the cooling one. I, indeed, am the inmost dweller. I, indeed, am the supreme Isvara.

9. Thus, in the manner declared, ever be of such conviction yourself. If you have wealth, never cheat the Supreme Guru of the offering to be made to him.

10. If you do, you will be consigned for eons to the horrible hell which bakes the errant like a potter's pots. Hearing this, Nidagha stood up and gave up his wife and children,

11. and also gave up his body like a son with all affection, and also wealth and grain and garments, and stood beside the Guru.

12. Giving his offerings to the Guru, Nidagha pleased Ribhu. Ribhu: O venerable one! I am forever pleased by your service.

13. You have now acquired Knowledge of Brahman. You are a blessed soul, indeed.[1] There is no doubt of this. Be ever of the certitude that this is the nature of Brahman.

[1]*You have very well accomplished your purpose, indeed*

14. Be of the certitude that there is no liberation other than having this certitude—none other. Certitude is the cause of Liberation. There is no other cause, indeed.

15. The essence of all the worlds, the essence of all Vedanta, the essence of the equanimous Guru, the essence of the meaning of all the Vedas, the essence of all the worlds, the essence of Existence-Consciousness-Bliss, the essence of the victory of equanimity—this is ever the essence of Liberation,

16. the Liberation from all births, the Liberation that is ever the Fourth State, the easiest Liberation of all, the Liberation from all domains, the Liberation without objects, the Liberation that dries up all wealth.[1] This is complete Liberation attained by just listening and reflection.

[1]*acquisition*

17. It is attained by that service and that listening. Hearing thus all the teaching disclosed to Nidagha, Suka and the other great ones attained the Supreme Brahman.

18. Ribhu, conveying this description of the Knowledge of Siva, addressed Nidagha thus, in the midst of the assembled sages. They, too, pleased on hearing this essence of the words of the Vedas, prostrated and spoke thus in great joy.

Sages:
19. You are the father, the mother, the brother, the Guru, the friend, and the well-wisher. You lead us across the ocean of ignorance to the shore. You are our refuge. Leading us by your power, you make us happy by the words of Siva, which mean: by the strength of my words alone is the attainment of the supreme way easy of access.

The Garland of 108 Names for Ribhu

ॐ

ध्यानम्

dhyānam

Meditation

स्वयं शाम्भुमुखोद्भूतं स्वात्मज्ञानरसामृतम् ।
निदाघवृन्दव्याख्यातं ऋभुनाथं नमाम्यहम् ॥

svayaṁ śambhu-mukhodbhūtaṁ
svātma-jñāna-rasāmṛtam |

nidāgha-vṛnda-vyākhyātaṁ ṛbhu-nāthaṁ
namāmy-aham ||

Expounding to the assembly of Nidagha and others
The nectar of the essence of the Knowledge of one's Self,
Coming out of Siva's words themselves,
To this Master Ribhu I bow.

ऋभ्वष्टोत्तरशतनामावलिः
ऋभु अष्टोत्तर शत नामावलिः

ṛbhvaṣṭottaraśatanāmāvaliḥ

ṛbhu aṣṭottara śata nāmāvaliḥ

The Garland of 108 Names for Ribhu

१ ॐ ओंकाराय नमः

om oṁkārāya namaḥ

1. Om, salutations to the one who is Pranava, what the letters AUM represent.

२ ॐ ऋभुमहर्षये नमः

om ṛbhu-maharṣaye namaḥ

2. Om, salutations to the great sage (great seer) Ribhu.

३ ॐ ब्रह्ममानसपुत्राय नमः

om brahma-mānasa-putrāya namaḥ

3. Om, salutations to the mind-born son of Brahma.

४ ॐ स्वयंशिवोपदिष्टाय नमः

om svayaṁ-śivopadiṣṭāya namaḥ

4. Om, salutations to the one who received instruction directly from Siva.

५ ॐ महोपनिषद्महर्षये नमः

om mahopaniṣad-maharṣaye namaḥ

5. Om, salutations to the great sage of the Mahopanishad.

६ ॐ अन्नपूर्णोपनिषदाचार्याय नमः

om annapūrṇopaniṣad-ācāryāya namaḥ

6. Om, salutations to the spiritual teacher of the Annapurnopanishad.

७ ॐ वराहोपनिषद्ऋषिवराय नमः

om varāhopaniṣad-ṛṣi-varāya namaḥ

7. Om, salutations to the revered sage of the Varahopanishad.

८ ॐ तेजोबिन्दूपनिषद्देशिकाय नमः

om tejo-bindūpaniṣad-deśikāya namaḥ

8. Om, salutations to the master (guide, guru) of the Tejobindupanishad.

९ ॐ जटाजूटमुकुटाय नमः

om jaṭā-jūṭa-mukuṭāya namaḥ

9. Om, salutations to the one with a crown of matted locks.

१० ॐ भस्मभूषिताङ्गाय नमः

om bhasma-bhūṣitāṅgāya namaḥ

10. Om, salutations to the one with limbs adorned with holy ashes.

११ ॐ त्रिपुण्ड्राय नमः

om tri-puṇḍrāya namaḥ

11. Om, salutations to the one wearing triple stripes of holy ashes.

१२ ॐ महातपस्विने नमः

om mahā-tapasvine namaḥ

12. Om, salutations to the one of great tapas (religious austerity, intense meditation).

१३ ॐ केदारशैलशिखरे वेदान्तसारप्रवाहकाय नमः

om kedāra-śaila-śikhare vedānta-sāra-pravāhakāya namaḥ

13. Om, salutations to the one who made the essence of Vedanta flow from the peak of Mount Kedara.

१४ ॐ ब्रह्मनिष्ठैरावृताय नमः

om brahma-niṣṭhair-āvṛtāya namaḥ

14. Om, salutations to the one surrounded by those established in Brahman.

१५ ॐ निदाघमुनिजनवन्दिताय नमः

om nidāgha-muni-jana-vanditāya namaḥ

15. Om, salutations to the one to whom Nidāgha and other sages bowed (whom Nidagha and other sages praised).

१६ ॐ विश्ववन्द्याय नमः

om viśva-vandyāya namaḥ

16. Om, salutations to the one to whom the world should bow (to whom the universe gives homage).

१७ ॐ ब्रह्मभावाय नमः

om brahma-bhāvāya namaḥ

17. Om, salutations to the one in the Brahman-conviction.

१८ ॐ ब्रह्मज्ञानिने नमः

om brahma-jñānine namaḥ

18. Om, salutations to the one who has the Knowledge of Brahman.

१९ ॐ अहंब्रह्मास्मि वाक्यार्थाय नमः

om aham-brahmāsmi vākyārthāya namaḥ

19. Om, salutations to the one who is the direct meaning of the aphorism, "I am Brahman."

२० ॐ महावाक्यविचारविशारदाय नमः

om mahā-vākya-vicāra-viśāradāya namaḥ

20. Om, salutations to the one who excels (is proficient) in the inquiry into the great aphorisms.

२१ ॐ तत्त्वमस्यादि निरूपणाय नमः

om tat-tvam-asyādi nirūpaṇāya namaḥ

21. Om, salutations to the one who defines "That you are" and others.

२२ ॐ स्वात्मनिरूपणसमर्थाय नमः

om svātma-nirūpaṇa-samarthāya namaḥ

22. Om, salutations to the one who is expert (very competent) in defining one's Self.

२३ ॐ आत्मानात्मविवेकाय नमः

om ātmānātma-vivekāya namaḥ

23. Om, salutations to the one who has the discrimination of the Self and the non-Self.

२४ ॐ सच्चिदानन्दस्वरूपाय नमः

om sac-cid-ānanda-svarūpāya namaḥ

24. Om, salutations to the one whose own nature is Existence-Consciousness-Bliss.

२५ ॐ अखण्डैकरसानुभवाय नमः

om akhaṇḍaika-rasānubhavāya namaḥ

25. Om, salutations to the one with the experience of the one undivided Essence.

२६ ॐ अद्वैताचार्याय नमः

om advaitācāryāya namaḥ

26. Om, salutations to the one who is the teacher of Advaita.

२७ ॐ सनकादि समानाय नमः

om sanakādi samānāya namaḥ

27. Om, salutations to the one who is a peer of Sanaka and others.

२८ ॐ ब्रह्मज्ञानतत्पराय नमः

om brahma-jñāna-tatparāya namaḥ

28. Om, salutations to the one whose goal (highest aim) is (who is totally devoted to) the Knowledge of Brahman.

२९ ॐ ब्रह्मानन्दमग्नाय नमः

om brahmānanda-magnāya namaḥ

29. Om, salutations to the one immersed in Brahman-Bliss.

३० ॐ दृश्यादृश्यविवेकाय नमः

om dṛśyādṛśya-vivekāya namaḥ

30. Om, salutations to the one with the discrimination of the seer (the unseen) and the seen.

३१ ॐ दृश्यरहिताय नमः

om dṛśya-rahitāya namaḥ

31. Om, salutations to the one with nothing to see.

३२ ॐ प्रपञ्चशून्यप्रदर्शनाय नमः

om prapañca-śūnya-pradarśanāya namaḥ

32. Om, salutations to the one who shows that the world is void.

३३ ॐ जगन्मिथ्या शतोपमदर्शकाय नमः

om jagan-mithyā śatopama-darśakāya namaḥ

33. Om, salutations to the one who shows that the world is false with a hundred examples.

३४ ॐ सर्वं शशविषाणं संदर्शिताय नमः

om sarvaṁ śaśa-viṣāṇaṁ saṁdarśitāya namaḥ

34. Om, salutations to the one who demonstrates (shows) that all is a rabbit's horn.

३५ ॐ हरिब्रह्मादिदेवनिराकृताय नमः

om hari-brahmādi-deva-nirākṛtāya namaḥ

35. Om, salutations to the one who rejects Hari, Brahma, and other gods.

३६ ॐ आत्मस्नानपरायणाय नमः

om ātma-snāna-parāyanāya namaḥ

36. Om, salutations to the one who is intent on a bath in the Self.

३७ ॐ ब्रह्मतर्पणतर्पिताय नमः

om brahma-tarpaṇa-tarpitāya namaḥ

37. Om, salutations to the one who pours a libation to Brahman.

३८ ॐ निराकारमानसपूजाविधायकाय नमः

om nirākāra-mānasa-pūjā-vidhāyakāya namaḥ

38. Om, salutations to the one who sets out the format of worship in the mind for the formless.

३९ ॐ चिदाकाशव्यापिने नमः

om cid-ākāśa-vyāpine namaḥ

39. Om, salutations to the one who pervades the space of Consciousness.

४० ॐ मायावरणविदारणाय नमः

om māyāvaraṇa-vidāraṇāya namaḥ

40. Om, salutations to the one who rends asunder the veil of maya (illusion).

४१ ॐ संसारसागरवितरणाय नमः

om saṁsāra-sāgaravitaraṇāya namaḥ

41. Om, salutations to the one who carries [one] across the ocean of the birth-and-death cycle.

४२ ॐ हृदयग्रन्थिच्छेत्रे नमः

om hṛdaya-granthic-chetre namaḥ

42. Om, salutations to the one who rends asunder the knot of the heart.

४३ ॐ करुणापाङ्गवीक्षिताय नमः

om karuṇāpāṅga-vīkṣitāya namaḥ

43. Om, salutations to the one with sidelong glances of compassion.

४४ ॐ कैवल्यदीक्षिताय नमः

om kaivalya-dīkṣitāya namaḥ

44. Om, salutations to the one who gives initiation into the state of being that which alone is.

४५ ॐ भवचक्रभञ्जनचक्रवर्तिने नमः

om bhava-cakra-bhañjana-cakravartine namaḥ

45. Om, salutations to the emperor who shatters the wheel of the birth-and-death cycle (worldly existence).

४६ ॐ ज्ञानार्णवाय नमः

om jñānārṇavāya namaḥ

46. Om, salutations to the one who is an ocean of Knowledge.

४७ ॐ ज्ञानभास्कराय नमः

om jñāna-bhāskarāya namaḥ

47. Om, salutations to the one who is the sun of Knowledge.

४८ ॐ स्वप्रकाशाय नमः

om sva-prakāśāya namaḥ

48. Om, salutations to the one who is self-luminous.

४९ ॐ चिन्मुद्रिणे नमः

om cin-mudriṇe namaḥ

49. Om, salutations to the one who holds the gesture of Consciousness.

५० ॐ निर्मलाय नमः

om nirmalāya namaḥ

50. Om, salutations to the one who is blemishless.

५१ ॐ निःसंशयाय नमः

om niḥ-saṁśayāya namaḥ

51. Om, salutations to the one who has no doubts.

५२ ॐ संशयहराय नमः

om saṁśaya-harāya namaḥ

52. Om, salutations to the one who removes doubts.

५३ ॐ निस्त्रैगुण्याय नमः

om nis-traiguṇyāya namaḥ

53. Om, salutations to the one who is without the triple qualities.

५४ ॐ निरुपाधये नमः

om nir-upādhaye namaḥ

54. Om, salutations to the one who is without conditionings (limitations).

५५ ॐ उपाधिघ्ने नमः

om upādhighne namaḥ

55. Om, salutations to the one who destroys conditionings (limitations).

५६ ॐ निर्ममाय नमः

om nir-mamāya namaḥ

56. Om, salutations to the one who is devoid of "my-ness."

५७ ॐ ममताहन्त्रे नमः

om mamatā-hantre namaḥ

57. Om, salutations to the one who destroys "my-ness."

५८ ॐ निर्भेदाय नमः

om nir-bhedāya namaḥ

58. Om, salutations to the one who is without differences.

५९ ॐ भेदनाशानाय नमः

om bheda-nāśanāya namaḥ

59. Om, salutations to the one who destroys differences.

६० ॐ निष्कामाय नमः

om niṣ-kāmāya namaḥ

60. Om, salutations to the one who is without desires.

६१ ॐ कामघ्ने नमः

om kāmaghne namaḥ

61. Om, salutations to the one who destroys desires.

६२ ॐ निष्क्रोधाय नमः

om niṣ-krodhāya namaḥ

62. Om, salutations to the one who is without anger.

६३ ॐ क्रोधशमनाय नमः

om krodha-śamanāya namaḥ

63. Om, salutations to the one who pacifies anger.

६४ ॐ निरहंकाराय नमः

om nir-ahaṅkārāya namaḥ

64. Om, salutations to the one who is without ego.

६५ ॐ अहंकारघ्ने नमः

om ahaṅkāraghne namaḥ

65. Om, salutations to the one who destroys the ego.

६६ ॐ निष्पापाय नमः

om niṣ-pāpāya namaḥ

66. Om, salutations to the one who is without sins.

६७ ॐ पापनाशनाय नमः

om pāpa-nāśanāya namaḥ

67. Om, salutations to the one who destroys sins.

६८ ॐ निःसंकल्पाय नमः

om niḥ-saṅkalpāya namaḥ

68. Om, salutations to the one who is without sankalpa (concept, volition, notion, will).

६९ ॐ निर्द्वन्द्वाय नमः

om nir-dvandvāya namaḥ

69. Om, salutations to the one without the pairs of opposites.

७० ॐ द्वैतवर्जिताय नमः

om dvaita-varjitāya namaḥ

70. Om, salutations to the one who is devoid of duality.

७१ ॐ ब्रह्मण्याय नमः

om brahmaṇyāya namaḥ

71. Om, salutations to the one who possesses Brahman-hood.

७२ ॐ केवलाय नमः

om kevalāya namaḥ

72. Om, salutations to the One who alone is.

७३ ॐ चिन्मयाय नमः

om cin-mayāya namaḥ

73. Om, salutations to the one who is full of Consciousness.

७४ ॐ चतुर्वेदविदे नमः

om catur-veda-vide namaḥ

74. Om, salutations to the one who knows the four Vedas.

७५ ॐ अनघाय नमः

om anaghāya namaḥ

75. Om, salutations to the one who is faultless.

७६ ॐ अघौघमर्षणाय नमः

om aghaugha-marṣaṇāya namaḥ

76. Om, salutations to the one who destroys the whole mass of sufferings (sins).

७७ ॐ तापत्रय विवर्जिताय नमः

om tāpa-traya vivarjitāya namaḥ

77. Om, salutations to the one who is devoid of the triple afflictions.

७८ ॐ असङ्गाय नमः

om asaṅgāya namaḥ

78. Om, salutations to the one who is unattached.

७९ ॐ भवदावसुधावृष्टये नमः

om bhava-dāva-sudhā-vṛṣṭaye namaḥ

79. Om, salutations to the one who is the nectarine rain for the burning fire of the cycle of birth-and-death (worldly existence).

८० ॐ भवारण्यकुठारिकाय नमः

om bhavāraṇya-kuṭhārikāya namaḥ

80. Om, salutations to the one who is an axe to cut through the forest of the cycle of birth-and-death (worldly existence).

८१ ॐ जाग्रत्स्वप्नसुषुप्त्यतीताय नमः

om jāgrat-svapna-suṣuptyatītāya namaḥ

81. Om, salutations to the one who transcends the waking, dream, and deep sleep states.

८२ ॐ जगज्जीवपरादि पराय नमः

om jagaj-jīva-parādi parāya namaḥ

82. Om, salutations to the one who is beyond the world, the individual, the Supreme, and such.

८३ ॐ स्थितप्रज्ञाय नमः

om sthita-prajñāya namaḥ

83. Om, salutations to the one who is established in Supreme Knowledge.

८४ ॐ तत्पदं दर्शिताय नमः

om tat-padaṁ darśitāya namaḥ

84. Om, salutations to the one who shows the state of "That."

८५ ॐ आत्मरमणाय नमः

om ātma-ramaṇāya namaḥ

85. Om, salutations to the one who sports in the Self (who is the delightful Self).

८६ ॐ आत्मानन्दाय नमः

om ātmānandāya namaḥ

86. Om, salutations to the one who is happy in the Self (who is the Bliss of the Self).

८७ ॐ आत्मविरामाय नमः

om ātma-virāmāya namaḥ

87. Om, salutations to the one who reposes in the Self.

८८ ॐ आत्मनिष्ठाय नमः

om ātma-niṣṭhāya namaḥ

88. Om, salutations to the one who is established in the Self (abides as the Self).

८९ ॐ शिवानन्दाय नमः

om śivānandāya namaḥ

89. Om, salutations to the one who is in the Bliss of Siva.

९० ॐ ज्ञानानन्दाय नमः

om jñānānandāya namaḥ

90. Om, salutations to the one who is in the Bliss of Knowledge.

९१ ॐ नित्यानन्दाय नमः

om nityānandāya namaḥ

91. Om, salutations to the one in eternal Bliss.

९२ ॐ आनन्ददाय नमः

om ānanda-dāya namaḥ

92. Om, salutations to the one who gives bliss.

९३ ॐ अविद्यारहिताय नमः

om avidyā-rahitāya namaḥ

93. Om, salutations to the one who is devoid of nescience.

९४ ॐ अविद्याहरणाय नमः

om avidyā-haraṇāya namaḥ

94. Om, salutations to the one who removes the primal ignorance.

९५ ॐ भवभयहराय नमः

om bhava-bhaya-harāya namaḥ

95. Om, salutations to the one who removes the fear of the cycle of birth-and-death (worldly existence).

९६ ॐ कलुषविदूराय नमः

om kaluṣa-vidūrāya namaḥ

96. Om, salutations to the one who casts afar any blemish (impurity).

९७ ॐ तुरीयाय नमः

om turīyāya namaḥ

97. Om, salutations to the one in the fourth state.

९८ ॐ जीवन्मुक्ताय नमः

om jīvanmuktāya namaḥ

98. Om, salutations to the one who is liberated while alive.

९९ ॐ भस्मधारणप्रेरकाय नमः

om bhasma-dhāraṇa-prerakāya namaḥ

99. Om, salutations to the one who urges the wearing of holy ashes.

१०० ॐ भस्ममहिमाप्रशंसाय नमः

om bhasma-mahimā-praśaṁsāya namaḥ

100. Om, salutations to the one who eulogizes (praises, lauds) the greatness of holy ashes.

१०१ ॐ नरनारीभेदनिराकृताय नमः

om nara-nārī-bheda-nirākṛtāya namaḥ

101. Om, salutations to the one who rejects differentiation (division, splitting, difference) between male (man) and female (woman).

१०२ ॐ जातिवर्णाश्रमातीताय नमः

om jāti-varṇāśramātītāya namaḥ

102. Om, salutations to the one who transcends class, caste, and order of life.

१०३ ॐ गुरुशिष्यनिर्भेदप्रकाशकाय नमः

om guru-śiṣya-nirbheda-prakāśakāya namaḥ

103. Om, salutations to the one who reveals no difference between the Guru and the disciple.

१०४ ॐ नित्यपूर्णस्वरूपाय नमः

om nitya-pūrṇa-svarūpāya namaḥ

104. Om, salutations to the one of the nature of the eternal and the complete (the eternal, perfect fullness).

१०५ ॐ आत्मोत्सवाय नमः

om ātmotsavāya namaḥ

105. Om, salutations to the one who is in the festivity of the Self.

१०६ ॐ आत्मसाम्राज्याभिषिक्ताय नमः

om ātma-sāmrājyābhiṣiktāya namaḥ

106. Om, salutations to the one who is anointed emperor of the empire of the Self.

१०७ ॐ नामरूपविवर्जिताय नमः

om nāma-rūpa-vivarjitāya namaḥ

107. Om, salutations to the one who is without name and form.

१०८ ॐ परमात्मस्वरूपाय नमः

om paramātma-svarūpāya namaḥ

108. Om, salutations to the one who is of the nature of the Supreme Self.

Glossary

ABLUTION. See BATH.

ABHISEKA. Holy ablution.

ACHAMANA. A sip of water, ritualistically taken during puja or worship.

ACHARYA. Teacher or preceptor; a spiritual guide; a proponent of a particular teaching. Also used as a title affixed to a proper name, meaning "venerable."

ACTIONS. See PENTAD OF ACTIONS.

ADHARMA. Contrary to dharma. See DHARMA.

ADJUNCTS. See FOUR ADJUNCTS.

ADHIBHAUTIKA. See TRIAD OF AFFLICTIONS.

ADHIDAIVIKA. See TRIAD OF AFFLICTIONS.

ADHYATMIKA. See TRIAD OF AFFLICTIONS.

ADVAITA. Nonduality. Nondualism. Most associated with Vedanta as Advaita Vedanta. Advaita reveals the identical nature of one's Self and the Absolute, that the Absolute is the Self, and that there is no separate or individual self or world.

AFFLICTIONS. See TRIAD OF AFFLICTIONS.

AGAMA-S. Divinely revealed teachings for which no human authorship is ascribed, but considered different than the Veda-s. Rituals and worship of deities in temples are founded mainly upon them.

AHAM. Aham means I. See I.

AHANKARA. Ego.

AJAHALLAKSHANA (Ajahal-Lakshana). See DIRECT MEANING/ IMPLIED MEANING.

AJNANA. Ignorance, lit., non-knowledge.

AKHANDAIKARASA. The one undivided essence.

ALL. The term *all* is used in the translation of the textual term *sarvam,* which occurs frequently. It collectively and comprehensively includes (subject to the context) everything in the universe: sentient, insentient, human, divine, demonic, past, present, future, concrete, or abstract, and all variety of things, qualities, forces, modes, and so on.

AMBIKA. The Mother.

ANTAHKARANA. The "inner organ" comprising manas, buddhi, chitta, and ahankara is known by four names according to different functions:

1. manas: mind—characterized by doubt and volition, or vikalpa and sankalpa. (The term *manas,* or mind, is often used as a general term to include buddhi or chitta also.)
2. buddhi: intellect—endowed with the power of discrimination and determination.
3. chitta: mind-stuff—the storehouse of past impressions.
4. ahankara: ego—characterized by "I" consciousness. See TATTVA-S.

ANUBANDHA. The four factors of a philosophical work: subject, aim, relation, for whom it is intended.

ANXIETIES. See SEXTET OF ANXIETIES.

APANA. See PRANA.

APHORISMS. See MAHAVAKYA-S.

APURVA. A term in philosophy meaning the unseen potency of an act of the remote past.

ARTHAVADA. Arthavada refers to an affirmation, declaratory assertion, or an explanatory remark that usually recommends a precept by stating the good arising from its proper observances and the evil arising from its omissions. A praise or eulogy. It is often used as a technical term in the interpretation of scriptural passages.

ARRAY OF DIFFERENCES. Refers to differences such as the difference between individuals, between God and matter, between individuals and matter, and between matter and matter itself in various forms.

ASHRAMA. See ASRAMA.

ASHTAKSHARA MANTRA. The eight-syllable mantra for Vishnu: Om Namo Narayanaya.

ASHTAMURTI. The octonary form of the Lord, so called because He is said to pervade the earth, water, air, fire, sky, sun, moon, and mankind.

ASHTANGA YOGA. The Raja Yoga of Patanjali (also called Ashtanga Yoga). A school of philosophy postulating a discipline to remove afflictions and lead to discriminative knowledge (between the Self and non-Self), which gives liberation. Ashtanga refers to eight limbs:

1. yama: abstentions, restraints (ethical)
2. niyama: observances, regulations (physical)
3. asana: postures
4. pranayama: control of breath
5. pratyahara: withdrawal of senses from objects
6. dharana: fixing one's attention
7. dhyana: meditation
8. samadhi: superconscious absorption in meditation (a super-conscious state in which there is complete absorption of the mind into the object of meditation). See SAMADHI.

ASRAMA. Stages of life. Also means hermitage, dwelling place of spiritual beings. See FOUR ASRAMAS.

ASVIN-S. Divine doctors.

ATHARVAVEDA. See VEDA-S.

ATMA. See ATMAN.

ATMALOKA. World of the Self.

ATMAN. The Self. The Self is one and universal, different from the body, sensory organs, senses, mind, intelligence, inner senses, and such others, remaining only as a witness to the activities of these and unsullied by them. The Self is of the nature of Being-Consciousness-Bliss, self-luminous, of the nature of knowledge, needing no other knowledge to know it. The Self is without desire or hatred, fear or sorrow, quality or activity, form, change or blemish. It is immaculate, indivisible, all-pervasive, and infinite. The Self and Brahman are one.

AVAHANA. Invocation.

AVIDYA (Ajnana). Generally translated as nescience or ignorance, it is the same as maya. Avidya is often used in relation to the conditioning as the individual self and maya in relation to the Absolute, or Brahman. Maya associated with Brahman is said to be controlled by Brahman, while avidya is associated with the jiva, or individual self. According to Advaita, when avidya disappears, the real nature of the individual soul, which is Brahman, is attained. See NESCIENCE.

AUM (Om). See PRANAVA.

BATH (Snana). Bath in holy waters, as a religious ablution, with muttering of appropriate mantra, and pouring of libation to deities; pilgrimages to sacred shrines and the observance of austere religious vows; taking up residence at hallowed spots and acts of charity traditionally held to be conducive to acquisition of merit. Bath as a religious ablution is one of the prescribed rites of purification in the traditional code of rituals. Tarpana is another rite, to be performed daily, consisting of an offering of libation of water to the gods, and on certain occasions, to rishi-s or the spirits of deceased ancestors. See UPACHARA-S.

BHAGATYAGA LAKSHANA (Jahad-Ajahallakshana). See DIRECT MEANING/IMPLIED MEANING.

BHAGAVAN. He who has bhaga is Bhagavan. Bhaga is said to consist of six guna-s or qualities: aisvaryasya samagrasya veeryasya yasasah sriyah jnana vairagyayos-chaiva shanna bhaga iteeranah. The sextet of qualities that entitle a person to be called Bhagavan are: aisvarya-samagra, veerya, yasas, sri, jnana, vairagya, defined as follows:

1. aisvarya: supremacy, sovereignty, might, power, sway, dominion, affluence, wealth, greatness, divine faculties of omnipotence, omnipresence, and so on. Samagra: all, whole, entire, complete.

320

2. veerya: prowess, valor, vigor, strength, virility, energy, firmness, courage, potency, splendor, lustre, dignity.

3. yasas: fame, reputation, glory, renown.

4. sri: prosperity, plenty, wealth, riches, affluence, royalty, majesty, dignity, high position, the marks or insignia of greatness or of dignity, beauty, grace, splendor, luster, and virtue or excellence.

5. jnana: knowledge, learning, cognizance, consciousness, sacred knowledge especially derived from meditation on the higher truths of religion and philosophy.

6. vairagya: absence of worldly desires or passions, indifference to the world, asceticism.

Another saying runs much to the same effect: bhagah sri kama mahatmya veerya yatnamsu keertishu, which means Bhaga is sri, kama, mahatmya, veerya, yatnamsa, keerti.

1. kama: wish, desire

2. mahatmya: greatness

3. yatnamsa: endeavor, diligence, perseverance, assiduity, zeal, watchfulness, vigilance, labour

4. keerti: fame

Another definition of Bhagavan is: utpattim cha vinasam cha bhootanam agatim gatim vetti vidyam avidyam cha sa vachyo bhagavan iti, which means Bhagavan also refers to one who knows creation and destruction, the arrival and departure of beings, and knowledge (vidya) and ignorance (avidya).

BHAKTA. Devotee.

BHAKTI. Devotion.

BHAVA (Bhavana). Bhava is not exactly represented by a single English equivalent, but is suggested by such terms as state, condition, attitude, manner, pose, mode, disposition of mind, nature, temperament, thought, opinion, supposition, feeling, emotion, sentiment, intense sense, resolution, determination, faith, conviction, abstract meditation, and contemplation. In the present translation of the *Ribhu Gita,* some of these terms have been used as suits the context, while sometimes it has been left untranslated.

BHAVANA. See BHAVA.

BHEDA. Difference. It is said to be of several types, including:

1. sajatiya bheda: difference that exists between two objects belonging to the same class, for example, between one type of tree and another.
2. vijatiya bheda: difference that exists between two objects belonging to different classes, for example between a tree and a stone.
3. svagata bheda: internal difference, for example, between the leaf and flower of a tree.

Bheda also refers to the differences between God and individuals, different individuals, God and matter, individuals and matter, and matter and matter itself in various forms.

BIJAKSHARA. Literally, "seed letters"; letters of the alphabet. They are sometimes used to denote the Absolute, particular deities, forces, and such. For example: kham for Brahman; ka for Siva; e for Sakti; ga for Ganesa; ham for Space; yam for Air; vam for Water; ram for Fire; lam for Earth

BILVA. A type of leaf used in worship of Siva.

BODIES. See TRIAD OF BODIES.

BRAHMA. The creator; the god who creates all manifestation. He is depicted with four heads (hence called Chaturmukha, "four faced") and as sitting on a lotus that rises from the navel of Vishnu.

BRAHMAN. A Sanskrit word formed from the root brmh, which means growth, and the suffix man, which signifies an absence of limitation (in space or time). Thus, Brahman means that which is absolutely the greatest. Brahman, according to Masters of Advaita, is said to be known through Vedic texts, primarily the Upanishad-s, which are considered a valid means of knowledge as a direct perception.

Brahman is the only Reality; it is beyond definition in words, the range of sensory perceptions, and the human mind. It is conceived to be boundless Being, ever existent, limitless in space and time, immutable, immaculate, devoid of qualities, attributes, name, or form. It is not subject to birth, continuation, growth, maturity, decay and dissolution, and has nothing similar to it and nothing different from it.

It is also described as pure Knowledge. It is also regarded as both the efficient and material cause of the visible universe, the all-pervading spirit of the universe, the essence from which all beings are produced and into which they are absorbed. The entire phenomenal world of beings, qualities, actions, all manifestations, and so on, is said to be an illusory superimposition on the imperishable substratum, which is Brahman.

The Upanishad-s also identify Brahman with the Universal Self. What Brahman, the only Reality, is and, more importantly, what Brahman, the only Reality, is not, is discussed in the entire text of the *Ribhu Gita.*

BRAHMANDA. Egg of Brahma; the "egg" of the cosmos. According to some accounts of creation, the self-existent Lord created the waters and deposited in them His seed, which became a golden egg in which He himself was born as Brahma, the progenitor of all the worlds.

BRAHMIN. See CASTES.

BUDDHI. See TATTVA-S (under Four Inner Senses).

CASTES. Hereditary classes into which Hindu society is divided. In a broad way, there are four castes:

1. Brahmin: learned, priestly class
2. Kshatriya: warrior, statesman class
3. Vaisya: merchant class
4. Sudra: laborer class

CHAITANYA. Used in contrast with "inert" (jada). Signifies sentience, intelligence, spirit, life, vitality, Supreme Spirit, All-Being, and the source of all sensations.

CHARACTERISTICS. See SEXTET OF CHARACTERIS-TICS.

CHITTA. See TATTVA-S (under Four Inner Faculties). Also see ANTAHKARANA.

CONCENTRATION. See DHARANA.

CONNECTIONS. See TRIAD OF CONNECTIONS.

CONSORT OF THE MOUNTAIN BORN. Refers to Siva, who is the consort of Parvati, the daughter of the mountain (Parvata) Himalayas, also called Himavan.

CRORE. One hundred thousand.

DAKSHINA. An offering to the Guru.

DAKSHINAMURTI. Siva, "southward-facing form," symbol of silent Wisdom and abidance; "wise and formless."

DARSHAN/DARSAN. Holy view.

DECAD OF VITAL AIRS. The prana, the apana, udana, vyana, samana, and the naga, kurma, krkara, devadatta, and dhananjaya, are the ten vital airs moving in all the nadi-s (subtle channels or "veins"). The principle vital airs are:

1. prana, whose work is said to be expiration, inspiration and coughing, standing in the heart, moving in the mouth, the nostrils, the throat, the navel, the two big toes of the feet, and above and below the kundalini.
2. apana, whose work is said to be evacuation of feces, urine and the like, moving in the entire body, the anus, the genitals, the thighs and the knees, the belly, the hip, the shanks, the navel, and so on.
3. vyana, whose work is said to be the acts of giving up, seizing, and the like, moving in the ears, the eyes, the hip, the ankles and heels, the nose, the neck and so on, that is, in the entire body.

4. udana, that which directs upward, whose work is said to be the carrying aloft and such other acts of the body, moving in the middle of the throat and having its place in all the joints.

5. samana, whose work is said to be the nourishment of the body in the navel, pervading the hands, feet, and all parts of the body, and throughout the 72,000 nadi-s (pathways), permeating it with its divisions and subdivisions.

The subsidiary vital airs are:

6. naga, whose work is belching and the like.

7. kurma, whose work is shutting and opening the eyelids.

8. krkara, whose work is producing hiccups.

9. devadatta, whose work is yawning and bringing sleep.

10. dhananjaya, whose work is producing phlegm, swelling, and the like. It pervades the entire body and, it is said, does not leave it, even if the body is dead.

DEITIES OF SENSES AND ORGANS. Different deities are said to be associated with different inner senses, sense organs, subtle senses (tanmatra-s), organs of action, and so on. Inner senses and their deities are: manas (mind): Moon; buddhi (intellect): Brahma; ahankara (ego): Rudra; chit (thought, intelligence): Vasudeva

Sense organs (gross), with corresponding subtle senses and their deities: ear (sound): Akasa (space, directions); skin (touch): Vayu (wind); eyes (form): Surya (sun); tongue (taste): Varuna (water); nose (smell): Asvinikumara-s (divine pair of apothecaries)

Organs of action and their deities: vak (speech): Agni (fire); pani (hands): Indra (chief of the gods); pada (feet): Vishnu (the sustainer); payu (excretion): Mrityu (God of death); upasta (generation): Prajapati (primal progenitor)

DEVI. Goddess.

DHARANA. Concentration of mind. This is otherwise translated as fixation, meditation, and so on. It is one of the eightfold steps of Patanjali's yoga. It is said to be of five possible kinds:

1. Repetition of the mantra Om
2. Concentration on a spiritual center within the body, such as the heart center or the lotus of the heart
3. Concentration on the heart of an illumined soul that is free from passion
4. Concentration on a dream experience about a holy personality or divine symbol or the experience of deep sleep
5. Concentration upon any divine form or symbol that appeals to one as good

DHARMA. The Sanskrit word *dharma* has a wide range of connotations, which include duty, righteous conduct, code of conduct, scripturally prescribed conduct, traditional conduct, law, natural law of life, usage, practice, custom, ordinance, statute, religious or moral merit, righteousness, good works, charity, right, justice, equity, piety, propriety, decorum, morality, ethics, natural disposition, natural characteristics, good company, association with the virtuous, devotion, and religious abstraction.

Dharma is generally understood as righteousness, referring to proper conduct according to the order of social classes (varna) and life-stations (asrama). Such conduct promotes prosperity and supports the emancipation of all living beings. Dharma is also said to arise from tradition, established usage, customary law, and usual social formality.

DIGAMBARA. Having space (literally, the directions) as one's vestment.

DIRECT MEANING/IMPLIED MEANING.
Jahallakshana (jahal-lakshana). A category of implied meaning wherein the implication of a sentence's meaning is other than the primary sense indicated by the words, but which is related to them, while the primary meaning is completely given up. For example, in the

326

phrase "the village on the river," the primary meaning of the word *river* is given up and *bank*, which is related to the river, is implied and accepted.

Ajahallakshana (ajahal-lakshana). When the primary meaning of a sentence is not adequate to convey the intended idea, then the secondary meaning is resorted to. In this case, the primary meaning is not totally rejected, but is retained and supplemented by the implied meaning. For example, "The red runs" means that the red horse runs. The primary meaning of *red* is retained, and clarified by adding the implied meaning, namely *horse*, to it.

Bhagatyaga lakshanah (jahad-ajahallakshana). A type of secondary implication in which part (bhaga) of the primary meaning of a word is given up (tyaga) and part of it is retained. In an identity statement, "This is that Ribhu," the meaning of the word *this* means Ribhu as qualified by present time, place, and such. The sense of the word *that* is this same Ribhu as qualified by past time, place, and such. In this type of identity, part of the meaning of the words *that* and *this* viz., "qualified by past time (conditioned) and place" and "qualified (conditioned) by present time and place" are rejected. This method is used by the nondualists to derive the meaning of identity statements, mahavakya-s, and such.

DOSA. Defect.

DVAITA. Dualism.

ELEMENTS. See PENTAD OF ELEMENTS.

ENEMIES. See SEXTET OF ENEMIES.

ESSENTIALS. See FOUR REQUISITES FOR REALIZATION OF BRAHMAN.

EYES. See TRIAD OF EYES.

FIFTY LETTERS OF THE ALPHABET. Refers to the letters of the Sanskrit alphabet, which are fifty in number.

FIVE ELEMENTS. See PENTAD OF ELEMENTS.

FIVE ORGANS OF ACTION, (karmendriya-s). See TATTVA-S.

FIVE ORGANS OF KNOWLEDGE, (jnanendriya-s). See TATTVA-S.

FIVE SENSE DATA (panca tanmatra-s). See TATTVA-S.

FIVEFOLD ACTIVITIES (pancakrtya). Activities of the gods: sristi (creation), sthiti (preservation), samhara (destruction), tirodhana (causing disappearance or removal), and anugraha (grace) corresponding respectively to Brahma, Vishnu, Rudra, Isana, and Sadasiva.

FIVEFOLD CONCENTRATIONS. See DHARANA.

FIVEFOLD DEITIES. See PENTAD OF GODS.

FORMS. See TRIAD OF FORMS.

FOUR ADJUNCTS (Tetrad of Adjuncts).
1. vishaya: subject matter
2. prayojana: aim
3. sambandha: relationship
4. adhikarin: the person for whom the work is meant

FOUR ASRAMAS (Stages or order of life).
1. brahmacharya: student stage
2. grihasta: householder stage
3. vanaprastha: retirement into the forest stage
4. sannyasa: renunciation

FOURFOLD BODY. Refers to the bodies associated with the four states of waking, dreaming, deep sleep, and turiya (the fourth).

FOURFOLD INSTRUMENTS.
1. manas (mind): Moon
2. buddhi (intellect): Brahma
3. ahankara (ego): Rudra
4. chitta (thought, intelligence): Vasudeva

See TATTVA-S. Also see DIETIES OF SENSES AND ORGANS.

FOUR MEANS. See FOUR REQUISITES FOR REALIZATION OF BRAHMAN.

FOUR MENTAL MODES. See FOUR QUALITIES.

FOUR QUALITIES (four mental modes).
1. maitri: friendliness toward those who are happy

2. karuna: compassion toward the suffering

3. mudita: happiness about the virtuous

4. upeksha: indifference toward sinners

   The four qualities are said to purify the mind and elevate men of knowledge from worldly sorrows, reveal the secrets of yoga, and urge them to transcend even the samadhi state.

FOUR REQUISITES FOR REALIZATION OF BRAHMAN. Sometimes called the four means or four requisites for spiritual practice (Sadhana Chatushtaya). They are:

1. viveka: the ability to discriminate between the Real and the unreal.

2. vairagya: a spirit of detachment from the enjoyment of the fruits of actions here and hereafter.

3. The sextet of essentials such as: a. sama: peacefulness, tranquility, composure; b. dama: self-control, control of the senses; c. uparati: renunciation, cessation of action, self-withdrawal, withdrawal of senses from the external; d. titiksha: forbearance, endurance, fortitude, ability to withstand opposites like pleasure and pain, heat and cold, and such, equally without struggling for redress or revenge, being always free from anxiety or lament over them; e. sraddha: clear understanding, faith, an affirmative attitude of mind, which includes humility, sincerity, earnestness, single-mindedness, reverence and an unwavering determination to find out the Truth at any cost; f. samadhana: profound meditation, abstract contemplation.

4. mumuksutva: surging desire for liberation.

FOURTEEN WORLDS. There are said to be fourteen worlds, seven upper and seven nether. The upper worlds (rising from earth, one above the other) are called bhuloka, bhuvarloka, svarloka, maharloka, janarloka, taparloka, satyaloka. The lower worlds (descending from the earth one below the other) are called atala, vitala, sutala, rasatala, talatala, mahatala, patala.

FRIENDLINESS AND OTHERS. See FOUR QUALITIES.

GANESA. Ganesa, also called Vinayaka, with an elephant face, to whom prayers are offered at the commencement of anything in order to clear away obstacles. He is one of the two sons of Siva. The other son is Skanda. Siva's consort is the Divine Mother, Uma. See SIVA. Also see SKANDA. Also see UMA.

GANGA. The holy river Ganges.

GARUDA. King of the birds; vehicle of Vishnu; said to be the slayer of snakes.

GAYA. A holy place in India where one performs sraddha, oblations to forefathers.

GITA. Song, spiritual text.

GODS. See PENTAD OF GODS.

GOTRA. Lineage.

GUNA-S. See TRIAD OF GUNA-S.

HARA. A name of Siva, meaning "the destroyer," the One who dissolves.

HARI. The God who sustains all creation; also called Vishnu. Of green-yellow color; of tawny color.

HARIH. "The Withholder," as He wards off samsara and its cause from His devotees. He who takes away one's ignorance, samsara, and sin. (cf. Sri Sankara's Visnusahasranama, verse 650).

HAVIS. See YAJNA.

HEART. The word *heart* (hrdaya) often appears in spiritual texts. The reference is to heart in the spiritual sense. It does not refer to any physical organ. According to some schools of thought, its location is defined as the source from which the "I" thought of all living beings issues forth. The heart is said to be of the nature of the one Consciousness and to exist both within and without.

HOMA. See YAJNA.

I. There is a profuse use of "I" in the English version of the *Ribhu Gita,* reflecting the word *aham* occurring in the Sanskrit text and the Tamil version. "I" arises chiefly in two contexts: the pseudo "I" which identifies itself with the body-mind complex, consisting of sense organs such as eyes, ears, nose, tongue, and skin; motor organs such as speech, hands, feet, and organs of evacuation and pro-creation; the vital airs; and also the inner faculties such as mind, intellect, thought, and ego; and the real "I" which, transcending these, identifies itself with the Self that is One, indivisible, all-pervasive, omnipresent, self-luminous, Existence-Consciousness-Bliss, the Self that is Brahman. It is the real "I," to which the teachings refer that speak of "I-am-Brahman" (or Existence-Conscious-ness-Bliss).

INDRA. Chief of the gods.

INNER SENSES AND THEIR DEITIES. manas (mind): Moon; buddhi (intellect): Brahma; ahankara (ego): Rudra chitta (thought, intelligence): Vasudeva. See TATTVA-S.

ISANA. See PENTAD OF GODS.

ISANA LINGA. See LINGA.

ISAVASYA MANTRA. Refers to the opening word of the *Isavasyopanishad*, "dwelt in by Isvara."

ISVARA. Isvara, meaning a Lord, a ruler, a king, a master, and the like, has been translated as Lord occasionally in the present text. According to Advaita, Isvara is Brahman as conditioned by maya. Isvara is said to be both the ma-terial and efficient cause of the world. Brahman is con-ceived of as both attributeless (nirguna) and with attributes (saguna). Isvara is the saguna Brahman with at-tributes such as omnipotence, omniscience, creation, and such. The term *Isvara* has varying connotations in other schools of philosophy such as in Visishtadvaita (qualified nonduality).

JAGAT-JIVA-PARA (world, individual soul, and Supreme). Many systems of philosophical and religious thought postulate the three principles, such as God, souls, and the world; or Isvara (God), chit (conscious beings), and achit (non-conscious objects); or pati (Lord), pasu (soul), and pasa (bondage); or God, Man, and Nature (in western philosophy); or Nature, Mind, and Spirit (Hegel); or world, souls, and God or Spirit (eastern philosophy). In this translation, the literal expression "world, individual soul, and Supreme" is used in this context. The Tamil version of the *Ribhu Gita,* as well as the Sanskrit, often uses the expression jagat-jiva-para.

JAHALLAKSHANA (Jahal-Lakshana). See DIRECT MEANING/IMPLIED MEANING.

JANARDANA. One who harrasses people, that is, gives trouble to bad people. Also one whom men seek for attaining the principle objects of human life, that is, dharma (conduct), artha (wealth), kama (desire) and moksha (liberation), for their welfare (*seek* in this instance indicates supplication). See *Visnusahasranama,* verses 27 and 126.

JAPA. Conscious repetition of a mantra for a period of time.

JIVA. Individual soul; ego.

JIVANMUKTA. One who has attained liberation even while tenanting a body. The usage of this term is said to be from the point of view of the unliberated and is not of significance from the point of view of the liberated.

JIVANMUKTI. Liberation while alive.

JIVATVA. Being an individual, individuality.

JNANA. Knowledge, wisdom.

JNANI. Knower, sage.

KAILASA (Mount Kailasa). A very tall mountain in the Himalayas, considered to be the sacred abode of Siva.

KAIVALYA(M). The State of being That which alone is; aloneness, the state of Liberation; Kevala means "the One," or "the Lone."

KALPA. A day of Brahma, consisting of 1,000 maha-yuga-s, is called a kalpa. Recurring in a cyclic manner constituting a maha-yuga of 4,320,000 years, there are said to be four yuga-s or epochs:

1. krita yuga: 1,728,000 human years
2. treta yuga: 1,296,000 human years

3. dvapara yuga: 864,000 human years

4. kali yuga: 432,000 human years

According to Hindu mythology, creation by Brahma starts afresh each morning of a Kalpa, and at the end of a Kalpa (his day), the universe dissolves into Him. Some texts also refer to a Kalpa being divided into the reign of 14 Manu-s (law givers or rulers) each consisting of 72 maha-yuga-s, the day of Brahma being equal to the 14 manvantara-s (epochs). See MANU.

KAM. See BIJAKSHARA (seed letters).

KARMA. See TRIAD OF KARMA.

KARMAKHANDA. Section of the Vedas that deals with sacrifices, rituals, and observances.

KARTIKEYA. Son of Siva, Skanda.

KEDARA. A mountain in the north of India, in the Himalayas, considered sacred to Siva and Sri Sankara (Adi Sankara).

KESAVA. Literally, "having luxuriant hair." A name for Vishnu. Kesava consists of *kesa*, hair, and *va*, beautiful and praiseworthy. Sri Sankara has stated in *Visnusahasranama, ka* means Brahma, *a* means Vishnu, *isa* means Rudra. So, Kesa denotes the trimurti (these three forms or gods) who are under His control (vasa). Sri Sankara also says that in the *Visnu Purana* 5:16:23 Vishnu is called *Kesava* because he slew the asura Kesin. Narada says to Krishna, "Because you have slain the impious Kesin, you will be known in the world by the name of *Kesava*."

In verse 648 of *Visnusahasranama*, Sri Sankara states that *Kesavah* means "one whose hair is effulgence" and that kesa-s are the rays of light "borrowed" by the sun and such. The *Mahabharata* (12:328:43) says, "The rays of Mine which illumine (the sun and such) are called *kesa-s*. The wise Brahmana-s call Me, therefore, by the name *Kesava*." Sri Sankara also states therein that the sakti-s or energies are called Brahma, Vishnu, and Rudra and are named *Kesa-s*; as He rules over them, He is Kesava.

KEVALA. The One, the lone; adjective form of kaivalya(m).

KNOT OF THE HEART. This knot is said to represent the nexus of the body, which is insentient and the Self, which is pure Awareness. The "knot of the heart" is referenced in many scriptural texts.

KOSA. See PENTAD OF SHEATHS.

KSHANA. A kshana is approximately 4/5 of a second, a lava is 1/2 of a kshana, a truti is 1/2 of a lava or 1/4 of a kshana.

KSHATRIYA. See CASTES.

LINGA. Mark; indication; characteristic. Also means the subtle body, the indestructible original of the gross body or visible body; the symbol used in the worship of Siva; phallus or phallic symbol; a means of proof, a proof or evidence; gender.

LOKA. World.

MAHADEVA. Great God. Refers to Siva.

MAHARLOKA. See FOURTEEN WORLDS.

MAHAT. Sri Ramana Maharshi states, in *Talks with Sri Ramana Maharshi,* Fourth Edition, 1968, p. 147-148: [Mahat is] the projected light from Absolute Consciousness. Just as a seed swells up before sprouting and then sprouts and grows, so also the Absolute Consciousness projects light, manifests as the ego and grows up as the body and the universe.

Chit	=	Absolute
↓		
Mahat	=	projected consciousness
↓		(swollen seed)
Ahankara	=	ego
↓		
Manas	=	mind
↙ ↘		
Aham (I) Idam (this)	=	body world

The Maharshi further states that it is the same as cosmic consciousness before the birth of the ego and the universe. It comprises all.

MAHAVAKYA-S. Great Sayings, Great Aphorisms. The Mahavakya- s or Great Aphorisms, as they are usually translated, are sayings of great import in the Upanishad-s (or elsewhere). Traditionally, these refer to the four pithy phrases:

1. Prajnanam Brahma, in the *Aitareya Upanishad* of the *Rig Veda:* Consciousness (or Knowledge) is Brahman.
2. Ayam Atma Brahma, in the *Mandukya Upanishad* of the *Atharva Veda:* This Self is Brahman.
3. Tat Tvam Asi, in the *Chandogya Upanishad* of the *Sama Veda:* That You Are.
4. Aham Brahmasmi, in the *Brhadaranyaka Upanishad* of the *Yajur Veda:* I am Brahman.

MAHESVARA. Great Lord. Refers to Siva.

MANANA. Reflection on what has been heard or studied to analyze why and how the teachings are true. See PROXIMATE AIDS TO LIBERATION.

MANAS. Mind. The term *manas*, or mind, is also often used as a general term to include buddhi or chitta. See TATTVA-S.

MANDALA. A kind of mystical diagram used to invoke a deity or for certain meditation purposes. The word can also mean a region, a division of the *Rig Veda,* or a circular shape.

MANMATHA. God of love, who was burnt to ashes by Lord Siva but was given life (but no form) by Uma.

MANTRA. A sacred formula, hymn, incantation, or spell, for chanting; a sacred word or phrase of spiritual significance and power; a charm; a formula of prayer sacred to any deity. Classified according to meters, according to whether they are given expression by the voice (kanthika), or to remain unuttered but repeated internally (ajapa). It means "that which saves one who reflects on it."

MANTRA-S FOR WEARING ASHES.

1. Agni mantra:
   agniriti bhasma
   vayuriti bhasma
   jalamiti bhasma
   sthalalmiti bhasma
   vyometi bhasma
   sarvam ha va
   idam bhasma
   mana ityetani
   chakshugumshi bhasma

This mantra is to be uttered while making a paste of ashes in water in the hand—invoking fire, wind, water, earth, space, all of this, the mind, and the eyes, in the ashes.

2. Tri-ayusha mantra:
   tri-ayusham jamadagneh
   kasyapasya tri-ayusham
   yat devanam tri-ayusham
   tan me astu tri-ayusham

"The tripled longevity of Sage Jamadagni, the tripled longevity of Sage Kasyapa, the tripled longevity that the gods have, may that tripled longevity be for me."

3. Tryambaka mantra:
   tryambakam yajamahe
   sugandhim pushti vardhanam
   urvarukamiva bandanath
   mrtyor mukshiya mamrtat

The well-known prayer to the triple-eyed god (Tryambaka, Siva) praising him and praying for deliverance from death and for immortality (death of the birth-death cycle).

MANU. Successive progenitors of the human race or sovereigns of the earth. The scriptures speak of fourteen of them, the reign of each constituting an epoch, and the total of the fourteen reigns making up one day of Brahma. The fourteen Manu-s are named:

1. Svayambhuva Manu
2. Svarochisha Manu
3. Auttami Manu
4. Tamasa Manu
5. Raivata Manu
6. Chakshusha Manu
7. Vaivasvata Manu
8. Savarni Manu
9. Daksha-Savarni Manu
10. Brahma-Savarni Manu
11. Dharma-Savarni Manu
12. Rudra-Savarni Manu
13. Rauchya-Deva- Savarni Manu
14. Indra-Savarni Manu

The present epoch is said to be that of the seventh, Vaivasvata Manu.

MAYA. Generally translated as delusion or illusion. It is the principle that causes the phenomenal world, which is only an appearance. Maya is also called the power of obscuration. In Advaita, maya is not considered a reality alongside or apart from Brahman, nor does it introduce any duality. Rather, maya is said to be neither real nor unreal. According to Sankara, because the world of plurality appears, maya is not unreal, and because maya disappears with the rising of knowledge of the nondual Self, it is not real. As it cannot be both real and unreal, and to indicate that it is neither real nor unreal, it is described as indeterminate (anirvacaniya).

Sankara also uses maya interchangeably with avidya (ignorance). This maya is not a real entity, being without any substance whatsoever, and is not an "unreal entity" either, as maya simply does not exist. Brahman, or the Self alone, is one without a second, and in Brahman, or the Self, there is truly no maya.

MEANS. See TRIAD OF MEANS.

MERU. An enormous mythological mountain regarded as the center of the "continent" on Jambu-dvipa, and thus regarded as the center of the world.

MISIDENTIFICATIONS. Confusion regarding what is the Self and what is not the Self. Superimposition of what is not the Self upon the Self, or not knowing the Self and consequent projection of identity upon what is not the Self. Misidentifications cause one to be subject to the sextet of anxieties.

MODE (Vrtti or Vritti). In the *Ribhu Gita,* mode refers to a state or a manner of existing or a way of acting. It indicates the state of being something, as apart from its substance. A vritti is a "mental mode," a modification or transformation of the mind. It is what makes the connection between the subject and the object in dualistic knowledge. It is a form of avidya (nescience), pervading the knowing and the known. In Advaita, all but the Absolute Reality (Brahman, the Self) is merely a vritti or result of vritti.

MODIFICATIONS. See SEXTET OF STATES.

MOKSHA. Liberation.

MUKTA. Liberated one.

MULAMANTRA. Root mantra; source mantra. There are specific mulamantra-s for individual god-forms. For example: om ugram viram mahavishnum. The mulamantra for Lord Nrsimha (lion man form) is:

> jvalantam sarvatomukham
> nrsimham bhishanam bhadram
> mrtyum-mrtyum namamyaham

MUNI. A Sage; a holy man.

NAIVEDYA. Offering consisting of cooked food.

NAMASIVAYA. Salutations, or obeisance, to Siva.

NESCIENCE. Ignorance. A key concept in the Advaita system. It is said to have the power to conceal the truth. It is also the power to project vikshepa (the false). See AVIDYA.

NIDIDHYASANA. Contemplation, meditation. It is used to remove contrariwise tendencies of the mind. See PROXIMATE AIDS TO LIBERATION.

NIRVIKALPA. See SAMADHI.

OCTONARY FORM. See ASHTAMURTI.

OMKARA. See PRANAVA.

ORGANS OF ACTION. See TATTVA-S.

PADYA. Washing of the feet.

PANCHA KOSA-S. See PENTAD OF SHEATHS.

PANCHAKSHARA MANTRA. Five-lettered mantra, Namah Sivaya, meaning, "salutations (obeisance) to Siva."

PANCHIKARANA. See QUINTUPLICATION OF ELEMENTS.

PAPA. Demerit, sin.

PARA. Supreme, the Supreme, the Absolute.

PARAMA SIVA. The Supreme Siva.

PARAMESVARA. The Supreme Lord.

PASA. Bondage.

PASU. Individual being or soul.

PASUPATA-S. Sect of worshippers of Siva.

PASUPATI. The Lord of souls; name for Siva.

PATI. Lord.

PENTAD OF ACTIONS. (Pancakrtya).
    1. srishti (creation)
    2. sthiti (maintenance)
    3. samhara (destruction)
    4. tirodhana (obscuration)
    5. anugraha (grace)

PENTAD OF ELEMENTS.
    1. earth
    2. water
    3. fire
    4. air
    5. space

PENTAD OF FUNCTIONS.
    1. srishti (creation)

2. sthiti (maintenance)

3. samhara (destruction)

4. tirodhana (obscuration)

5. anugraha (grace)

PENTAD OF GODS. Brahma, Vishnu, Rudra, Isana, and Sadasiva. Sometimes this pentad is also referred to as the five Brahma-s. Isana means reigning, ruler, or master and is one of the forms of Siva. These are also sometimes said to be the presiding deities of the pentad of elements:

1. earth: Brahma

2. water: Vishnu

3. fire: Rudra

4. air: Isana

5. space: Sadasiva

PENTAD OF GREAT SINS.

1. brahmahatya: killing of a brahmin

2. surapana: consumption of alcohol

3. steya: stealing

4. gurvanganagamana: adultery with teacher's wife

5. samsanga: association with anyone guilty of these

PENTAD OF SHEATHS (Pancha-kosa-s). The individual soul is said to be enclosed in five sheaths which, considering the physical body first, are conditionings of increasing degrees of subtlety:

1. annamaya kosa: sheath of food, physical body

2. pranamaya kosa: sheath of prana or "vital air" with its instrumentality of "vital airs" and nervous system

3. manomaya kosa: sheath of mind with its patterns of desires and motives, which form the complexity called mind

4. vijnanamaya kosa: sheath of intellect and intellectual knowledge

5. anandamaya kosa: sheath of bliss

The above are also grouped as a triad of bodies.

1. gross body: stula sarira, being the first of the above, consisting of the sheath of food, annamaya kosa, composed of the five elements in fractional proportions

340

2. subtle body: sukshma sarira, being the group of second, third and fourth above
3. causal body: karana sarira, being the fifth above, the cause of the other two

According to Advaita, the sheath of bliss is enveloped in ignorance. According to some other schools, it is infinite, transcendent, and perfect, the very essence of the Self. See TRIAD OF BODIES.

PRAJAPATI. Progenitor, an epithet of Brahma; also an epithet of the ten lords of beings created by Brahma.

PRAJNANA. Variously translated as intelligence, knowledge, wisdom, awareness, consciousness. Jnana, or knowledge, is a term that denotes learning, erudition, understanding, information, cognizance, or wisdom. Special categories of knowledge are sometimes meant, for example, scientific knowledge (systematized knowledge of natural and physical world) and intuitive knowledge (instantaneous apprehension without conscious use of reasoning). The term "Absolute Knowledge" or "Highest Knowledge" is used in the translation of the mahavakya "Prajnanam Brahma" to denote knowledge relating to the highest truth of religion and philosophy, which is that of union with the Supreme. The term has been used keeping in view the author's statement in this gita that "Knowledge" (Jnana) itself is called Prajnana. Prajnanam Brahma is also translated as "Consciousness is Brahman."

PRAKRITI/PRAKRTI. Primal nature. This has different connotations in different Indian philosophies:

In Samkhya, it is one of the two categories basic to its system, fundamentally active, but non-conscious, one and imperceptible, infinite, the source of the universe, inferable from its effects, a composite of three constituents called guna-s (sattva, rajas, and tamas).

In Dvaita (dualism), it is the material cause of the world and one of the twenty categories of substances.

In Visishtadvaita (qualified monism), it is one of the six substances, guna-s being the qualities of prakriti and not its constituents, inseparable therefrom but not identical with it, related to Isvara and dependent on the dwelling place of the individual, not infinite but limited by a nitya-vibhuti, or eternal manifestation, which is infinite and immaterial.

In Advaita (nondualism), it is all phenomena, being purely illusory (maya) and not actually real.

PRAMATHA-S. Attendants in the retinue of Siva.

PRANA. Vital air; life breath; vitality. Prana is said to be five-fold:
1. prana: the air; that which rises upward
2. apana: that which moves downward
3. vyana: that by which prana and apana are held
4. samana: that which carries the grosser material of food to apana and brings the subtler material to each limb
5. udana: that which brings up or carries down what has been drunk or eaten

See DECAD OF VITAL AIRS.

PRANAVA. Om, Aum. Pranava refers to the word *Om,* which represents the Eternal, the Absolute. The syllable *Om* is explained in some Upanishad-s as being composed of the letters A, U, and M, denoting a set of triads such as the waking, dream, and deep sleep states. *Omkara* can denote the sound of Om, the symbol Om, and also the word *Om (Aum)* as written. Om is also a syllable uttered as a holy exclamation at the beginning and end of a reading of the Veda-s, or at the commencement of a sacred work or spiritual function or a prayer, or in calling out the names of a deity in archana as in a list of 108 and 1,000 names. As a particle, it implies a solemn affirmation and respect-ful assent (so be it, amen!) or assent or acceptance (yes, all right), a command, or auspiciousness.

PRARABDHA. See TRIAD OF KARMA.

PROXIMATE AIDS TO LIBERATION. Three main steps (or main proximate aids to Liberation) in the path of knowledge according to Advaita are:
1. sravana: learning, listening, and study

342

2. manana: reflection on what has been heard or studied (to analyze why and how the teachings are true), and consideration

3. nididhyasana: profound contemplation and meditation (to remove contrariwise tendencies of the mind)

PUNYA. Merit.

PURANA-S. Hindu texts of a certain type, which include mythology, history, spiritual teachings, and other topics of an encyclopedic nature. They are said to be eighteen in number and composed by Vyasa. Eighteen of the following twenty are found in various lists.

1. *Brahma Purana*
2. *Padma Purana*
3. *Bhagavata Purana*
4. *Narada Purana*
5. *Markendeya Purana*
6. *Agni Purana*
7. *Bhavisya Purana*
8. *Brahma Vaivarta*
9. *Linga Purana*
10. *Varaha Purana*
11. *Skanda Purana*
12. *Vamana Purana*
13. *Kurma Purana*
14. *Matsya Purana*
15. *Garuda Purana*
16. *Brahmanda Purana*
17. *Vishnu Purana*
18. *Siva Purana*
19. *Vayu Purana*
20. *Devi Bhagavata*

PURNA. Fullness, perfection, perfect fullness.

PURUSHA. The word *purusha* means man. *Purusha* also means spirit or individual soul. It has different connotations in different schools of Indian philosophy:

According to the Samkhya system, it is one of the two basic categories. It is pure Consciousness, unattached, unrelated to anything, nonactive, unchanging, eternal and pure. There is an infinite number of individual souls.

According to Kashmir Saivism, it is the universal Self appearing under limitations as the many individual souls enveloped in the five sheaths of kala (time or mortality, temporal order), niyati (limitation by cause and effect relation, limitation of what ought to be done and what not), raga (limitation by desire, attachment), vidya (limited knowledge), and kala (limitation of the power of action).

According to Advaita, it is fundamentally One, the eternal witness, the motionless, the modificationless, the one who knows the field of experience. The Paramatman (Supreme Self) is considered to be the one and only Purusha.

The *Purusha Sukta* describes the Cosmic Purusha as thousand-headed, thousand-eyed, thousand-footed, immanent and transcendent, covering the earth on all sides, and extending beyond another length of "ten fingers," all that has been and will be. One-fourth of Him is all beings, threefourths of Him is what is immortal in heaven.

PURUSHARTHA. Aim of life.

QUALITIES. See FOUR QUALITIES.

QUINTUPLICATION OF ELEMENTS. (Panchikarana). The world is said to be formed by the five elements by a process of each of the elements combining with the others in various proportions.

RABBIT ON THE MOON. A phrase that alludes to the spots or shadings of the moon's surface that are visible to the eye.

RAHU. "Shadow planet." Considered as a separate planet, it is the dark disk of the moon obscuring the sun during a solar eclipse. The earth's shadow covering the moon during a lunar eclipse.

RAJAS. Agitation. See TRIAD OF GUNA-S.

RAKSHASA-S. Demons.

REQUISITES. See FOUR REQUISITES FOR REALIZATION OF BRAHMAN.

RIBHU. The Sage whose expositions of the sublime Truth are preserved in the *Ribhu Gita* and certain Upanishad-s. Ribhu is pronounced in Sanskrit as denoted by Rbhu, which is phonetically intermediate between Ribhu and Rubhu.

RIBHU GITA. The Ribhu and Nidagha dialogue about the Self and Brahman that forms a portion of the epic *Sivarahasya*. The dialogue between Ribhu and Nidagha on the Self and Brahman is also found in ancient texts such as the traditional anthology of 108 Upanishad-s enumerated in the *Muktikopanishad*, that is, in the *Tejobindu Upanishad* of *Krishna Yajurveda* (37th in the list), *Mahopanishad* of *Sama Veda* (61st), *Annapurnopanishad* of *Atharva Veda* (70th) and *Varahopanishad* of *Krishna Yajurveda* (98th).

RISHI. Seer; Sage.

RUDRA. Name associated with Siva, first appearing in the *Rig Veda. Rudra* means terrible, howling, roaring, dreadful, strong, bestowing power, red, shining, glittering, praiseworthy, and driving away evil.

RUDRAKSHA. Literally, "The eye of Siva." A type of berry used for beads of a mala (rosary) by devotees of Siva. There are several types. They are also worn on the body and are considered sacred. *Siva Purana* contains chapters detailing the glory and holiness of rudraksha, the different types of rudraksha, and the effects and advantages of each kind. It is said the rudraksha are the manifestation of Siva's tears of compassion for all beings.

SADASIVA. Siva, who is always Himself. Siva, who is always at peace. The state of Siva as pure Being.

SADGURU. (Sat Guru). The true Guru. An enlightened Guru; one who can reveal the Truth of the Self to the disciple. The Guru who reveals that there is only one Absolute and that That is the Self. Can also be translated as "good Guru."

SADHANA CHATUSHTAYA. See FOUR REQUISITES FOR REALIZATION OF BRAHMAN.

SAHAJA. Natural state, innate, effortless state.

SAIVA. Pertaining to Siva.

SAKSHATKARA. Sakshat: direct, evident, visible kara: what has been made evident. Sakshatkara means one's direct experience, personal realization.

SAKTI, SHAKTI. Power, energy, feminine counterpart of Siva, consort of a God.

SAMA. Peacefulness, tranquility, composure. See FOUR REQUISITES FOR REALIZATION OF BRAHMAN.

SAMADHANA. See FOUR REQUISITES FOR REALIZA-TION OF BRAHMAN.

SAMADHI. Absorption in meditation, super-conscious state. Sextet of samadhi-s. There are two categories:

I. Savikalpa Samadhi, in which the meditator does not lose such distinctions as the knower, knowledge, and the known, in which the mind is functioning. It is a prelude to nirvikalpa samadhi and has four subcategories:

1. Objective: associated with cognizable objects of thought (desire and such, centered in the mind are treated as cognizable objects). Thoughts appear in the mind and are regarded as objects, and the meditator remains indifferent to them, thinking of the Self as his real nature.
2. Subjective: associated with abstract thought. Here, the meditator thinks, "I am the witness," "the innermost Self," "I am unattached," and such. The object of meditation is the Nondual Self free from ideas of desire and such. Only a current of self-consciousness of the Self remains.
3. Objective: associated with external objects, such as the sun. Here the meditator separates changing aspects of name and form from what is pure Existence of the object by concentrating on the Existence-Consciousness-Bliss nature of the object of meditation.
4. Objective: similar to the subjective savikalpa but associated with an external object.

II. Nirvikalpa Samadhi, in which the meditator makes himself free from all thoughts of distinctions, free of all differentiations as the knower, knowledge, and the known, and in which the mind ceases to be active. It may be divided into two subcategories:

1. Subjective: Here the mind is steady like an unflickering flame in a windless place, indifferent to both objects and sounds and in which the ideas that arise in savikalpa samadhi are absent. It is likened to an empty pitcher placed in the sky having nothing inside or outside.

2. Objective: Here the meditator, plunged in bliss, perceives no external objects. He is completely absorbed in the contemplation of Brahman; all illusory phenomena are merged in Brahman; he is indifferent to the manifest world and also to such ideas as akhanda (the undivided), eka rasa (the single essence), and such. It is likened to a pitcher placed in the sea with water inside and outside.

Sri Ramana Maharshi refers to nirvikalpa samadhi, complete absorption in the Self with resultant oblivion to the manifested world, as a state of blissful trance but not permanent, like a bucket of water lowered into a well. In the bucket there is water (the mind) that is merged with the water in the well (which is the Self), but the rope and the bucket still exist to draw it out again. The Maharshi declares that Sahaja Samadhi is pure, uninterrupted Consciousness, transcending the mental and physical plane, yet (to an observer), with awareness of a manifested world, and full use of mental and physical faculties; Sahaja is a state of perfect equilibrium, perfect harmony, beyond even bliss, comparable to the waters of a river merged in those of the ocean. Sahaja signifies what is effortless, natural, and innate. It is the state of being the Self and the Self alone.

In *Talks with Sri Ramana Maharshi,* p. 359, 1984, seventh edition, the following chart elucidates the samadhi-s given as thus:

SAVIKALPA SAMADHI

(Bahya) External	(Antar) Internal
(Drisyanuvidha) The mind jumps from one object to another. Keep it steady, fixed on the Reality behind them.	The mind is afflicted by kama, krodha, etc., See wherefrom they arise and how they have their being. Hold on to their source.
(Sabdanuvidha) There are external phenomena which are said to have their origin from the Single Reality. Search for It and hold on to it.	There are all manner of thoughts which rise up from the Reality within and manifest themselves. Hold on to that Reality.

All these four kinds of savikalpa samadhi
are attended with effort.

NIRVIKALPA SAMADHI

(Bahya) External	(Antar) Internal
Merging in the one Reality underlying all the phenomena and remaining unaware of the transitory manifestations.	Merging in the Inmost Being which is the One Reality giving rise to all thoughts, etc., and remaining unaware of anything else.
This state is compared to the waveless ocean whose waters are still and placid.	This state is compared to a flame unagitated by currents of air, but burning quite steady.

When these kinds of nirvikalpa samadhi are not attended with effort and it is realised that the waveless ocean of external samadhi and the steady flames of internal samadhi are identical, the state is said to be Sahaja Nirvikalpa Samadhi.

348

SAMASHTI. Coalesced, integrated, the collective, the cosmic whole. Macrocosmic, virat.

SAMAVEDA. See VEDAS.

SAMBAMURTI. Name for Siva, especially in the form along with Divine Mother.

SAMBHU. The bestower of happiness, name for Siva.

SAMKHYA/SANKHYA. A philosophical system of thought of Hindu Sanatana Dharma. It is dualistic, for it postulates two ultimate realities: Purusha and prakriti.

In many respects, the Purusha resembles Atman (the Self) of Vedanta, but with a fundamental difference. In Vedanta the changeless, omnipotent Self, which is said to be one with the all-pervading Brahman, is One with nothing apart from it. In Samkhya the Purusha-s are many, infinite in number, though formless, omnipotent, beyond mind and senses and intellect, beyond time and space and causation, unborn, undying, uncreated, beginningless, endless, perfect, and free.

The jiva (individual soul), according to the Samkhya system, is the individualized spirit distinguished from the Purusha by connection with the ego, the intellect, the mind, and the senses and limited by the body. There are in Samkhya a multitude of jiva-s.

By wrong identification of the Purusha with the intellect, there arise experiences of limitation and ignorance, pleasure and pain, bondage and death, which can be got over by knowledge of Reality.

Prakriti has as its constituents the three guna-s (triple strand of qualities): sattva, rajas, and tamas—energies or forces that are never at rest. They are broadly understood as: sattva, inspiring all that is pure and fine; rajas, the active principle; and tamas, causing stolidity and resistance.

The above explanation of Samkhya has been given by Sri Suresvara, who promptly negated it.

Samkhya, along with five others, forms the six main types of Hindu philosophical systems:

1. Vaiseshika of Kanada
2. Nyaya of Gotama
3. Samkhya of Kapila
4. Yoga of Patanjali
5. Mimamsa of Jaimini
6. Vedanta of Vyasa

The above Sages were not always the original founders of the philosophical systems, but were those who systematically formulated them. The systems are astika, or orthodox, because they accept the authority of the Veda-s on all questions pertaining to the nature of the universe. Vaiseshika basically relates to the qualities or properties of substances. Nyaya is notable as a system of logic, and Mimamsa for Hindu law and ritual portions. See YOGA. Also see VEDANTA.

SAMRAT. The sovereign of the external. The sutratma (the Self running through all). Hiranyagarbha. Ever-luminous.

SAMSARA. The cycle of birth and death. Also referred to as transmigration, metempsychosis, and succession of births. Also means the circuit of worldly life, secular life, mundane existence, and the world.

SANGHA. Connection. An assembly.

SANKALPA/ VIKALPA (Volition/Indecision, misapprehension). The meaning of these is not always expressed by a single English word equivalent. *Sankalpa* denotes various shades of ideas such as will, volition, mental resolve, solemn vow to perform an observance, purpose, aim, intention, determination, wish, desire, thought, ideation, reflection, and imagination. *Vikalpa* is often used as a contrast or reverse of this, expressing doubt, uncertainty, indecision, hesitation, suspicion, option, error, misconception, ignorance, and differentiation. Sankalpa and vikalpa refer, in essence, to contrasting functions of the internal instrument of perception, generally designated as the mind.

The words *sankalpa* and *vikalpa* have generally been left untranslated in this present work. Occasionally, the terms *volition* and *indecision* have been used to translate *sankalpa* and *vikalpa*, respectively; sometimes other equivalents, depending on the context, are used.

SANKARA. The beneficent One, name for Siva.

SASTRA-S. Scriptures.

SATSANG. Association or connection with Sat (the true or good). Being in the company of Sat, of Being itself, or in the company of those who have realized Being.

SATTVA. See TRIAD OF GUNA-S.

SAVIKALPA. See SAMADHI.

SEASONS. See SEXTET OF SEASONS.

SEED LETTERS. See BIJAKSHARA.

SENSES. See TATTVA-S.

SETU. The bridge that Rama built over the sea between Sri Lanka and India.

SEXTET OF ANXIETIES (shad-urmi-s). Six kinds of suffering: hunger, thirst, sorrow, despondence, old age, and death.

SEXTET OF CHARACTERISTICS (shad-linga). Six linga-s or marks to be noticed in understanding the Veda-s:

1. upakrama and upasamhara (beginning and conclusion)
2. apurvata (novelty)
3. abhyasa (repetition)
4. phala (result or fruit)
5. arthavada (praise or censure)
6. upapatti (intelligibility in the light of reason)

SEXTET OF ENEMIES. The six enemies or obstructions to spiritual development and peace are desire, anger, greed, infatuation, arrogance, and jealousy.

SEXTET OF ESSENTIALS. See FOUR REQUISITES FOR REALIZATION OF BRAHMAN.

SEXTET OF MODIFICATIONS. See SEXTET OF STATES.

SEXTET OF SAMA. See FOUR REQUISITES FOR THE REALIZATION OF BRAHMAN.

SEXTET OF SAMADHI-S. See SAMADHI.

SEXTET OF SEASONS (shad-ritu). The sextet of the seasons of the year with their approximate correspondence (in the northern hemisphere) are as follows:

1. vasanta: spring; mid-April to mid-June
2. grishma: summer; mid-June to mid-August
3. varsha: monsoon, rainy season; mid-August to mid-October
4. sarad: autumn; mid-October to mid-December
5. hemanta (hima): winter (snowy); mid-December to mid-February
6. sisira: cool; mid-February to mid-April

SEXTET OF SHEATHS (shad-kosa-s). These components of the body are sometimes called the "six sheaths," not to be confused with the pentad of sheaths. They are marrow, bone, seminal fluid, blood, skin, and flesh.

SEXTET OF STATES. The six changes that occur for all beings in illusion are origination, existence, growth, maturity, decay, and death.

SEXTET OF SUPPORTS (shad-adhara). Six chakra-s or centers in the path of the kundalini. These are said to be associated with:

1. muladhara: cohesion, stimulating sense of smell
2. svadhishthana: contraction, stimulating sense of taste
3. manipura: expansion, producing heat, stimulating sight-sense of color and form
4. anahata: general movement, stimulating sense of touch
5. visuddhi: space-giving, stimulating sense of hearing
6. ajna: mental faculties

SEXTET OF TIMES (shad-kala). The sextet often referred to is predawn, early morning, forenoon, midday, evening, and late night. Worship to the temple deity is offered at these times.

SEXTET OF WAVES. See SEXTET OF ANXIETIES.

SHANMUKHA. Six faced one, Skanda.

SHEATHS. See PENTAD OF SHEATHS AND SEXTET OF SHEATHS.

SIDDHA. A spiritual being of great purity and power said to be particularly characterized by possession of eight supernatural faculties called siddhi-s:

1. anima: power to become as small as an atom
2. laghima: power to become light at will
3. prapti: power to obtain anything
4. prakamyam: power of irresistible will
5. mahima: power of increasing in size at will
6. isitva: power of superiority
7. vasitva: power to subjugate others
8. kamavasayita: control of desire

SIDDHI-S. Accomplishments; miraculous powers.

SINS. See PENTAD OF GREAT SINS.

SHISHYA/SISHYA. A disciple of a Guru. One who is taught.

SIVA. The Good, the Auspicious One, the Absolute. Siva is worshipped in connection with various elements at certain sacred places:

1. earth, at Kancipuram
2. water, at Jambukesvaram
3. fire (light), at Arunachala
4. wind, at Kalahasti
5. space, at Chidambaram

SIVAGAMA-S. Scriptures regarding Siva.

SIVARAHASYA. Secret of Siva, mystery of Siva.

SIVASANKARA. Same as Sankara; means "auspicious Sankara." See SIVA. Also see SANKARA.

SIVOHAM. Siva am I.

SIX CHANGES. See SEXTET OF STATES.

SIXFOLD. See sextet headings.

SIXTY-FOUR ARTS.

1. Knowledge of the 18 scripts
2. Ability to write them
3. Ability to read them properly
4. Painting
5. Knowledge of several languages

6. Study of these languages
7. Speaking of these languages
8. Gambling
9. Study and knowledge of the *Rig Veda*
10. Study and knowledge of the *Yajur Veda*
11. Study and knowledge of the *Sama Veda*
12. Study and knowledge of the *Atharva Veda*
13. Ayurveda: subsidiary to *Rig Veda*
14. Dhanurveda: military sciences, subsidiary to *Yajur Veda*
15. Gandharva Veda: music, subsidiary to *Sama Veda*
16. Sthapatya Sastra Veda: mechanics, carpentry, architecture, subsidiary to *Atharva Veda*
17. Vedanta Sastra: knowledge of the Upanisad-s and the Teaching contained therein; the "science" of the knowledge of Brahman. See VEDANTA.
18. Mimamsa Sastra: science of investigation or inquiry, especially of interpretation of Vedic rites and the meaning of Vedic texts
19. Nyaya/Tarka Sastra: science of logic, abstract reasoning, argumentation, and supposition
20. Yoga Sastra: science of union, especially with the Divine. See YOGA.
21. Dharma Sastra: science of jurisprudence
22. Artha Sastra: science of wealth and politics
23. Niti Sastra: science of ethics
24. Kama Sastra: science of love and eroticism
25. Jyotisha Sastra: science of astronomy and astrology
26. Natya Sastra: science of drama, dramatics
27. Alankara Sastra: science of rhetoric and poetics
28. Ganita Sastra: science of mathematics
29. Tantra-s, Purana-s, Smriti-s
30. Poetry, poetics (rhetoric), drama
31. Santi: application of the means for tranquilizing
32. Vasya: application of the means for subduing
33. Akarsna: application of the means for attracting
34. Vidveshana: application of the means for creating enmity

35. Ucchatana: application of the means for ruining one's enemy
36. Marana: application of the means for causing death
37. Paralyzing gait
38. Stopping the flow of water
39. Freezing the sight
40. Immobilizing fire
41. Arresting a weapon
42. Benumbing speech
43. Stopping seminal fluid
44. Sculpture
45. Training of or with elephants
46. Training of or with horses
47. Training with chariots
48. Training of or with infantry
49. Science of physiognomy
50. Wrestling
51. Cooking
52. Taking poison out of the body by application of Garuda charm
53. Instrumental music
54. Playing on wind instruments like flute and such
55. Playing on percussion instruments like drums and such
56. Playing on metallic instruments like gongs and such
57. Magic
58. Dancing
59. Singing
60. Alchemy
61. Scrutiny of precious gems
62. Oratory
63. The study of nadi-s, pulses in the wrists, and such
64. Disappearing from view

Alternatives listed:

Making jewelery, making flower garlands and displays, making perfumes, puppetry, quiz, antakshari (making up words or verses beginning with the last letter of another word or verse, etc.), samasya completion (composing a verse so that the last line is a given phrase or sentence, or proposing part of a stanza for someone else to complete), house building, hair styling, massaging, cockfighting, predictions based on flowers, thought reading, make-up (disguise), kite flying, toy making, machine building, treatment of trees, training parrots to talk, and preparation of beds.

SKANDA. Younger son of Siva, also called Shanmukha (with six faces), Kartikeya, Kumara, and Murugan.

SOULS. See TRIAD OF SOULS.

SPACE OF CONSCIOUSNESS /SPACE OF THE SELF. These terms indicate the infinite and all pervasive nature of Consciousness and Self.

SPHERE OF THE EGG OF THE COSMOS. See BRAH-MANDA.

SPHURANA. A throbbing vibration; a flashing.

SRADDHA. See FOUR REQUISITES FOR REALIZATION.

SRAVANA. Learning, listening, and study. See PROXIMATE AIDS TO LIBERATION.

STATES. See SEXTET OF STATES.

STOTRA. Hymn of praise or eulogy.

SUPPORTS. See SEXTET OF SUPPORTS.

SURYA. The sun.

SUTRA. Brief, terse aphorisms; a brief phrase that acts as a thread by which one can remember a point; any work or manual containing such rules. Literally, sutra means thread, string, line, cord, or fiber; short rule or precept; a short or concise sentence used for recollective purposes. The following are said to pertain to sutra-s: having few words, not a sentence, contain much substance, having faces in all directions, faultless.

SUTRATMA. Literally, "thread of the Self," the Self that pervades the universe like a thread (sutra) through a garland; the vital force before manifestation.

SVANUBHAVA. One's own experience.

SVARAT. The ruler of oneself, of the inner senses. Also said to denote Isvara, the experiencer of the unmanifest state, being the only independent Reality and causing all other dependent categories. Also said to denote self-luminosity, or he who is shining in his own glory.

TAIJASA. Individual cognizer of the subtle in the dream state.

TAMAS. Inertia, darkness. See TRIAD OF GUNA-S.

TANMATRA. Sense data. See TATTVA-S.

TANTRA. Rules, rituals, religious treatises for modes of worship, and such. Principle, doctrine, or treatise teaching magical and mystical formulas for the worship of deities or the attainment of superhuman power.

TAPAS. Penance, religious austerity, mortification, or meditation connected with the practice of personal self-denial or bodily mortification, moral virtue, merit, special duty or observance of any particular caste. *Tapah* means heat, warmth, fire, the sun, the hot season and the like: *tapas* has been translated also as intense, fiery practice.

TARPANA. Libation of Water. See UPACHARA-S.

TATTVA-S. Generally called "verities"; these are the factors that constitute manifest experience. A verity (tattva) may be defined as that which gives scope for functioning to all orders of creation until their final dissolution. Sometimes the verities are classified into three groups, characterized by: (1) insentience, (2) both insentience and sentience, (3) sentience. The twenty-four verities mentioned here are as follows:

Five gross elements (bhuta-pancaka):

1. prithvi: earth, possessed of solidity
2. ap: water, possessed of fluidity
3. tejas: fire, possessed of heat
4. vayu: air, of the character of perpetual motion
5. akasa: ether, of the character of space

Five sense data (panca tanmatra-s):

6. gandha-tanmatra: smell, in the form of subtle earth
7. rasa-tanmatra: taste, in the form of subtle water
8. rupa-tanmatra: form, in the form of subtle fire
9. sparsa-tanmatra: touch, in the form of subtle air
10. sabda-tanmatra: sound, in the form of subtle ether or space

Five sense organs, also called the organs of knowledge (jnanendriya-s):

11. srotra: the auditory sense that perceives sound (ear)
12. tvak: the tactile sense that perceives touch (skin)
13. chakshus: the optic sense that perceives form (eye)
14. jihva: the gustatory sense that perceives taste (tongue)
15. ghrana: the olfactory sense that perceives smell (nose)
    Five organs of action (karmendriya-s):
16. vak: speech, the motor organ of articulate expression
17. pani: the hand, the motor organ of prehension, grasping and leaving
18. pada: the foot, the motor organ of locomotion, movement
19. payu: the motor organ of evacuation
20. upastha: the organ of generation and sexual pleasure

Four inner faculties (antah-karana):

21. manas: the mind; the inner sense that is attained when rajas, the mobility of misery, preponderates over sattva and tamas, the rhythm of happiness and the inertia of delusion, and that is the root of all sankalpa and vikalpa (volition and doubt).
22. buddhi: the intellect; the inner sense that is attained when rhythm preponderates over mobility and inertia, that is endowed with the power of discrimination and determination, and as such is the root of all conviction.
23. ahamkara: egoism. The inner sense that is attained when inertia preponderates over rhythm and mobility, characterized by "I" consciousness and which is the root of all fancy, converging toward the self.

24. chitta: mind that is attained by the equipoised state of rhythm, mobility and inertia, the storehouse of past impressions, the mind-stuff. The term manas or mind is often used as a general term to include buddhi or chitta also.

Other groups of thirty-six tattva-s or ninety-six tattva-s are also mentioned. Refer to the Varahopanisad.

TETRAD OF RELATED ADJUNCTS. See FOUR AD-JUNCTS.

THAT. *That* has been used in the translation of the Sanskrit term *tat* which denotes Brahman, the impersonal Absolute, devoid of any conditioning such as maya (delusion).

THIS. *This* has been used in the translation of the Sanskrit word *idam*. The expression encompasses, subject to context, all things except the first person and the second person.

THREE CONNECTIONS. See TRIAD OF CONNECTIONS.

THREE-EYED LORD. Reference to Siva.

THREE PRINCIPLES. Many systems of thought, philosophical and religious, postulate the three principles: God, souls, and the world. For example: Isvara (God), chit (conscious beings), and achit (non-conscious objects); or pati (Lord), pasu (soul), pasa (bondage); or God, Man, and Nature (in western philosophy); or Nature, Mind, and spirit (Hegel); or world, souls, and God or Spirit (eastern philosophy). In this translation, the expressions *world, jiva* (individual soul), and *supreme* are used in this context. See JAGAT-JIVA-PARA.

TIME. See TRIAD OF TIME.

TITIKSA. See FOUR REQUISITES FOR REALIZATION OF BRAHMAN.

TRIAD OF AFFLICTIONS (tapa traya).

1. adhyatmika: due to intrinsic nature; bodily and mental afflictions such as presence of bile, phlegm, desire, anger; caused by inner senses.

2. adhibhautika: due to extrinsic nature; inflicted by external natural influences, by other individuals, beasts, birds,
and inanimate objects.

3. adhidaivika: due to the supernatural; inflicted by extrinsic supernatural influences such as spirits, demons,
ghosts; and by the deities presiding over heat, cold, wind,
rain, etc.

TRIAD OF BODIES.

1. Gross body (stula sarira) consisting of the sheath of
food (annamaya kosa): composed of the five elements
in fractional proportions

2. Subtle body (sukshma sarira) consisting of:
   a. sheath of vital airs (pranamaya kosa): of vital airs
   and organs of action
   b. sheath of mind (manomaya kosa): of mind along
   with sensory organs
   c. sheath of knowledge (vijnanamaya kosa): of intellect
   along with sensory organs

3. Causal body (karana sarira) consisting of sheath of
bliss (anandamaya kosa): of ignorance, the cause of
the other two bodies

The five sheaths are referred to as the pentad of
sheaths (pancha kosa-s). See PENTAD OF SHEATHS.

TRIAD OF CONNECTIONS. Three types of connections:
conjunction, inseparable inherence, and identity.

TRIAD OF EYES. Siva and his consort Uma, son Skanda,
and other divinities, are said to have three eyes; which
are often referred to as three luminous entities, the sun,
the moon, and fire. See TRIAD OF LIGHTS.

TRIAD OF FORMS. Forms of Brahma (creator), Vishnu
(sustainer), and Siva (destroyer).

TRIAD OF GUNA-S. *Guna* means quality, attribute, characteristic. There are three guna-s.

1. sattva: buoyant, illuminating, light, knowledge, happiness

2. rajas: agitation, stimulating, mobile, pain, action

3. tamas: heavy, enveloping, dark, indifferent, laziness, inertia

Guna also means a rope; the three constituents are said to be like strands of a rope that bind the individual.

TRIAD OF KARMA. Karma means the results of actions or action itself. The triad of karma refers to results. The triad of karma is:

1. sanchita karma: residue of results of acts in this or previous life, but latent during this life.
2. agami karma: result of acts during present life that will mature in the normal course.
3. prarabdha karma: residue of results of acts that has fructified and started working itself out during present life.

It is held sometimes that sanchita karma is destroyed through Self-Knowledge, or that for one who has realized the Self there is neither Agami karma nor Sanchita karma, but that the remaining portion of the prarabdha will be worked out in this body. However, Sri Ramana Maharshi and Sri Sankara, in expounding the pure non-dual Truth, declared that Self-Realization liberates one from all three kinds of karma.

Apart from the word *karma* being used to denote the results or fruit of action, the word is also used to denote action itself.

Karma, in the sense of action, is of several kinds. There is kamya-karma (optional deeds), which one need perform only if one wishes for their fruit, such as desiring heaven; nitya-karma (daily obligatory duties), which one performs because they have to be done, such as offering twilight prayers; naimittika-karma (obligations which are occasional) such as performance of rites on the birth of a son; also pratishiddha-karma (prohibited actions) such as killing or doing injury to living beings. Other classifications of karma are: laukika (secular), and vaidika (sacred).

TRIAD OF LIGHTS. Sun, moon, and fire. See TRIAD OF EYES.

TRIAD OF MEANS. Mind, speech, and body.

TRIAD OF SOULS. (triad of jiva-s). Different triads of jiva-s (souls) are mentioned:

One triad is:
1. nitya: ever free
2. mukta: having attained freedom
3. baddha: bound

Another triad is:
1. sakala: subject to the three mala-s or impurities
   a. anava: due to innate ignorance
   b. karma mala: result of anava
   c. mayika: due to karma mala
2. pralayakala: subject to anava mala and karma mala
3. vijnanakala: subject only to anava mala

TRIAD OF STATES. Waking, dream, and dreamless sleep. These are also known as the three states of mind or the three states of the jiva.

TRIAD OF TIME. Past, present, and future.

TRIAD OF WORLDS. (1) svarga (heaven), (2) prithvi (earth), and (3) patala (netherworld).

TRIPURA-S (three cities). Mythology has it that three sons of the demon Taraka named Tarakaksha, Vidyunmali, and Kamalaksha, by engaging in severe penance over several centuries, had boons granted to them by Brahma, the Creator. The boons were that they would each be blessed with a well-nigh impregnable fortress of gold, silver, and iron respectively. The fortresses were created by the arch-architect, maya, and were of incomparable grandeur and wonder. The boons included that the three sons would be invincible. They came to possess untold power. Though great worshippers of Mahadeva, they strayed, in the course of time, into unrighteous action, particularly in the harassment of the gods, who ultimately prevailed upon Lord Siva to subdue them.

The colossal chariot, weaponry, and accouterments of the Lord were provided by the gods and sages, encompassing the various forces of heaven and earth, and as the Lord set out on this behemoth for the onslaught of the three cities, the three cities fused as one, losing their unique powers and were totally burnt. In the *Siva Purana* it is stated that the three cities came into alignment, and Siva destroyed them with a single arrow. This is referred to in mythology as the destruction of the three cities. The entire episode is considered an epic exploit of Siva.

The event is explained allegorically in various ways. The chariot symbolizes the body, or the universe, or all experience. The three cities symbolize the triad of desire, anger, and covetousness, or attachment, hatred, and infatuation, the three states, or other triads, in various ways. It is also explained as the destruction of the three differentiated states, each a realm unto itself, all originally for only the glory of Siva, Absolute Consciousness, destroyed as different states by the single arrow of nondual Knowledge when the three are "aligned" to see their only essence.

TURIYA. The fourth state; the underlying substratum of the three states of waking, dream, and deep sleep; sometimes used as a synonym for Self-Realization and sometimes used as a synonym for samadhi.

TVAM. You.

UMA. The consort of Siva; the daughter of the mountain king Himavan and Mena. One version of the story that explains the origin of her name says that as she set out to practice severe penance to obtain the hand of Siva, her mother said, "Hey! (U), don't (Ma) (practice severe penance)." Thus the name Uma has come to stay.

UPACHARA-S. Courtesies and honors in worship (puja). There are several courtesies and honors accorded to the deity in a ritual worship. They vary from about five to sixty-four or more according to the tradition practiced and the details of worship. Other sets of upachara-s, for example forty-four as listed in Sri Sankara's *Mrtyunjaya Manasika Puja Stotram,* and sixty-four listed in the *Sixty-four Upachara-s to Devi Stotram,* exist. The same are extended mentally in mental worship. The various items dealt with in this text are:

Invocation (in the icon or picture or otherwise) (avahana)
Offering of a seat (asana)
Water for feet washing (padya)
Respectful oblation (arghya)
Sips of water (achamana)
Formal ablution (snana)
Garments (vastra)
Triple strands of sacred thread (yajnopavita) (upavita) (over left shoulder and under right arm)
Ornaments (abharana)
Sandal paste (chandana)
Rice grains, unbroken (akshata)
Flowers (pushpa)
Incense (dhupa)
Light on a wick (deepa)
Cooked food (naivedya)
Seasonings (vyanjana)
Water for hand washing (hasta prakshalana)
Betel leaves (tambula)
Scattering of flowers (pushpanjali)
Waving of camphor light (nirajana)
Circumambulation (clockwise) (pradakshina)
Prostration (namaskara)
Singing of names (nama kirtana)
Release (visarjana) (udvasana)

UPANISHAD-S/UPANISAD-S. These are the concluding portion of the Veda-s, and hence referred to as Vedanta (end of the Veda-s) also. The word *upanishad* has been held severally to mean: sitting near, devotedly; the instruction received by sitting near the Guru (which gives) certitude and cleanses (sorrow); secret teaching; knowledge of the Absolute.

The Veda-s have four broad classifications: *Rig, Yajur, Sama,* and *Atharva.* There are several branches in the Veda-s called "sakha-s." Each sakha has a karma khanda (which deals with the holy action to be performed) composed of mantra-s, and brahmana-s, the latter dealing with upasana or meditation, and containing aranyaka-s (particularly for study by those who have taken to the path of a recluse and resorted to the forests for a devoted pursuit of knowledge). The Upanishad-s are said to form part of the aranyaka-s.

According to traditional accounts, the four Veda-s have been codified by Vyasa into 1,180 sakha-s, and each sakha is said to have had an Upanishad. Thus, according to the *Vishnupurana,* there should have been 21 sakha-s for *Rig Veda,* 109 for *Yajurveda,* 1,000 for *Samaveda,* and 50 for *Atharva Veda.* Most of these have been lost with the lapse of time, and only 108 are said to be extant.

A list of the 108 Upanishad-s is given below, with the Veda to which each pertains, namely, R for *Rig Veda,* KY for *Krishna Yajurveda,* SY for *Sukla Yajurveda* (KY and SY being two versions of *Yajurveda*), S for *Samaveda,* and A for *Atharva Veda.*

1. *Isavasya* (SY)
2. *Kena* (S)
3. *Katha* (KY)
4. *Prasna* (A)
5. *Mundaka* (A)
6. *Mandukya* (A)
7. *Taittiriya* (KY)
8. *Aitareya* (R)
9. *Chandogya* (S)
10. *Brhadaranyaka* (SY)
11. *Brahma* (KY)
12. *Kaivalya* (KY)
13. *Jabala* (SY)
14. *Svetasvatara* (KY)
15. *Hamsa* (SY)
16. *Arunika* (S)

17. *Garbha* (KY)
18. *Narayana* (KY)
19. *Paramahamsa* (SY)
20. *Amrtabindu* (KY)
21. *Amrtanada* (KY)
22. *Atharvasira* (A)
23. *Atharvasikha* (A)
24. *Maitrayani* (S)
25. *Kaushitaki* (R)
26. *Brhajjabala* (A)
27. *Nrsimhatapini* (A)
28. *Kalagnirudra* (KY)
29. *Maitreyi* (S)
30. *Subala* (SY)
31. *Kshurika* (KY)
32. *Mantrika* (SY)
33. *Sarvasara* (KY)
34. *Niralamba* (SY)
35. *Sukharahasya* (KY)
36. *Vajrasuchi* (S)
37. *Tejobindu* (KY)
38. *Nadabindu* (R)
39. *Dhyanabindu* (KY)
40. *Brahmavidya* (KY)
41. *Yogatattva (KY)*
42. *Atmabodha* (R)
43. *Narada-parivrajaka* (A)
44. *Trisikhibrahmana* (SY)
45. *Sita* (A)
46. *Yogachudamani* (S)
47. *Nirvana* (R)
48. *Mandalabrahmana* (SY)
49. *Dakshinamurti* (KY)
50. *Sarabha* (A)
51. *Skanda* (KY)
52. *Tripadvibhutimahanarayana* (A)
53. *Advayataraka* (SY)
54. *Ramarahasya* (A)
55. *Ramatapini* (A)

56. *Vasudeva* (S)
57. *Mudgala* (R)
58. *Sandilya* (A)
59. *Paingala* (SY)
60. *Bhikshuka* (SY)
61. *Maha* (S)
62. *Sariraka* (KY)
63. *Yogasikha* (KY)
64. *Turiyatita* (SY)
65. *Sannyasa* (S)
66. *Paramahamsaparivrajaka* (A)
67. *Akshamala* (R)
68. *Avyakta* (S)
69. *Ekakshara* (KY)
70. *Annapurna* (A)
71. *Surya* (A)
72. *Akshi* (KY)
73. *Adhyatma* (SY)
74. *Kundika* (S)
75. *Savitri* (S)
76. *Atma* (A)
77. *Pasupatabrahma* (A)
78. *Parabrahma* (A)
79. *Avadhuta* (KY)
80. *Tripuratapini* (A)
81. *Devi* (A)
82. *Tripura* (R)
83. *Katharudra* (KY)
84. *Bhavana* (A)
85. *Rudrahrdaya* (KY)
86. *Yogakundalini* (KY)
87. *Bhasmajabala* (A)
88. *Rudrakshajabala* (S)
89. *Ganapati* (A)
90. *Jabaladarsana* (S)
91. *Tarasara (SY)*
92. *Mahavakya* (A)
93. *Panchabrahma* (KY)
94. *Pranagnihotra* (KY)

95. *Gopalatapini* (A)
96. *Krishna* (A)
97. *Yajnavalkya* (SY)
98. *Varaha* (KY)
99. *Satyayani* (SY)
100. *Hayagriva* (A)
101. *Dattatreya* (A)
102. *Garuda* (A)
103. *Kalisantarana* (KY)
104. *Jabali* (S)
105. *Saubhagyalakshmi* (R)
106. *Sarasvatirahasya* (KY)
107. *Bahvrchi* (R)
108. *Muktika* (SY)

The Upanishad-s are also sometimes compiled into groups by topic as follows:

a. The ten major Upanishad-s: 1, 2, 3, 4, 5, 6, 7, 8, 9, 10. Called thus because they are the first ten according to the order in the Muktikopanisad and because only these ten bear commentaries by the great acharayas (teachers), such as Sri Sankara.

b. The Samanya Vedanta Upanishad-s: 14, 17, 24, 25, 30, 32, 33, 34, 35, 36, 42, 51, 57, 59, 61, 62, 69, 70, 71, 72, 73, 75, 76, 94, 108. Called thus because they all deal with the teachings of a general interest.

c. The Saiva Upanishad-s: 12, 22, 23, 26, 28, 49, 50, 67, 85, 87, 88, 89, 93, 104. Called thus because they deal predominantly with Siva.

d. The Sakta Upanishad-s: 45, 80, 81, 82, 84, 105, 106, 107. Called thus because they deal predominantly with Sakti.

e. Vaisnava Upanishad-s: 18, 27, 52, 54, 55, 56, 68, 91, 95, 96, 100, 101, 102, 103. Called thus because they deal predominantly with Vishnu.

f. Yoga Upanishad-s: 15, 20, 21, 31, 37, 38, 39, 40, 41, 44, 46, 48, 53, 58, 63, 77, 86, 90, 92, 98. Called thus because they deal predominantly with Yoga.

g. Sannyasa Upanishad-s: 11, 13, 16, 19, 29, 43, 47, 60, 64, 65, 66, 74, 78, 79, 83, 97, 99. Called thus because they deal predominantly with sannyasa (renunciation).

UPASANA. Meditation, worship.

VAISVANARA.

1. The cosmic experiencer of the waking state: The one whose sphere of experience is the waking state. Sri Sankara says: Vaisvanara is the "enjoyer of the gross. He is called Vaisvanara because he leads in diverse ways all (visva) beings (nara)" and "He is called Vaisvanara (all beings) because He encompasses all beings by virtue of His being nondifferent in reality from the Self comprising all experiencers (Virat)." In his commentary on Gaudapada's Karika, Sankara equates Visva with Virat, (the cosmic experiencer of all that is gross).

   Gaudapada states in the *Mandukya Upanisad Karika,* "Visva experiences the external things and is all-pervading." (1:1) and "Visva ever enjoys the gross" (1:5).

   Virat is the all-pervading cosmic experiencer and is used to indicate the gross, collective context.

   Vaisvanara is used to indicate the gross individual context, or individual experiencer of the waking state. The Advaita view is that there is no difference between vaisvanara, visvan, and virat.

2. The fire of digestion in the stomach: Vaisvanara is used in another context in the *Bhagavad Gita* (15:14) as the digestive fire in the bodies of living beings. "As the fire vaisvanara, I enter into the bodies of all living beings and mingling with the prana and apana (upward and downward pranas), I digest the four kinds of food."

VANAPRASTHA. One who has taken to the forest. See ASRAMA. Also see FOUR ASRAMAS.

VARNAM. Caste.

VASANA. Knowledge derived from memory, particularly the impression unconsciously left on the mind by past good or bad actions, which, therefore, produce happiness or grief; fancy, imaginations, ignorance, ignorant tendency, desire, inclination, or wish. The residue of past impressions, tendencies of delusion.

VASUDEVA. The God who is present everywhere; name of Vishnu.

VEDANTA. Literally, "end of the Veda-s." Vedanta is a term applied to the Upanishad-s and the teaching contained therein. Vedanta also means a teaching or "school of philosophy" founded upon the knowledge expounded in the Upanishad-s. The major "schools" or types of Vedanta are: Advaita (Nonduality), Visistadvaita (Qualified Nonduality) and Dvaita (Dualism). Vedanta of all kinds consider the Upanishad-s, the *Bhagavad Gita,* and the *Brahma-Sutra* (also called *Vedanta-Sutra)*—referred to as prasthana-traya, or the triple canon—as the basic, foundational texts, though there are many other texts such as treatises, dialogues, and scriptures composed on Vedanta. Vedanta is considered one of the traditional six schools or types of spiritual philosophy of Hinduism. See SAMKHYA.

Advaita Vedanta, or the Teaching of Nonduality, is that which is expounded by Ribhu, Sri Dattatreya (the Avadhuta), Sri Ashtavakra, Sri Sankara, Sri Ramana Maharshi, and many other great sages. It reveals the utter absence of any differentiation between Atman (the Self) and Brahman. It is the revelation of Reality without even a trace of notional superimpositions. The entire *Ribhu Gita* is an exposition—a veritable scripture—of Advaita Vedanta.

VEDA-S. The most ancient and foundational scriptures of Hinduism, usually counted as four in number *(Rig, Sama, Yajur,* and *Atharva),* though sometimes only three, the Atharva being excluded, are accepted as actual Veda-s (cf. 3:45).

VERITIES. See TATTVA-S.

VIBHUTI. Sacred ashes.

VIDEHAMUKTA/VIDEHAMUKTI. Videhamukta means one who ·has attained liberation outside the body (videhamukti). The distinction between jivanmukta and videhamukta is sometimes declared by sages of Advaita to be an unreal distinction. There is also a three-fold classification of liberation sometimes described:

1. with form
2. without form
3. with and without form

The first two are the same as jivanmukta and videhamukta, respectively. The third, with and without form, is said to be the release in the case of the adhikarika (qualified person) mukta, whose mission is to save the world. After shedding the physical body, they live in the subtle body for the welfare of humanity for a further period.

In Advaita, all these differences are negated and only the one state of Mukti is regarded as real. Sri Ramana Maharshi, in his *Truth Revealed (Sad-Vidya)* verse 40, states:

If it is said that Liberation is of three kinds, with form, or without form, or with and without form, then let me tell you the extinction of the ego which inquires into the three forms of liberation is alone Liberation.

VIKALPA. See SANKALPA/VIKALPA.

VIKARA. Change of nature, modification.

VINAYAKA. The remover, Ganesha.

VIRAT. The Cosmic waker, the Cosmic form of the Self, functioning through the aggregate of all bodies in the waking state. Also said to denote, "shining as the manifold."

VISHAYA. Subject matter.

VISHNU. Literally, "all pervading." Refers to Lord Vishnu or to any One who is all pervading.

VISVA(M). The entire world, the universe, the entire, all.

VISVAN. The totality of the individuals in the waking state.

VITAL AIRS. See DECAD OF VITAL AIRS.

VIVARTA. An illusory form and unreal appearance caused by avidya (ignorance). For example, a snake is a vivarta of a rope.

VRATA. Vow.

VRITTI. See MODE.

VYANJANA. Seasonings used as an offering during puja or worship.

VYASTI. The individual, the discrete, the separate; collection in which the components retain their individuality; microcosmic.

WORLDS. See FOURTEEN WORLDS.

YAGA. See YAJNA.

YAJNA, YAGA, HOMA, HAVIS. These generally refer to a sacrificial act, often to a sacrificial offering in a fire, but have various connotations.

Yajna may mean (appropriate to the context) a sacrifice, sacrificial rite, an act of worship, any pious or devotional act, or spiritual offering or endeavor. A fivefold yajna daily is enjoined on householders, particularly on a Brahmin, as:

1. bhootha yajna: oblation or offering to all created beings
2. pitr yajna: obsequial offerings, daily libations of water to the deceased ancestors
3. deva yajna: sacrifice to the superior gods made by oblations to fire or through fire to other gods (commonly called homa)
4. manushya yajna: offerings to people, hospitality, hospitable reception of guests
5. brahma yajna: teaching and reciting Veda-s

The word *yajna* may be used in an extended sense for other pious, devotional, spiritual endeavors, projects, observances, and such.

Repeating or muttering a mantra numerous times may be called a "Japa Yajna." In the *Bhagavad Gita,* the Lord says: "Of the yajna-s, I am the Japa Yajna."

The writing down of the name of the Lord ten million times as a devotional offering is termed "Koti Nama Likhita Yajna."

The exposition and dissemination of the knowledge of the *Bhagavad Gita* may be termed "Gita Jnana Yajna."

The publication and propagation of the *Ribhu Gita* may be spoken of as the "Ribhu Gita Yajna."

Yajna is also associated with fire sacrifices for various purposes.

Yaga is a term used generally (but not exclusively) for elaborate performance of fire sacrifices on a large scale, following various Vedic injunctions, employing special priests for specified duties in the conduct of the Yaga, such as Adhvaryu (officiating priest), Hotr (for reciting the *Rig Veda)* Udgata (for chanting the hymns or samans of the *Sama Veda*), Brahman (presiding priest, often employed at a Soma sacrifice), up to sixteen different priests in a grand ceremony. A Yaga is usually attended by a large number of people, members of the public. Various types of Yaga are also classified, such as, a Kratu in which a sacrificial post is erected to which the object of sacrifice is fastened.

Homa is generally (but not exclusively) on a smaller scale, domestic in nature, performed with oblations to propitiate deities, and often by way of the daily Deva Yajna mentioned above.

Sometimes the recitation of scriptural passages is offered in the format of a Homa, such as, "Purusha Sukta Homa," "Sri Sukta Homa," and "Bhagavad Gita Homa." Havis is the term used for the oblation or burnt offering poured into, or tossed into, the sacrificial fire.

YAJURVEDA. See VEDAS.

YAKSHA-S. Demi-gods.

YAMA. see ASHTANGA YOGA

YANTRA. Mystic diagram.

YOGA. Yoga is a general term for a path or discipline leading to union or oneness with the Divine, such as the path of breath control, the path of kundalini, the path of mantra or other concentrations, the path of mind control, the path of bhakti (devotion), the path of action, and the path of jnana (knowledge).

WE. In Sanskrit and Tamil literature, and certain other languages, it is customary for a person of authority, high rank, or divine power to use the word *we* to represent the first person singular.

WORSHIP. See UPACHARA-S.

27056122R00221

Printed in Great Britain
by Amazon